C000184512

Howzat?

To Stephen

Best wishes

Graheme Lloyd

Chester-le-St, Oct 2014

For Frank Keating (1937–2013)

A wizard of a wordsmith who loved a good yarn

Howzat?

The *Six Sixes* Ball
MYSTERY

Grahame Lloyd

Foreword by Matthew Engel

Published by Celluloid Ltd,
12, Chargot Road, Llandaff,
Cardiff CF5 1EW
grahameatcelluloid@btinternet.com

The right of Grahame Lloyd to be identified as the author of this work
has been asserted in accordance with the Copyright,
Designs and Patents Act, 1988.

ISBN 978-09545961-5-6

Printed in Garamond by Jellyfish Print Solutions Ltd

By the Same Author

Daffodil Days: Glamorgan's Glorious Summer
Jan the Man: From Anfield to Vetch Field (with Jan Molby)
C'mon City! A Hundred Years of the Bluebirds
One Cap Wonders: The Ultimate Claim to Football Fame
One Hell of a Season: Imps, Pilgrims and Tales of the Unexpected
Hard Man, Hard Knocks (with Terry Yorath)
Six of the Best: Cricket's Most Famous Over

Contents

Foreword

There is an old story about the Irish travelling fair that was exhibiting what it claimed to be the skull of Oliver Cromwell. A passing Englishman started to get snotty about this and upbraided the man in charge of the booth. Cromwell's head was known to be elsewhere; this one was the wrong shape; and it was far too small. "Ah, well, y'see," said the shameless showman, "this was Cromwell's skull when he was a boy."

When we go to the fairground we have a vague expectation of being gently chiselled: fake skulls, sickly goldfish, useless toys, whatever. Day-to-day, though, we try to be more sensible: we don't deliberately pick out rotten apples in a supermarket. But when it comes to buying something intangible, even the most careful buyer can get a little lost. Consumer groups no longer focus on rotten apples or exploding TV sets; nowadays the problems are caused by intangibles. How do you know if your electricity bill is correct or your pension is phoney?

Then again, what happens when we pay £26,400 for something that it is intrinsically worth only a few quid, like an old cricket ball? Ah, that's when things really get complicated.

The sporting memorabilia market is a very odd one. Normally shrewd people will, after a few drinks, pay large sums for a signed cricket bat they would never dare spoil by wielding on the field. But they usually do that for charity. When it becomes serious business we risk not just opening cans of worms but treading on nests of vipers.

There was a story a few years back about a man who paid several thousand pounds for the sweater Brian Lara wore for one of his record-breaking innings of the 1990s. It was only when he sat back to watch his proud new possession on the video that he discovered Lara wasn't actually wearing one. He had bought... a sweater.

The ball Garry Sobers hit six times for six off Malcolm Nash in 1968 perhaps deserves to be the most famous ball in history. It has certainly become the most controversial. Or at least that's true of the ball Sobers allegedly hit.

Grahame Lloyd has spent years trying to unravel the truth about this ball. One might say his quest has become as obsessive as the urge to own such an object. But it is an absolutely fascinating tale. It centres on one of the most famous moments in cricket's history, made more resonant because – by pure fluke – it was filmed and televised by the BBC.

The story, however, is not really about cricket. It is about the real people who play the game, watch it, love it and cling to it. It is about the mysterious business of collecting. It is about the strange and glamorous world of the international auction houses. Above all, it is about the most important and intriguing subject that any writer can tackle: human nature.

Matthew Engel
Herefordshire, September 2013

Willow, King Willow, thy guard hold tight;
Trouble is coming before the night;
Hopping and galloping, short and strong,
Comes the Leathery Duke along;
And down the palaces tumble fast
When once the Leathery Duke gets past.

E.E. Bowen, 'Willow the King'

Introduction

It was a truly remarkable year – and not just because of an unforgettable Olympics or the England rugby team's unexpected humiliation of New Zealand or Captain Cook's cricketers recording a first Test series win for almost 28 years in India, the land of temples, tigers and turning wickets and, incidentally, the current resting place of a battered leather ball reputedly bowled during one of the game's most memorable moments.

Away from the sporting arena, 2012 saw the re-election of the first Afro-American president of the United States for a second term, proposals to overhaul the British press via the Leveson Inquiry, the Eurozone economic crisis and the discovery of Higgs boson, the world's most sought-after particle which gives all elementary particles mass. As Hurricane Sandy wreaked havoc across the other side of the Atlantic, Britain experienced its second wettest year since records began in 1910 amidst a timely stream of dire warnings about global warming and climate change. A skydiver jumped from a balloon 24 miles above the earth to break the speed of sound in freefall and a very famous former astronaut died – 43 years after taking his "one giant leap for mankind" to become the first man to walk on the moon.

But it was British sport that bequeathed enough special memories to last us a lifetime during 2012. After Manchester's two football clubs had produced the most exciting climax to a Premier League season in the competition's 20-year history, our athletes were inspired by the Queen's Jubilee and a fanatical home crowd to collect a record haul of medals at the Olympics and equally joyous Paralympics. Tennis gold medallist Andy Murray then made history by winning the US Open – his first Grand Slam title and the first by a British male for 76 years – before Europe's golfers retained the Ryder Cup thanks to a scarcely believable comeback. As 2012 drew to a close, England beat the seemingly insuperable All Blacks at Twickenham and the apparently invincible Indians were humbled in their own back yard.

2012 was also the year the truth came out – about Jimmy Savile and two sporting scandals. After nearly a quarter of a century of lies, damned lies and altered statements, the full horror of the Hillsborough tragedy and its subsequent cover-up was exposed. A rogues' gallery – including the football authorities, the local council, the coroner and, most importantly, the police – stands accused of incompetence, negligence or collusion and, in some cases, a combination of all three. The Hillsborough Independent Panel's report also criticised some media coverage of the disaster and politicians from all parties had to admit their share of the blame for, in the words of Prime Minister David Cameron, not doing enough "to challenge publicly the unjust and untrue narrative that sought to blame the fans." The revelation that 41 of the 96 victims might have been saved if the emergency services had responded quicker simply compounded their loved ones' grief. As Trevor Hicks, the chair of the Hillsborough Families Support Group who lost two daughters in the tragedy, remarked in response to the report's publication: "The truth is out today, justice starts tomorrow."

The uncovering of another truth – that the all-conquering cyclist, Lance Armstrong, was using performance-enhancing drugs – also occurred during 2012. A 13-year investigation by the *Sunday Times* reporter David Walsh, with more than a little help from some of the American rider's former friends and colleagues, was completely vindicated when the winner of seven successive Tour de France titles was finally forced to come clean. The United States Anti-Doping Association's report into the "most sophisticated, professionalised and successful doping program that sport has ever seen" was followed by Armstrong's public confession on a television chat show in 2013 which confirmed him as a bully, a liar, a doper and a cheat.

While Operation Howzat?, my 18-month search for the truth about a red cricket ball, could never be compared with the Hillsborough and Armstrong exposés in terms of either gravity or longevity, I must admit to drawing huge inspiration from the dignified stoicism shown by both a maligned community and an indefatigable journalist. They knew the facts were being obscured and distorted but they refused to be bowed by malevolent mendacity. On a much, much smaller scale, I strongly identified with their indomitable determination to keep going.

When Garry Sobers hammered his way into the record books by hitting Malcolm Nash for six successive sixes at Swansea in 1968, the feat rightly passed into sporting legend. The West Indian captain went on to secure his status as the game's greatest all-rounder while the England triallist, despite enjoying a successful county career, found his name inextricably linked with those fantastic five minutes of mayhem. As I was writing my 40th anniversary celebration of the event, *Six of the Best: Cricket's Most Famous Over*, it saddened me to discover one indisputable, incontrovertible fact: the ball sold by Christie's for £26,400 in 2006 was not the actual one bowled by Nash. It couldn't have been the genuine article because it was the wrong make – a Duke rather than a Surridge – and I was also aware that only one ball had been used in the over, not three as claimed by Christie's. Their crucial but incorrect lot notes, along with a certificate of provenance signed by Sobers, had been instrumental in securing a world record price for a cricket ball. When the same Duke ball was consigned to Bonhams in May 2012, I knew this controversial chapter of cricketing history just had to be re-written – to set the record straight and to attempt to put right a most blatant wrong. On the strength of my evidence, Bonhams withdrew the Duke from their sporting memorabilia auction and during the second half of 2012, Operation Howzat? developed into a dual-purpose investigation: to solve the mystery surrounding the sold ball and to clear Sobers' name. His mistaken and misleading ratification of the Duke meant his integrity had been impugned and his reputation sullied but I couldn't believe that he'd been involved in anything underhand. As my evidence piled up, I failed to understand how a Duke could have supplanted a Surridge – especially as the BBC TV footage of the extraordinary event showed the same ball being used throughout the over. Operation Howzat? was firmly based on fact, supported by personal recollection. The camera doesn't lie and, neither does Nash. If anyone should know the make of the ball, it is undoubtedly him – and he has steadfastly insisted that he bowled the same Surridge ball six times to Sobers 45 years ago this summer.

With more than one reputation on the line, I knew it wasn't going to be easy but I hadn't anticipated the amount of time and effort

I'd have to spend trying to unravel the riddle. For the most part, my investigation into the ball's movements from England to the Indian subcontinent resembled an obstacle course. As soon as I had negotiated one hurdle, another one appeared. Some of those involved were so keen to absolve themselves of any responsibility that one or two ran for cover and refused to speak to me. Others were downright unhelpful – even obstructive – and one in particular seemed incapable of telling the truth. At times, my frustration forced me to consider abandoning Operation Howzat? but when a handful of the saga's key players chose the route of openness and honesty, I felt duty bound to continue. The investigation was re-invigorated and finally concluded.

What happened to the original Surridge ball used in the famous over? The answer to the question most frequently asked during the course of my quest is simple: I'm afraid I don't know. It could have been lost in the re-development of Trent Bridge in Nottingham or perhaps it was inadvertently left lying in a cricket bag somewhere inside the ground. While it has disappeared without trace, the Duke ball has come to rest in India, bought first by one citizen of that country for a sporting memorabilia collection and then by another cricket-mad fan who retrieved it from a mass of airport flotsam and jetsam three years later; it has achieved nebulous notoriety in the most Indian of Indian summers.

I'd like to think that the late Frank Keating would have enjoyed this book. When he died in January 2013, the warmth of the tributes – from fellow journalists, the sportsmen and women he wrote about and especially his readers – was suitably respectful, even touching. A former *Guardian* colleague and close friend, Matthew Engel, recalled how Frank "simply tore up the rulebook, reinventing the language, turning adjectives into nouns and nouns into adjectives, and making everything fizz with the sheer joie de vivre of word play". David Hopps, another ex-*Guardian* writer and now UK editor at Cricinfo, focused on Frank's ability to explain "either in a single phrase or a lengthy alliterative flight of fancy, just why we all spent so much of our lives watching people compete with bat and ball". The *Mail on Sunday*'s Patrick Collins, a multi-award-winning journalist himself, described Frank as "the most gloriously readable sports writer these islands have ever produced."

Frank Keating not only influenced a generation of writers through his linguistic imagination; to me personally, he was a reassuring source of encouragement when I began reporting football for the *Guardian* 30 years ago and an incredibly supportive reviewer of my books over the last 15 years. I have a feeling he would have loved the broad sweep of the Six Sixes ball story as it moved from Swansea to Nottingham and London before taking in New Delhi and then Faridabad. He would have chuckled at the antics of its motley crew of characters: the antiquarian book dealer, the art impresario, the solar energy expert with a penchant for the poetry of a Nobel Prize winner – not to mention the world's finest cricketer, his agent and the sporting memorabilia specialists who failed to spot that the ball being sold by their auction house was the wrong make.

I'm delighted to dedicate this book to a wizard of a wordsmith who loved a good yarn – or, as his friend and fellow journalist, David Miller, described Frank after his death, "a one-man party of anecdotes – some of them naughtily apocryphal." As you will discover, parts of this story are both naughty and apocryphal but, in the end, it will be up to you to decide how much of it to believe. I have simply sought to shine the torch of transparency onto the business of buying and selling sporting memorabilia – an increasingly popular activity dependent on truth, trust and fair play – all the while believing that what happened to that scuffed and scruffy red cherry before it was sold in 2006 was "just not cricket." Howzat? Who knows? Conspiracy or cock-up? Probably a perfect call for the third umpire and DRS – the problematic decision review system. I may not have completely cracked the Six Sixes Ball Mystery but I hope you'll agree I've had a jolly good go. Enjoy the journey.

A knockabout with Basher

Nothing was delivered
And I tell this truth to you
Not out of spite or anger
But simply because it's true

Bob Dylan, 'Nothing Was Delivered'

At the time, the significance of the short, unexpected conversation largely passed me by. In March 2008, I was sitting in my study writing *Six of the Best: Cricket's Most Famous Over* when the telephone rang. I didn't recognise the voice at the other end of the line.

"Is that Grahame?"

"Speaking. Who's that?"

"It's Basher here."

Basher? Ah yes. Basharat Hassan, the former Nottinghamshire cricketer and now Garry Sobers' agent. I hadn't spoken to him for nearly two years – not, in fact, since the only time I'd ever met him in May 2006 at St Helen's in Swansea – the ground where Sobers had hit Malcolm Nash for six sixes off a single six-ball over for the first time in the history of the game on 31st August 1968. With the 2006 cricket season in full swing, I had discussed the idea of marking the 40th anniversary of Sobers' feat with Peter Walker, the former Glamorgan and England all-rounder and a fellow journalist and broadcaster. Peter had been fielding during Nottinghamshire's first innings in 1968 and had also worked with Sobers subsequently. As part of our forward planning, we had then conducted, through Hassan, two interviews with Sobers while he was on an after-dinner speaking tour of South Wales – one for use in my book and the other as part of a possible TV programme.

"Oh…hello Basher. How are you?"

"Fine thanks. How's the book going?"

"Not bad – I'm making good progress."

"Yes. I hear you've been speaking to a few of the Notts boys."

Indeed I had. After recently going to Nottingham to interview Brian Bolus, I'd then travelled north to the village of Kimberley to meet John Parkin, the non-striking batsman during the iconic over. The other three members of The Not-So-Famous Five, Bob White, Graham Frost and Mike Smedley, the team-mates who had provided Sobers with the platform to launch his extraordinary assault, had all kindly given me their recollections of the day via the telephone.

"Yes…they've all been very helpful – especially John. I spent a couple of hours with him at his home."

"Good. Have you spoken to Jose Miller?"

Jose – pronounced Josie – Miller was the former secretary of the Nottinghamshire Supporters' Association who'd kept the Six Sixes ball in her make-up drawer before selling it in 2006. Two days after the historic over in 1968, after Nottinghamshire had won the match by 166 runs, the ball was reported to be on its way to Trent Bridge via Nottinghamshire's scorer, Arthur Wheat. It was destined to be put on display in the county's museum but according to Peter Wynne-Thomas, Nottinghamshire's archivist, a museum wasn't created there until the 1980s and he had never seen the ball. The received wisdom was that it was given by Sobers to Miller's predecessor, John Gough, and then put behind the bar in the Eddie Marshall lounge in The Tavern pub at Trent Bridge where the association used to meet. When Gough retired, it had passed into Miller's hands and then, via Sobers and Hassan, it was sold for £26,400 by Christie's at their South Kensington saleroom in November 2006. Once Malcolm Nash had agreed to be interviewed for my book in the summer of 2007, I'd visited Trent Bridge to photocopy the match scorecard when I learned of Miller's connection with the ball from Wynne-Thomas.

"Yes, I contacted her last year," I told Hassan, "to confirm that she was the person who had sold the ball at Christie's."

"Right. Garry wouldn't like it if you talked to Jose."

"Pardon?"

"Garry wouldn't like it if you talked to Jose about the ball."

"Why not?"

"She's been ill recently and it would only upset her. Garry wouldn't like it."

"Oh. Well…I don't need to speak to her again."

And with that, the conversation rather abruptly ended. It left me scratching my head a little and I later mentioned it in passing to a couple of friends before returning to writing the book. But as I continued collecting material for later chapters – including one covering the whereabouts of the players, umpires, bat and ball – I became intrigued by, and then suspicious about, the authenticity of the ball sold at Christie's in 2006. I came across an *Independent on Sunday* article written by Andrew Tong just over two weeks after the auction which raised doubts about the ball's provenance: it was made by Duke & Son but Glamorgan only used Stuart Surridge balls at that time. Peter Walker was quoted as saying he thought the ball was "phoney" and Nash claimed that he'd bowled only one ball during the over and that was a Surridge. Peter later told me that he'd spoken to Christie's on the telephone before the auction to express his concern but it appeared that his view had been ignored in favour of a signed Sobers certificate of provenance. I then read a BBC News online report of the auction which revealed that according to the Christie's lot notes, the ball was the last of three used in the over – the first two having been hit into the crowd and reportedly returned to the umpires.

In early May, I rang Nash in California to record my main interview for the book. He was adamant that only one ball had been used during the over and cited the BBC Cymru Wales footage of the feat which showed the same one coming back to him after every six. He also confirmed the Stuart Surridge connection. Glamorgan had used only Surridge balls – rather than Duke or any other make – because the county's scorer, Bill Edwards, through his own sports shop near St Helen's, had a suppliers' contract with the equipment company run by the former Surrey captain, Stuart Surridge. Another Glamorgan opening bowler who played in the Six Sixes match, Tony Cordle, told me exactly the same thing when I contacted him at his home in Canada.

I then had a rather strange conversation with Glamorgan's archivist, Dr Andrew Hignell, who was providing some photographs for my book. In conjunction with Peter Walker, he had also given me vital information about the 1967 law change which had enabled Sobers to make history in Swansea. The experimental rule meant that if any part of a fielder's body went over the boundary while "making the catch and afterwards" then it was not out. As a result, when Roger Davis 'caught' the fifth six and tumbled over the rope at St Helen's, the umpire eventually awarded a six. Hignell had also supplied me with a newspaper cutting about the 30 minutes which former Welsh football international Trevor Ford had spent fielding during Nottinghamshire's first innings because of an injury to Ossie Wheatley. I'd already found the article myself but it was nice of him to think of me. We'd always had a good working relationship and I'd written a chapter about his role as archivist, scorer and webmaster in *Daffodil Days: Glamorgan's Glorious Summer*, the official celebration of the county's 1997 county championship win. In 2008, Hignell told me that he'd been invited to London by Christie's before the auction of the ball but, after revealing details of the meeting, he then resolutely refused to allow me to include any of them in the book – other than his verification of the match details when he'd been shown the ball. I was at a loss to understand his attitude – why was he being so secretive? – but because his role was such an important part of the Christie's authentication process which I needed to refer to in the book, I agreed to his request by including two factual sentences.

By the early part of June, my writing was going well but I was still looking for some more Glamorgan photos circa 1968. So I asked the players who'd taken part in the Six Sixes match to bring any individual memorabilia to their annual reunion lunch being held at the SWALEC Stadium in Cardiff. As my son, Tom, a keen photographer, whizzed around the room taking pictures of players for the book's 'then and now' section, Brian Lewis handed me an envelope. In doing so, the former off-spinner inadvertently bowled the delivery that would sneak through the defence of anyone who had claimed that the ball sold by Christie's was the real thing.

When I opened the envelope later at home, I found, among Brian's handful of photos, a Glamorgan members newsletter from December 1968 which contained a review of the previous season. Under the headline "A World Record clutch of Sixes", the tale of the feat and the ball's return to St Helen's was re-told. Beneath a photograph of Wilf "Mr Glamorgan" Wooller standing alongside Sobers and Richard Lewis, the 17-year-old schoolboy who found the ball in St Helen's Avenue where the last six had landed, I came across this crucial sentence in the report:

> Glamorgan presented this ball, which was made at the firm of Stuart Surridge, the former Surrey captain, to Nottingham to reside in a place of honour in their Sporting Museum.

Four months after Sobers had made history, a contemporaneous report on his achievement had confirmed what the former Glamorgan players had been saying all along: the Christie's ball cannot have been genuine because it was the wrong make.

Anecdotal rather than documentary evidence would surface later in June. Ten days after the ex-players' lunch, the Cardiff Institute for the Blind held a special 40th anniversary Six Sixes dinner – again at the SWALEC Stadium. Sobers was guest of honour. Some of his former Nottinghamshire team-mates, including Basharat Hassan, attended and Peter Walker was asked to interview Sobers and then chair a question-and-answer session with him. A few days before the event, Walker attended a briefing with the organisers where he was specifically told not to mention the ball while speaking to Sobers. As an experienced broadcaster, he wasn't happy – "it was none of their business what I was going to say to Garry" – and, putting two and two together, I immediately recalled my telephone conversation with Hassan the previous March. I began to ask myself one or two questions. Why had he taken the trouble to ring me out of the blue? What was the point of his mentioning Sobers during the conversation? Why would Sobers have been so concerned about Jose Miller becoming upset if I'd spoken to her about the ball? Suddenly, a conversation which, at the time, I'd found a little baffling now appeared a lot less so. In retrospect, I realised that Hassan, not very subtly, had been warning me off talking to Miller. My not unreasonable inference was that by using Sobers' considerable standing in the game to emphasise his point, Hassan had, in effect, been saying to me: 'If you don't want to upset the world's greatest all-rounder, then don't speak to this woman about the ball.' But why? What lay behind his phone call to me and the later instruction to Peter Walker? I wasn't invited to the Six Sixes dinner but I went to the ground beforehand to interview one of the guests, Herschelle

Gibbs, the then Glamorgan and South African batsman who had joined the 'Six Sixes Club' during a World Cup match against Holland in 2007. The next day, Peter told me that, following the briefing, he'd arranged for a friend to raise the subject of the ball a little way into the Q & A session. But instead of waiting until a couple of questions had been answered, the friend had stuck his hand up and asked about the ball straightaway. Although Peter recalled that Hassan hadn't looked too pleased, he said Sobers had quite happily explained the story involving John Gough, Jose Miller and Christie's before moving on to the next question.

Richard Lewis was another of the invited dinner guests and, four days later, I decided to ring him as I searched for another piece of valuable evidence. Since 1974, he'd been teaching history and politics at Bourneville School in Birmingham and was thrilled to meet – and be photographed with – one of his cricketing heroes 40 years after they'd last met. We discussed the dinner and the famous day before I raised the subject of the souvenir or replacement ball which Glamorgan had given him as a thank-you present for returning the actual one used in the over. He said it had been reserved a special place on his mantelpiece, alongside the picture taken with Sobers at St Helen's in 1968. I asked him if he would mind bringing the ball to the phone and then, when he was holding it in his hand 30 seconds later, I popped the question:

"Could you just tell me what make the ball is please Richard?"

"It's a Stuart Surridge."

I was now faced with a dilemma. As a journalist, my sole concern was finding out the truth. Because I considered *Six of the Best* to be the definitive record of one of sport's most iconic moments, I had meticulously pieced together Nottinghamshire's first innings, ball by ball and run by run, to make sure it was 100 per cent correct. Accuracy had always been my guiding watchword. As a huge cricket fan, Garry Sobers had been a hero of mine ever since I'd seen him play for the West Indies against England in 1966 on a school day trip to Trent Bridge. He was renowned for his honesty – he was a walker and proud of it – so could one of the world's legendary cricketers actually be involved in the controversy surrounding the ball's sale? I re-examined the facts. On the one hand, Sobers had signed the certificate of provenance. It was there for all to see. On the other, the evidence suggesting that something wasn't quite right was pretty overwhelming. The ball wasn't the correct make, it was the only one bowled in the over – and not the last of three as claimed by Christie's – and, although I didn't want to believe it, there was more than a hint of suspicion about the circumstances in which the ball had been sold. A few more questions came to mind: could Sobers really have been expected to know the make of the ball he'd smashed around St Helen's 38 years earlier? Was I prepared to tarnish the reputation of cricket's greatest ever player or should I sweep all the evidence under the covers and opt for a quiet life? As I sat down to write 'Forty Years On', the book's "whatever happened to?" chapter, I did so with a heavy heart.

In the end, I decided to follow my journalistic instincts and simply report the facts as I'd uncovered them. I would leave it to the readers to draw their own conclusions. So the chapter ended with a series of straightforward statements – ranging from the pre-auction disquiet to the Richard Lewis revelation. Not surprisingly, my concern over the ball's authenticity provided the *Nottingham Evening Post* with a front-page story when the paper serialised the book in late August 2008.

Under the headline "It cost £26K but is this the real Six Sixes ball?", the report detailed my doubts and carried denials from both Miller and Sobers. "I can assure you 150% that this was the ball," declared the former Nottinghamshire Supporters' Association secretary. When Sobers was asked by the paper's reporter if he could remember the brand of the ball he'd given to John Gough, he replied: "How can I? That was 40 years ago. I never saw it until two years ago when she brought it." Presumably, that was about the time he'd signed a certificate of provenance stating that the ball had been bowled during the Six Sixes over. In response to my revelations, a spokeswoman for Christie's said the auction house made every effort to "thoroughly examine and research every object that is sold. This is the first time we have heard of the matter and we will take the necessary action that we deem appropriate in the circumstances." She obviously wasn't aware of the concerns about the ball's make raised by Peter Walker before it was auctioned in 2006. The exact details of whatever "necessary action" Christie's deemed appropriate have not yet been revealed.

On the day the story broke, I had just delivered some copies of *Six of the Best* to John Ellison, the Trent Bridge club shop manager, when Basharat Hassan was back on the phone. I wasn't surprised to hear that, after reading that evening's *Post*, he was very annoyed about a small section of the Forty Years On chapter – one of the most carefully crafted sentences I'd ever written:

> In 2006, the ball was passed to Christie's in London via Garry
> Sobers' agent, Basharat Hassan, a former Nottinghamshire player
> who now runs an events promotion company.

Hassan had arrived in Nottingham from Nairobi and made his county debut as a batsman in 1966. He was unfortunate in having to sit out the 1968 season when the qualification rules for overseas cricketers were finally relaxed. In an attempt to revive a moribund county championship, each side was now allowed to field two such players: one had to serve a two-year qualification period but the other could be registered straightaway. As West Indies wicket-keeper Deryck Murray had completed his qualification by residence, his newly-arrived fellow countryman Sobers immediately became Nottinghamshire's second overseas player and Hassan, as a less established Kenyan, was forced to drop to the seconds. But he went on to carve out a respectable career – scoring 1,000 runs in a season five times and hitting 15 centuries – including a highest score of 182 not out. Hassan was a genuine all-rounder – bowling right-arm medium-pace – and an outstanding close fielder who, at times, also kept wicket. He won his county cap in 1970 and, almost as a reward for services to the game, was chosen as twelfth man for England when the Australians played at Trent Bridge in 1985 – the year he retired. He had a spell as a first-class umpire and then spent a decade working in the commercial department at Trent Bridge before setting up Basher Promotions, a company specialising in corporate hospitality, event management and after-dinner speakers, from his home not far from his former stamping ground. Good-natured and gregarious, Hassan can still be seen around Trent Bridge – either in his role as a general committee member or trying to promote the occasional golf day or dinner. He's also chairman of the Trent Bridge Taverners, a director of the Nottinghamshire Cricket Board and the current president of the Nottinghamshire Premier League.

My aim in giving Hassan his only mention in *Six of the Best* was simple: I wanted to publically link him to the sale of the ball. In an initially heated phone conversation about my single sentence in the book, Hassan denied playing any part in the ball's arrival at Christie's – until I pointed out that he must have been involved in the process because, as Sobers' agent, he'd arranged for the certificate of provenance to be signed, sealed and then delivered. He reluctantly agreed and I politely suggested he should read the book as a whole and then contact me if he was still unhappy. He didn't.

But I did have another conversation with Hassan during the late summer of 2008. Again, it was on the phone but, this time, it had nothing to do with the book's revelations. He wanted to know if I still had a copy of the contract I'd drawn up to enable Peter Walker and I to interview Sobers at St Helen's in 2006. He'd apparently lost his and just wanted to check a couple of things so I agreed to dig out the original and send him a photocopy. After putting down the receiver, I started to wonder why Hassan had rung. Might it have something to do with the fee paid to Sobers? To refresh my memory, I quickly found the contract of employment which Hassan had signed on his client's behalf two years earlier. It revealed that Sobers had been engaged to provide material for use in "video format or book form at an unspecified date in the future". The £500 cash fee – split 50/50 between myself and Peter Walker – was a "full and final settlement on the terms and conditions" of the agreement. I'd deliberately included that clause in the contract because, apart from the initial interview, no other input from Sobers in the *Six of the Best* project was required. As the main man, his recollections of the event were obviously crucial but I knew the book was going to be much more than that – in fact, it would be focusing on the effect his feat had had on those people who'd witnessed it, especially Malcolm Nash. I was happy to pay Sobers for his memories but the fee was a one-off: there would be no further payment. I sent a photocopy of the contract to Hassan and, again, I heard nothing more from him.

I can't deny that I was disappointed by the lack of interest shown in my revelations about the ball's authenticity by the national cricket press corps – whether they worked in the print, broadcast or internet sections of the media. All the major movers and shakers had received a complimentary copy of the book yet only one had mentioned the Christie's sale. In his column in the *Independent*, Brian Viner noted that I'd talked to all the major protagonists – "as well as an impressive number of the minor ones, but the whereabouts of the celebrated ball challenges even his investigative skills." He then summarised the ball-makers disparity and highlighted the 1968 Glamorgan newsletter. In truth, I wasn't really interested in the original Surridge – I just assumed it had disappeared sometime during the extensive redevelopment of Trent Bridge and it would probably never be found. What concerned me was the way in which the Duke ball was unmistakeably masquerading as the Surridge. It was clearly not the Six Sixes ball and it seemed to me that the more mainstream cricket writers had passed up the opportunity to investigate a dispute involving one of the game's most lauded legends and the world's leading auction house – despite the story being handed to them on a plate. Perhaps, like me, they just couldn't entertain the idea of the former West Indian captain with such a formidable reputation for fair play being mixed up in such an unedifying business. I later learned that this attitude wasn't restricted to the nation's cricket writers: many ordinary followers of the game also refused to think the unthinkable about the man who had achieved the unthinkable. But there were quite a few enthusiasts who were prepared to publicise the puzzle – like Douglas Miller who reviewed the book for the Association of Cricket Statisticians and Historians. At the end of his generous article, he wrote that I had "provided convincing evidence to challenge the provenance of the ball purportedly used in the historic over and recently sold at Christie's for £26,400. Whose ball, one might ask, was it to sell in the first place?" Good question – and one that I kept being asked. The controversy was also raised by sportspages.com, a website which specialises in autographed books, *Wisden*s and a wide range of collectable material. Its review included the observation that "a particularly intriguing sub-plot involves doubts over the authenticity of a ball purported to have been used during the over, which was auctioned in London recently for an obscene amount of money." Another good point equally well made. The ball had sold for £26,400 – nearly four times its guide price. In his review for The Cricket Society, John Symons hinted at the controversy by noting that my detailed approach had given the event the "most rounded coverage possible. Even the bat and ball have a history and the ball, in particular, a chequered one at that."

My concerns about the ball's authenticity were also mentioned by Chris Waters in the *Yorkshire Post* and I was heartened by a remark in another review by Mark Whiley in the *Lincolnshire Echo*. After revealing that he'd been born long after Sobers had hung up his bat, he said he'd heard about the Six Sixes but that was about it. He commented on the fortuitous fluke by which the feat had been filmed by BBC Cymru Wales – thanks to the actions of a cricket-mad cameraman in Swansea and an engineer in Cardiff. Even though the *Grandstand* sports programme had gone off the air and no longer required any coverage of the game, the cameraman continued to follow Sobers through a fixed lens and the engineer kept his recording machine running back at base. Whiley then wrote that he was "unaware of the bizarre, almost laughable, story of the ball from the over being sold at auction for thousands of pounds – before it was discovered that the ball in question was most likely not the one used." Forget the "almost"; the word "laughable" beautifully summed things up. What surprised me most was the sheer audacity of the situation: the discrepancy between the balls was so blindingly blatant. It simply beggared belief that a Duke could have been substituted for a Surridge without anybody in the auction world, apparently, noticing.

Five weeks after *Six of the Best* was published, Malcolm Nash was given a second opportunity to vent his spleen, again by the *Nottingham Evening Post*. Having read the paper's coverage of the ball controversy, he contacted the reporter in question, Chris Birkle, by email from his home in America:

> I find it very interesting that nobody from Nottingham CCC, the supporters club, Christie's, the purchaser of the ball or members of the press have bothered to ask me about the facts concerning the

'ball'. Having had it my hands not just for that over but many overs previously, I know what I was bowling with. I should also like to point out that at no time was the ball replaced.

If you are really interested, I am probably the best person in the position of being able to authenticate or refute the ball in question. The event is still very clear in my mind and I have talked about the over annually for 40 years. Please contact me and I will do my best to solve some of the mystery that surrounds this story.

In another prominent article, this time written by Marcus Boocock, Nash made it clear that the ball sold at Christie's wasn't "the right one" because it was the wrong make. "Whenever we played at home," he said, "we used a Surridge ball. People believe this is the real ball but there is no possibility that it is." In response to his accusations, Christie's this time declined to comment but did cite the signed certificate of provenance as evidence of authenticity and the paper repeated the earlier protestations of innocence by both Miller and Sobers. Following the initial burst of publicity, mainly in Nottinghamshire and South Wales, I decided to contact *Private Eye*, the satirical magazine which delights and specialises in exposing less than honourable behaviour. As usual, Lord Gnome pulled no punches. Under the headline "Christie's and a lot of balls", their report in October 2008 colourfully re-told the story before declaring that the Duke was "almost certainly bogus."

I was elated when *Six of the Best* was later nominated for the 2009 MCC/Cricket Society Book of the Year and just as deflated when, despite a raft of very favourable reviews, it failed to make the final short list. The blow was softened by the incredibly enthusiastic reception I received from those cricket fans who bought the book and its continuing steady sales. I really appreciated an unofficial note of commiseration from John Symons who expressed his surprise at *Six of the Best*'s omission from The Cricket Society's shortlist. "Don't let it deter you from continuing to write on cricket" he wrote. Although I had no more book ideas in the pipeline, I must admit to thinking that, because of the ball controversy, there remained some unfinished business with the Six Sixes saga. I felt a little like the not out batsman who's in sight of a century when bad light stops play. Sobers may have declared the Nottinghamshire innings closed on that hot August Bank Holiday Saturday in 1968 but I sensed that one or two of us, at some future date, might be batting on. Or to paraphrase one of sport's most memorable sayings: "They think it's all over – but it isn't."

And that's where the matter rested until April 2012 when John Parkin, the non-striking Nottinghamshire batsman during the Sobers onslaught, rang me. Had I heard? The Six Sixes ball was up for sale again – this time at Bonhams in Chester rather than Christie's in London. John had become a good friend since *Six of the Best*'s publication by agreeing to accompany me on a speaking tour of cricket societies around Britain. I would give a short talk, play part of a BBC radio programme I'd made about the Six Sixes and then interview John as the man standing at the other end during the over. His memories of the day proved the highlight of a number of extremely enjoyable evenings as we travelled around the country – from Leicester to Liverpool, Sheffield to Southport and Chelmsford to Cleethorpes, as well as up to Glasgow and Edinburgh. Sometimes, my star guest would be Roger Davis, who'd explain his key part in the historic over by recalling how he fell over the boundary clutching the fifth six. Whoever accompanied me, the question of the actual ball's whereabouts would always be raised and I relished the opportunity to express my disquiet. The revelations about the ball's make, the Christie's lot notes and the 1968 Glamorgan newsletter – not to mention the thoughts of Malcolm Nash – inevitably proved intriguing to our knowledgeable and attentive audiences. John's phone call proved the catalyst for what would become Operation Howzat? To return to an earlier cricketing analogy, I was now that not out batsman waiting to resume his innings. As the clouds parted and the sun came out, I strapped on my pads, picked up my bat and gloves and made my way out to the middle. A regular flow of runs, in the form of evidence, had kept the scoreboard ticking over and a ton – perhaps more – was now there for the taking. I sensed that a particularly sticky wicket was about to start turning and the ball would be moving around all over the place. Flight and guile, perhaps some reverse swing and the odd bouncer or two were all likely to figure in the opposition's attack but with my defence bordering on the Boycottesque, I was confident of eventually amassing a competitive total, before, as captain, declaring the innings closed. And I was quite content to be bowling last; wickets would start tumbling on a strip that was crumbling.

I knew the Duke wasn't the right ball otherwise it would have been a Surridge; it was a 'wrong 'un', in effect, a 'no-ball'. But was it the one being sold by Bonhams? Not long after John Parkin's phone call, I received a national newspaper cutting about the impending sale in the post from Bill Tansell, a member of the Worcestershire Cricket Society. "Can it be the ball or not?" he asked in an accompanying note. I didn't know – but I would certainly try to find out. If it was, then it was time to unmask the imposter.

Let the buyer beware

Auctions and controversy do seem to go together. In November, Christie's auctioned what was definitely a cricket ball. It was said to be the one that Garry Sobers clobbered for the last of his six sixes in an over at Swansea in 1968. But how do we know it was that ball?

David Rayvern Allen, Wisden Cricketer's Alamanck 2007

Although most media reports suggested that the Duke & Son ball being auctioned by Bonhams was the same one sold at Christie's in 2006, I needed confirmation. My first port of call was the company's website which revealed that full details of the lots would be available about a month before the sporting memorabilia sale was held on 29th May. In the meantime, I decided to leave nothing to chance. Although I was supremely confident of my case, I felt it was important to go back to basics and re-check my source material: the Christie's lot notes, the BBC TV footage, newspaper reports of the day and interviews with some of the key players carried out 40 years after the event. I was also on the look-out for any new evidence but I decided to start by re-examining the three-ball theory. The Christie's catalogue had – with the air of authority associated with the world's leading auction house – unequivocally spelt out the situation:

> Three separate balls were used in the over. The first two balls were hit into the stands and allegedly returned to the umpires. The third ball was used throughout the rest of the over and was hit out of the ground for Sobers' last triumphant six.

But as I trawled through my material again, I could find no mention of more than one ball being used – either in the newspapers or the 1969 edition of *Wisden* or a number of books about Sobers, two of them autobiographies. The national and local press coverage at the time naturally revolved around the feat itself and the subsequent return of the ball to Nottingham. As I moved from the *Observer* to the *Daily Telegraph* and from the *Western Mail* to the *Nottingham Evening Post*, I kept drawing a blank: one over, six sixes but only one ball. Two months after the event, an article in the *Playfair Cricket Monthly* magazine declared that the ball would be given "pride of place" at Trent Bridge while the 1969 *Wisden* report of game referred to the first two sixes being "slashed out of the ground and when the last six landed in the street outside, it was not recovered until the next day." Neither publication made any reference to three balls being used in the over. An extremely detailed account of the event was included in the 1969 Glamorgan yearbook – complete with a diagram showing where each ball had disappeared to. Again, I searched in vain for any acknowledgement of more than one ball being bowled by Malcolm Nash. In his book, *Sir Gary: A Biography*, Trevor Bailey included a section on the historic over by recalling that Sobers "simply hit each ball on the rise into various sections of the delighted crowd, who had never seen such a burst of controlled hitting before and are never likely to see it again" but made no suggestion that Nash had bowled three balls.

All these accounts had come from journalists and writers but what about the man himself? Some cricketers enjoy sufficiently successful careers to warrant one autobiography – not too many are able to draw on enough material for two. But then, as the world knows, Sobers was no ordinary cricketer. As my research continued, I reckoned, quite reasonably I think, that such a significant moment in such an historic event – i.e. the replacement of the original Six Sixes ball – would have been included somewhere in the Garry Sobers life story. Despite his later ambivalence to the feat, surely it would merit a mention – however brief and passing? The over featured prominently in both *Sobers: Twenty Years at the Top*, written with Brian Scovell in 1988, and 2000's *My Autobiography*. As I leafed through the respective chapters, "Lost Ball in Swansea" and "Six of the Best", I read how Sobers recalled his approach to the famous over as he eyed up the short boundary on the Gorse Lane side of the St Helen's ground. He revealed that he was only interested in quick runs and a declaration and his intention was "to swing so hard at each ball that even a mishit would clear the rope." After describing the first four sixes, Sobers explained that he'd then decided to "give it a go" and aim for the complete set. He referred to the controversy surrounding the fifth six which was 'caught' by Roger Davis just before he'd tumbled over the boundary and revealed that he'd known that Nash would bowl a quicker ball to finish off the over. As a result, Sobers said he was waiting for the final, short-pitched delivery and the rest was history – quite literally – as the ball went, in BBC Cymru Wales TV commentator Wilf Wooller's immortal words, "way down to Swansea!" Sobers accepted that he'd been on course to complete the season's fastest hundred but, with no interest in personal records, had decided to declare instead. He later confirmed that the ball was found by a young boy – "battered and torn, still rolling down the street" – before being taken to Trent Bridge. So, in summary, Sobers had provided a pretty comprehensive account of the Six Sixes in both his autobiographies but, for some reason, had not mentioned that three balls rather than just one had been used in the over.

So much for the man at the centre of the drama. What about some of the other players who'd taken part in the match and written their autobiographies? I wondered if one of them had included the use of three balls in their recollections of the over. The Glamorgan captain on the day, Tony Lewis, has produced two accounts of his career, *Playing Days* in 1985 and *Taking Fresh Guard* in 2003. Not surprisingly, the Six Sixes featured in both with Lewis, in *Playing Days*, describing Sobers as "furious" when he came down the long flight of steps to the St Helen's square because of the slow run rate. "A benign Sobers is not an animal to taunt," he wrote, "and a mad Sobers is a species to be avoided." Lewis, fielding at mid-off, said he was left with "images of the ball being blitzed with a coil of the body and lash of the bat to all directions" but the need for a second or third ball wasn't referred to in either of his books. Fielding at mid-on, Peter Walker was the closest Glamorgan player to Nash and during the penultimate over of the afternoon session, had been hit by Sobers for 15 runs – including the only other six in the Nottinghamshire captain's innings. In his 2006 autobiography, *It's Not Just Cricket*, Walker gave an amusing account of the event but, again, didn't allude to more than one ball being used in the over.

The Glamorgan v Nottinghamshire game at St Helen's in 1968 was included in *The Daily Telegraph's Century of County Cricket: The 100 Best Matches*, published in 1990. The report of the first day's play said Sobers hit Nash "for six sixes in one over, three of them out of the ground" but there was no reference to more than a single ball being used. Following the auction of the Duke ball for £26,400 by Christie's in November 2006, the *Sunday Times* ran a feature on the over in its "Caught in Time" series. The last six and the ball's discovery in St Helen's Avenue was included in the first paragraph but during a detailed analysis of the over, no mention was made of any other balls being involved. Finally, I turned to the official programme for the special 40th anniversary Six Sixes dinner which was organised by the Cardiff Institute for the Blind in Cardiff in June 2008. After the order of events and the menu – a mixture of Welsh and West Indian, including lamb rump steak and Caribbean bread and butter pudding with a rum sauce – the programme included a two-page account of the over which contained no reference to more than one ball being bowled.

I then listened again to the interviews that Peter Walker and I had conducted with Malcolm Nash and Tony Cordle for a BBC Radio Wales documentary about the famous over in 2008. Both the former Glamorgan opening bowlers had repeated their initial claims which were included in my book that one ball was used and it had been made by Stuart Surridge. I re-visited the BBC Cymru Wales television interview Nash and Sobers had done with reporter Brian Hoey immediately after the Six Sixes match in 1968. After introducing them as "the vanquished and the victor", Hoey closely questioned the pair about the over and mentioned the controversial fifth six but not the number of balls bowled by Nash. It was while I was viewing our day's filming with Sobers at St Helen's in 2006 that I made the most startling and significant of discoveries. I happened to light upon a conversation between Sobers and Roger Davis as they stood near the spot where the Glamorgan fielder had fallen over the boundary rope while clutching the fifth six. They were being recorded as our cameraman collected some cutaway shots – general views of the pair talking and the St Helen's ground for editing purposes – and their discussion ranged across a variety of subjects: former Glamorgan players, the Six Sixes over and the whereabouts of the ball used. Sobers explained that he'd given it to John Gough, the then secretary of the Nottinghamshire Supporters' Association, in 1968 and revealed that Gough's successor, a "young lady", was currently trying to auction it. Towards the end of their chat, this exchange took place:

RD: So there must have been two or three balls used in that over, mustn't there? Or was it the same ball?

GS: The same ball.

RD: The same ball came back all the time?

GS: The same ball – except the last one. A little boy brought it back three days later. He said he found it rolling. (Laughter all round)

For me, it was no laughing matter but a defining moment. I played back the conversation to make sure I wasn't hearing things. Six months after his revelation to Davis at St Helen's, Sobers had put his name to a certificate of provenance stating "that this signed cricket ball was bowled during the over in which I [Sobers] hit six sixes off Malcolm Nash." In doing so, he had been party to a categorical and unequivocal assertion in the Christie's lot notes that three balls had been used. Yet the BBC footage – and now Sobers himself – had confirmed that just one ball had been bowled. I felt distinctly uneasy as I returned to the lot notes to re-visit the question of the sold ball's manufacturer:

> No records of the ball suppliers exist from the match. However, Duke & Sons were supplying balls to Glamorgan County Cricket Club during this period.

While the first part of that statement might have been true – why should any such records still exist? – the second half seemed highly dubious so I resolved to examine the Stuart Surridge connection in greater detail by contacting the former Surrey captain's son and Bill Edwards' widow. Both Stuart "Tiger" Surridge, who'd helped his father run the family firm, and Elizabeth Edwards explained the strong link between the two families – a fact confirmed by an obituary written by Glamorgan's archivist and scorer, Andrew Hignell, following Edwards' death in 2009 which I found on the cricket club's website:

> By this time he had built up a good friendship with Surrey captain Stuart Surridge, and it was Bill who acted as Surridge's agent in Wales, selling a wide range of the company's products, both to club cricketers and Glamorgan Cricket, who always used Surridge balls when they played their games at St Helen's.

Not much room for doubt there then. The business relationship between the Stuart Surridge company and Glamorgan was also corroborated by an advert which I discovered on the inside page of the cricket club's 1968 yearbook:

BILL EDWARDS

THE COUNTY SPORTS SHOP
59a KING EDWARD ROAD
SWANSEA
Suppliers to Glamorgan County Cricket Club

BATS AUTOGRAPHED BY
**Gilbert Parkhouse, Peter May, Ken Barrington, Tony Lewis,
Alan Jones, and other world-famous players**

* Stockists of the famous **"Perfect"**, **"Coil Spring"** and **Peter May
"Test" Selection** Cricket Bats and the entire range of Stuart Surridge
sports equipment, including the **David Evans** Wicket-keeping gloves.

So the confident claim in the Christie's catalogue that Duke & Son had been supplying balls to Glamorgan at the time was simply not true. "The entire range of Stuart Surridge sports equipment" meant everything – including bats, gloves and, crucially in this case, balls. When I then returned to the Christie's lot notes, I came across a little phrase which I hadn't spotted before – towards the end of a section about the final delivery and the ball's last known movements in Swansea:

> From studying video footage…it seems the ball was hit out of the ground…

This was the first time I'd been aware of the TV recording of the event being used during the Christie's verification process. Surely, I reasoned to myself, if someone from the auction house had studied the BBC Cymru Wales footage, they would have seen the first two balls being returned to Nash? The notes claimed they were "allegedly" returned to the umpires but, from what I could remember of my forensic analysis of the event while writing *Six of the Best*, the word "actually" should have been used. It's claimed that the camera never lies but I wondered, in this particular instance, if it had? To make sure my imagination wasn't playing tricks on me, I put on the DVD of the Six Sixes and sat back to watch the over for the umpteenth time. I needn't have worried – it was as plain as day. The footage confirmed that three sixes were smashed out of St Helen's during the over but only one ball was used. The first two deliveries had been hit, not as stated by Christie's, "into the stands" but right out of the ground. After the first six, Wilf Wooller had remarked when referring to Sobers:

> He's smiling all over his face. The ball's been returned…

Nash is then seen picking it up and coming back to bowl the second ball of the over. After the next six, the footage clearly shows the ball being thrown back from the other side of the Gorse Lane wall at St Helen's – over the heads of the spectators – within seconds and, as it bounces onto the field of play, Glamorgan's Brian Lewis goes to pick it up. Nash himself has come to the edge of the square to collect it and is seen walking back to his mark to bowl the third ball. There is no footage of any replacement balls being chosen by the umpires in consultation with the captains following the alleged disappearance of the first two balls. There was no doubt about it: one ball – and only one – had been bowled by Nash. I started to ask myself a series of questions. Just what was going on here? How could the return of the first two balls have been completely ignored by the writer of the lot notes? Just how thorough had Christie's been in carrying out what, in legal jargon, would have been "due diligence" on the ball before it was auctioned? How could a Duke have been mistaken for a Surridge? It seemed to me that fundamental questions about the actual ball's make and the number of balls used in the over just hadn't been asked – and if they had, then they hadn't been answered properly. If Christie's had followed their stated procedure to "thoroughly examine and research every object that is sold", then surely the sale would have been aborted? The devil – not to mention the truth – was indeed in the detail. As a result of all my research, I was now convinced that only one ball was bowled by Malcolm Nash to Garry Sobers in 1968 and it was made not by Duke & Son but by Stuart Surridge.

Towards the end of April, I began logging onto the Bonhams' webpage on a daily basis. A week of anxious anticipation passed before I clicked onto their site on Tuesday 1st May to discover that the catalogue for the sporting memorabilia auction had at last been printed and was also available online. Two crucial questions remained: would the ball's lot entry rely at all on the erroneous Christie's catalogue notes and, more importantly perhaps, would potential buyers be referred to the 2006 sale if they wanted to examine the item's provenance? If the answer to both these questions was negative then my attempt to have the ball effectively declared null and void would fall at the first hurdle: there would be nothing to link the Bonhams' sale with the Christie's one. I scrolled down the lot 32 entry. Along with a description of the Duke ball, it included the signed certificate of provenance and a detailed diagram showing the line each ball had taken after being hit. The estimated value was put at £20,000–£25,000 and there followed a brief summary of the 1968 event, shorter than the Christie's version, and containing no reference to the number of balls used. I was just beginning to despair when a single line right at the bottom of the lot entry caught my eye:

Provenance: Christie's sale 4101 lot 173

Bonhams were indeed relying on the 2006 sale and that single referral meant that anyone interested in checking the ball's authenticity would have to consult the Christie's lot notes. Because they were riddled with inaccuracies, I would now be able to use my existing material to try to persuade Bonhams to withdraw the ball. Armed with my mountain of evidence, I felt ready for action: as coiled as one of the springs in those Peter May cricket bats being sold by Bill Edwards in The County Sports Shop in 1968. I'd reached my hundred – time to declare. Operation Howzat? was up and running.

The next day, I wrote to Christopher Hayes, the sports memorabilia expert at Bonhams, to voice my concerns. The letter was sent by recorded delivery and I confirmed online that it had arrived in Chester. When his emailed reply pinged into my inbox almost a week later, it was clear I was being fobbed off. He'd noted my comments, pointed out that the number of balls used in the over hadn't been mentioned in the Bonhams catalogue and expressed his satisfaction with the item's provenance – which he described as "very good." But Hayes did say he would pass on my concerns to the company's sports consultant, Dan Davies, when he returned to the office four days before the auction was due to be held.

I was very disappointed and intensely irritated by this reply so I decided to aim a little higher than the boys in the backroom. Although I generally like to give people the benefit of the doubt, I felt, in this particular instance, that Hayes had dismissed my case a little too easily. My evidence was impressive yet his perfunctory response appeared to suggest that he hadn't given it even the most cursory of glances. I simply couldn't afford to wait around for Dan Davies to become involved on his return to work. Via the Bonhams website, I identified the saleroom director at Chester as Alexander Clement – as well as three of the company's top brass in London. Four days later, I sent an email to Clement. It was similar to my original letter to Hayes but this time I attached some evidence: the 1968 Glamorgan newsletter, the unchallenged extract from *Six of the Best* questioning the ball's authenticity and three articles about the book and ball from the *Nottingham Evening Post*. I mentioned my more recent research involving the Surridge and Edwards' families and my determination to protect my reputation as a journalist. After repeating my willingness to share all the evidence, I noted that Bonhams prided themselves on being the only international auction house to hold dedicated sporting auctions. I concluded by explaining that I was very keen to prevent a second controversial sale of the ball taking place, so if Bonhams didn't take action, then I would:

> If this matter is not addressed satisfactorily within the next 48 hours,
> I will have no alternative but to make my concerns public.

I also sent a copy of the email to Bonhams' chairman, Robert Brooks, their UK chief executive officer, Malcolm Girling, and their chief financial officer, Hugh Watchorn – and then waited. I heard nothing during that afternoon or the next morning but then, about 24 hours after sending the email, Alexander Clement rang me to say they were "extremely grateful" for my getting in touch about the ball. He acknowledged the particular importance of the Glamorgan newsletter and we then arranged for me to visit Chester four days later.

The meeting went very well in that I was allowed to present all my evidence in an ordered and orderly fashion – punctuated by a series of pertinent questions from Clement, a self-confessed non-cricket fan. We discussed the wording of the certificate of provenance – he noted that it didn't say 'it is the ball that was hit for six' – and the origins of the incorrect information in the lot notes. He asked about the make of balls that Nottinghamshire would have brought with them to St Helen's, the umpires – I explained they'd both died in 1990s – and the procedure for choosing the match balls after the captains had tossed up. I told him the story of the last six being hit out of the ground and Richard Lewis finding the actual ball before returning it to St Helen's two days later. I mentioned the make of Lewis' thank-you present ball from Glamorgan, we examined a copy of the club's 1968 newsletter and I then showed him the Bill Edwards sports shop advert from the same year's club yearbook. My flow of evidence was then politely interrupted when Clement asked me a couple of questions as "an outsider not familiar with cricket." Because Nottingham were playing at St Helen's, he raised the possibility of one of their balls, stamped "Duke & Son, Nottingham", finding its way into the pool of balls being used during the match and being handed to Malcolm Nash. He wondered if it was conceivable that Nash had bowled a Duke ball without realising it? No, I replied. If he'd found himself about to bowl with a Duke, would he have taken it to the umpire and pointed out the discrepancy? Yes, I said – and offered to give him Nash's number in America to confirm my answer. I explained that bowlers were – and still are – very particular about the balls they use and it was their job, rather than the captain's, to choose the ones they wanted to start an innings with. We then watched a DVD of the Six Sixes over on his laptop – noting that the ball came back after the first two – and listened to Peter Walker's BBC Radio Wales interviews with Malcolm Nash and Tony Cordle on CD.

After an hour and a half of diligent examination, Alexander Clement announced that he would be withdrawing the ball from the auction immediately because of what he called my "compelling and conclusive" evidence. He said Bonhams had already received one bid for it and there were other potential buyers who needed to be told of his decision as soon as possible. The announcement would be posted on the company website and by the time I arrived home three hours later, it was indeed there. First wicket down.

Less forthcoming was any public acknowledgment by Bonhams of my role in their decision to withdraw the ball. To be fair to him, Julian Roup, Bonhams' director of press and marketing, had insisted from the outset that the auction house would be making no comment – other than that the ball had been removed from the auction. He said it was company policy not to explain such decisions. But having saved Bonhams what I believed would have been a considerable amount of public embarrassment, I felt very frustrated. I couldn't understand why they weren't prepared to include even a single paragraph in a press release simply thanking me for my part in the ball's withdrawal. So I rang Malcolm Girling in London to discuss the matter and, in a heated exchange of views, Bonhams' UK chief executive officer made it clear that the "no comment" policy was for legal reasons – "in our interests and the interests of the client." When I raised the question of my helping Bonhams to avoid a second controversial auction of the ball, he insisted that "we have no duty of responsibility to you at all – you have an agenda." So much for journalists being seekers after truth and justice…

My next task was to secure some publicity for the first successful part of Operation Howzat? Because of their invaluable support when *Six of the Best* had been published, I thought it only right to give the *Nottingham Evening Post* an exclusive. I also decided to contact Lawrence Booth, the editor of *Wisden*, who also writes a cricket column for the *Daily Mail*. He'd kindly allowed me to use his description of Sobers as "a master of all trades and a jack of none" in *Six of the Best* and I asked him if he thought his paper might be interested in a national exclusive, to run simultaneously with a similar one in the Nottingham paper. The problem was that the *Post* wanted to hang on to the story for almost a week until the start of the Second Test between England and the West Indies at Trent Bridge on Friday 25th May. I was worried about a journalist picking it up from the Bonhams' website because keeping a story under wraps in this internet age is nigh on impossible. Although I understood the paper's reasoning, I would have preferred them to have run it earlier – on the Thursday, perhaps even on the

Wednesday. I was right to be concerned. Lawrence said he'd contact the *Mail*'s sports desk and then texted me an offer of £100. "I'd still be happy to write the story but it's entirely up to you if you're prepared to sanction it for that amount," his message read. I was thinking over the offer when he rang me early the next day and revealed that the *Times* had broken the ball withdrawal story – 48 hours earlier than I'd planned to via the *Nottingham Evening Post* and the *Daily Mail*. Not surprisingly, the *Mail* were now no longer interested. "Collectors believe history of 'Sobers' ball is over the top" read the headline as Julian Roup confirmed that Bonhams had pulled the Duke "for further research." He also explained that "an auction house has to have the history and provenance right. In this case, the provenance has been questioned quite seriously and once that happens, the automatic response is to withdraw." The report also quoted Nottinghamshire's archivist, Peter Wynne-Thomas, who described the latest situation as a "very tangled web." He said "it was thought they replaced a ball during the over when Sobers hit one a long way with the nearest thing. I guess the mystery will go on." Far be it from me to disagree with such an esteemed authority on the game but the TV footage makes it clear precisely what happened during the famous over; the only ongoing mystery now – and I suspect for ever more – is the whereabouts of the actual ball bowled by Malcolm Nash. Following the *Times* scoop, other national newspapers weren't interested in the ball's withdrawal or my part in it but I did manage to arrange a couple of radio interviews and the *Nottingham Evening Post* ran a page-lead story under the headline "Disputed ball is dropped". I was left to rue the view that a week is a long time in journalism as well as in politics. The vagaries of both professions mean that situations do indeed change very quickly.

But my contact with Lawrence Booth proved a fruitful one. On the day before the Trent Bridge Test, I travelled to his hotel in Nottingham to show him my evidence. For over an hour, we looked at the DVD of the over, the interview transcripts and documents such as the 1968 Glamorgan newsletter – as well as the Sobers-Davis conversation at St Helen's which had been caught on camera in 2006. Lawrence then confirmed that he'd like me to write an article about the ball sale for the 150th edition of *Wisden* due to be published in April 2013.

The *Post*'s involvement with the Six Sixes story turned out to be crucial because their enquiries strengthened my belief that something disturbingly suspicious had happened before the sale of the ball. I'd given one of their reporters, Dominic Howell, the contact details of David Convery, Christie's head of sporting memorabilia in 2006, who was now running his own company, Convery Auctions, in Blackburn, about 20 miles from Edinburgh. A self-confessed Celtic fanatic, Convery had been working in the Scottish Art department of Christie's Glasgow branch when their first specialist football auction was held in 1989. It raised about £50,000 but a decade later, that figure had risen to just over £2 million from two major sales a year. On the back of the explosion in the football market – and as collectible items from golf, cricket and tennis started to sell well too – Convery moved with the Christie's sporting memorabilia department to London as business boomed. While researching his background, I was particularly struck by the importance he'd always seemed to attach to the verification process. In one *Herald* newspaper article in 2001 about the local Glasgow boy made good, Convery said the shirt worn by England's captain, Bobby Moore, in the 1966 World Cup Final would be "a great find." He was asked, if it were found, how he would know for sure that it was the genuine article. "There is a lot of detective work involved," replied Convery. "There would be the shirt badge, for a start – and the label. We have contacts at Umbro who keep records and we can check against them. We could also check on the history of the shirt itself. Where it has been kept, who has had it, and how it got there." Convery would follow this exacting and thorough process in 2002 when the second of three shirts worn by Pele against England at the 1970 World Cup was sold by Christie's for a world record £157,750. He even met the owner, Brazilian defender Roberto Rosato, in England, as part of his research. The message was clear: no stone would be left unturned by the world's leading auction house when it came to checking the provenance of any sports-related item offered for sale.

Convery's career at Christie's ended in 2007 when, in the wake of a cost-cutting exercise, their sporting memorabilia and teddy bear departments were closed. The South Kensington saleroom bore the brunt of the redundancies as the result of a feeling that the fun departments were putting off more serious collectors. Sotheby's also closed a similar high-volume, low-value operation at Olympia in 2007 as the economic climate worsened. So Convery returned to his native Scotland to set up Convery Auctions, specialising in "a wide range of sporting memorabilia." As Dominic Howell was writing his story about the ball's withdrawal by Bonhams, I rang him to ask how his enquiries were going. He explained that Jose Miller had, once again, denied any wrongdoing by insisting that "it was the genuine ball – end of story." And what about David Convery? What did he have to say for himself? I nearly fell off my chair when Dominic gave me Convery's response:

> I had nothing to do with the sale of that cricket ball. I worked in a
> completely different side of things.

What? I couldn't believe what I was hearing. How on earth could Convery be denying any involvement with selling the ball when he was head of the sporting memorabilia department at Christie's? I immediately recalled an email I'd received from another journalist, Ed Baker, who was working for the Bournemouth News and Picture Service when *Six of the Best* was published in 2008. He'd expressed an interest in following up the book's authenticity revelations and a quick trawl through my inbox immediately paid off. Dated 6th November 2008, Ed's email read:

> Just to let you know, I spoke to the auctioneer who sold the ball. He
> is David Convery, who now runs his own sports memorabilia
> auction house in Edinburgh. Oddly, I had done a story about him
> selling Beckham's boots just this week.

> I asked him about the ball and, needless to say, claims all was fine;
> letter of provenance, checked with people involved etc etc. He did
> say there was a five year "bring back" clause with the sale. So the
> buyer could return it if he found it was not "right" within five years.

There was certainly something not quite right about Convery's response. Who were the people Christie's had checked with? Two days after speaking to Dominic Howell, I decided to ring Max Dunbar, the chief executive officer of the Manchester Jewish Museum who'd also been working in the Christie's sporting memorabilia department in 2006. He refused to take my call so, through another person in his office, I asked if Convery had sold the ball. "No comment" came the reply from the third party. Curiouser and curiouser...

I then spoke to Mike Scott, an independent television producer who used to run sportspages.com. I'd known him since 2008 when his collectibles website had written a generous review of *Six of the Best* and ordered three copies of the book. Mike had become aware of the growing disquiet about the ball's authenticity within the sporting memorabilia world. His sportspages.com colleague, Giles Lyon, had attended the sale in 2006. Mike kindly sent me the Christie's catalogue for the auction which listed Convery, Dunbar and Rupert Neelands as "specialists." I knew Neelands was the only one of the three still working for Christie's and their website described him variously as "director and head of sale, "books specialist" and "senior specialist and auctioneer."

By this time, I was being assisted by Chris Davies, an independent filmmaker, cricket enthusiast and part-time antiques collector living in Lancaster who had really bought into Operation Howzat? After working as a squash professional – mainly in Germany – he'd become a cabaret juggler and circus entertainer before making a film celebrating the life of his great-grandfather, Eugen Sandow, the bodybuilding icon. Fittingly, in view of his lineage, Chris proved a pillar of support from day one and through a contact in the British Library, he managed to obtain a flyer which had been distributed at the 2006 auction. It directed anyone with any enquiries to Convery through an email address and a telephone number.

When I visited the Convery Auctions website, I was staggered to find no mention of the Six Sixes ball in a long list of notable sales – both during and after Convery's time at Christie's. As well as the Pele shirt, these included:

> * The private treaty sale of The Bobby Moore Collection to West Ham United (July 2000) and the sale of the collection of Sir Geoff Hurst, which set a then world auction record of £91,750 (September 2000) for Sir Geoff's shirt worn during the 1966 World Cup final game.

* Other world auction record prices achieved under David's charge include Alan Ball's 1966 World Cup Winners Medal which sold for £164,800 and his 1966 World Cup Cap which sold for £43,200 and the 1888 F.A. Cup Final ball which sold for £45,000.
* One of the many highlights from David's Christie's career was selling the Football Association Challenge Cup (1896-1910) which sold for a world auction record price of £478,000, the highest price for a piece of football memorabilia sold at auction.
* Other pre-eminent football related property sold recently includes the single-owner collections of Sir Alf Ramsey, Tommy Taylor, Phil Neal, Ray Wilson, Bobby Murdoch and Jimmy Delaney. Other successful sporting sales include the Eagar and Guy Curry Cricket Libraries and the Railing Real Tennis Library.

Again, something wasn't quite right. It just didn't ring true. Why was the sale of the world's most expensive cricket ball not included in Convery's very impressive list of achievements? Surely, if you'd have been in any way involved in this historic auction, you'd have wanted people – and especially potential customers – to know about it via your CV on your website? Although Convery was now claiming he'd had nothing directly to do with the sale, the Six Sixes ball had been sold under his watch, when he was head of the Christie's sporting memorabilia department. It was a huge feather in his cap and, quite inexplicably, he'd now chosen to airbrush it from his career. With all my newly acquired evidence – plus Dunbar's refusal to discuss his former head of department's role in the sale – I found Convery's response to Dominic Howell's enquiries even more perplexing. But dealing with his defiant denial could wait for another day. My next task was to find out more about the Duke ball. Where had it been since being sold at Christie's in 2006 and who had consigned it to Bonhams in 2012?

Stonewalling on a sticky wicket

Falsehood and delusion are allowed in no case whatever: but, as in the exercise of all the virtues, there is an economy of truth. It is a sort of temperance, by which a man speaks truth with measure that he may speak it the longer.

Edmund Burke

There was no doubt about the time, the place or the price. Those undisputed details were all to be found on the Christie's website: 15th November 2006, the South Kensington saleroom and £26,400 – or just under a tenth of the total receipts from the sporting memorabilia auction. But, as I scrolled up and down the relevant page – pausing only briefly to glance in wonderment at the infamous lot notes – I knew that the human flesh to cover the bare bones of this particular transaction would be much harder to find. The one question I needed to answer concerned the identity of the anonymous buyer. Who had paid a world record price for a piece of cricketana that was, quite palpably, not the real thing? Through Giles Lyon, formerly of sportspages.com and now the owner of The Worlds End Bookshop in Chelsea, I'd learned in 2008 that Bernard Shapero, a London antiquarian book dealer, had been the man on the mobile bidding for the ball at Christie's nearly two years earlier. In fact, I'd passed on Shapero's contact details to Marcus Boocock at the *Nottingham Evening Post* in the wake of Malcolm Nash's allegations about the ball's authenticity a month after *Six of the Best*'s publication. After explaining that the ball's new owner lived abroad, the paper had quoted a spokesman for Shapero Rare Books who had outlined their position in unequivocal terms:

> As far as we are concerned, Christie's guaranteed it was 100%
> genuine. Both ourselves and the ball's owner still believe that.

I wondered if Shapero or his client had changed their minds about the provenance of the ball in the intervening four years? How would they react to the news that it had just been withdrawn from the Bonhams sale because it wasn't the genuine article? There was only one way to find out but, before I rang Shapero, I decided to re-establish contact with Giles Lyon who'd attended sale 4101 on behalf of sportspages.com. He recalled the crowded saleroom, the growing anticipation as the auctioneer worked his way towards lot 173 and the sense of unease surrounding the provenance of the Six Sixes ball. He remembered the way in which the bidding war intensified as the staggering hammer price of £22,000 was reached – and the subsequent gasp of astonishment from all those present when the gavel finally came down.

Armed with this first-hand account of the sale, I felt ready to speak to Shapero so, a couple of days after the Bonhams auction – minus the Duke ball – in Chester, I put in a call to the headquarters of Shapero Rare Books in St George Street in Mayfair, directly opposite the back of Sotheby's in Bond Street. On its website, the company was described as an internationally recognised dealer in antiquarian and rare books which specialised in "travel books with an emphasis on Russia and Eastern Europe, natural history and colour plate books, cartography, literature, and Baedeker travel guides." From the outset, Shapero was helpful – in fact, he later became an ally in my search for the Duke ball – but he was also determined to protect his client's identity at all times. As a result, certain relevant facts were held back simply because he didn't want to reveal too much information about the ball's overseas owner. Of course, I understood why – he had a duty of care to his client who'd made it clear he wanted to stay anonymous – but it didn't lessen my frustration. In the first of what turned out to be a series of exasperating phone calls, Shapero confirmed his original purchase of the ball but not the name of his client. In fact, he steadfastly refused to identify him throughout all of our conversations – until I'd finally discovered it through my own devices. In the absence of a name, I decided that the client would from now on be known as "The Mystery Man" while Shapero himself would become "The Book Man." After I'd explained my role in Bonhams' decision to withdraw the Duke ball, Shapero said he hadn't heard about it but he promised to contact his client and get back to me. Over the next month or so, I rang him at least half a dozen times but, on every occasion, Shapero said his client's phone had remained unanswered whenever he'd tried to contact him.

As Operation Howzat? started to pick up speed, I became aware that a peculiar pattern – almost a common denominator – was beginning to emerge: the truth was being obscured either through salient points being skipped over or key facts being omitted. As I dug deeper, I would discover that some of the protagonists either couldn't find or had mislaid certain information, they couldn't remember the exact details of a particular event or, in some cases, they didn't even want to talk to me. At least one of them would prove to be a downright liar. My research had enabled me to produce a treatise of truth about the Six Sixes saga and uncover facts which even the most skilful city lawyer could never refute so I usually had a good idea when I was being lied to. I also noticed that some of the principal players seemed a little uncomfortable, even embarrassed about their role in the whole affair. There was Glamorgan archivist Andrew Hignell's unusual behaviour when I'd first mentioned his 2006 meeting at Christie's, ex-Christie's sports specialist Max Dunbar's refusal to discuss the ball sale on the phone and David Convery's denial of any involvement in it – despite his prominent position as head of sporting memorabilia in South Kensington.

In early June, I re-established contact with Hignell, who's also the club's first X1 scorer, statistician and webmaster. When I rang him on his mobile, he was in Colwyn Bay preparing for Glamorgan's four-day county championship match against Yorkshire. Essentially, I was hoping he would confirm that David Convery had been his point of contact when he'd viewed the ball in London. After explaining my role in the Bonhams withdrawal, I said I was trying to find out more about the way it had been authenticated by Christie's for both my *Wisden* article and this book. At no time during the conversation did Hignell repeat the request for confidentiality that he'd made while I was writing *Six of the Best* and neither of us referred to it. He spoke freely and without conditions as we talked about his trip to London in 2006 and then the possible consignment by Richard Lewis of his Stuart Surridge ball to the new Museum of Welsh Cricket, of which Hignell was curator-elect, in 2012. Lewis had been given the ball in return for bringing back the actual one used in the Six Sixes over in 1968. I'd heard, via Chris Davies, my co-investigator on Operation Howzat? that, soon after the Duke ball had been withdrawn by Bonhams, Lewis had decided to have his Surridge valued by the same auctioneers.

When I mentioned Convery, Hignell said he couldn't remember the name of the Christie's person who he'd dealt with. He and his wife, Debra, had gone into a viewing room to look at the ball and were also shown the certificate of authenticity signed by Sobers. He'd explained that the balls used by Glamorgan in 1968 were made by Stuart Surridge and not Duke & Son and they'd discussed the number of balls bowled by Nash. Hignell told me that Bill Edwards, the late Glamorgan scorer and ball supplier, had often talked about there being three balls used in the over and he said that he'd mentioned his discussions with Edwards to the Christie's contact. He said he could find out who he'd met in London because he had a file on the visit back at the SWALEC Stadium in Cardiff. Hignell also told me that he might be able to identify the contact from some emails of the time. I said I would be in touch the following Monday after Glamorgan's trip to North Wales had ended with their 40-over game against Durham in Colwyn Bay on the Sunday.

I then mentioned the dilemma facing Richard Lewis after he'd asked Bonhams to value his thank-you present from Glamorgan: should he sell the Surridge ball at auction or donate it to Hignell's pride and joy, the Museum of Welsh Cricket, which would be opening in September 2012? Hignell was very enthusiastic about the idea of the ball residing in Cardiff and I asked him how much Glamorgan might be willing to pay for it. He said he'd need to look at the ball first and I offered to act as the go-between. After unsuccessfully trying to contact Hignell by phone on the following Monday and Tuesday, I emailed him with one simple question: who was his contact when he'd gone to Christie's to examine the ball? I asked him if he could look in his file on the meeting and help me out. His reply set me thinking:

> As I mentioned, I have a folder on Sobers' 6 sixes. It doesn't though contain any of my notes from the 2006 meeting up in London. I'll continue looking to see if I can find them and confirmation of the name you require.

I then asked about the emails from the time of the Christie's meeting which Hignell had mentioned during our phone conversation the week before. Again, his reply wasn't particularly promising:

Have deleted them but will look on my other machines at home.

I then decided to nudge his memory by revealing that I knew the sporting memorabilia sale was organised by David Convery and "I suspect he was the person you met." I received no reply and had no further contact with Hignell until I emailed him two months later.

Towards the end of June and in early July, I started to make some progress. Ten days after my trip to Bonhams in Chester, an unfortunate dispute over travel expenses had been amicably settled – thanks to the intervention of Bonhams' press and marketing director, Julian Roup. A month later, I felt my relationship with the auction house was good enough for me to ask for their help with the next part of Operation Howzat? I wanted to track down the person who had consigned the ball to their sporting memorabilia sale – along with an antique bat, signed by, among others, W.G. Grace, C.B. Fry, Ranjitsinhji, A.C. MacLaren and J.B. Hobbs. It had been made by G.G. Hearne sometime between 1890 and 1920 and I suspected it had also been bought by Bernard Shapero on behalf of his mysterious client. Roup suggested I should contact Bonhams' saleroom director at Chester, Alexander Clement, so, whilst acknowledging the importance of client confidentiality, I asked Clement if he'd be prepared to forward my contact details via email to the ball's current owner.

On the same day, I also had a long phone conversation with Richard Lewis who, as a 17-year-old schoolboy, had found the actual ball used in the famous over lying in St Helen's Avenue in Swansea in 1968. Unlike Hignell, Dunbar and Convery, Lewis was very forthcoming. Unlike Shapero, he had no client's identity to protect. He was more than happy to talk about his association with the match and his plans for the unexpected memento he'd acquired as a result of it. Here was a batsman who was fully prepared to play his shots – rather than drop anchor and descend into defensive mode by stonewalling every delivery. Now a semi-retired history and politics teacher in Birmingham, Lewis had consigned his thank-you ball from Glamorgan to the Bonhams saleroom at Knowle in

Warwickshire, not far from his home, soon after the Duke ball was withdrawn in May. Lewis explained that he'd taken it – along with the relevant verification material – to the auction house for safe-keeping and we discussed the possibility, however incredible, of it being stolen and then substituted for the Duke by some unscrupulous person or persons. After all, it was the same make as the actual ball used in the over – a Stuart Surridge – it was from the same era and it had also been signed by Sobers. Lewis wondered if "reputations stand or fall on the authenticity of the Six Sixes ball, there might be people who would want my ball to disappear?" He admitted to feeling under a certain amount of pressure following the Duke ball's withdrawal by Bonhams – all the conjecture about the actual ball's make was "debasing the moment" for him.

Lewis said the ball had been examined by the Bonhams staff at Chester but he'd not been too impressed by their less than enthusiastic response. He didn't feel they appreciated that his ball, "by association", was the closest thing to the actual one. "I'm yet to be convinced that they'll see its true worth," he told me. Lewis said that although his Surridge ball hadn't been involved in the Six Sixes over, it had the same sort of feel and shape as the one he'd found in the street. He clearly remembered Sobers signing the souvenir ball before it was given to him by Glamorgan. He told me that a full valuation would be made by Bonhams in August, its sale was scheduled for late September and we discussed the possibility of his donating the ball to the Museum of Welsh Cricket. For my part, the auction of his ball at that stage was nothing more than a side dish to the main course.

The next day, Bernard Shapero rang. I must admit I was about to draw a line under this particular avenue of enquiry because it seemed to be going nowhere. But his phone call from the Masterpiece Antiques Fair in Chelsea changed all that. Shapero explained that he'd now spoken to his client who had definitely not consigned the ball to Bonhams. He confessed that the ball's original owner had been a little "cryptic" during their phone conversation and when I asked if the ball had been stolen, he replied: "You'll have to draw your own conclusions." Shapero said that after buying the ball, he'd personally given it to his client at a meeting in London

– and that was the last he saw of it. He said they both wanted me to continue my enquiries because they would like their money back. Not for the first time – or the last – a conversation with Shapero left me shaking my head in bewilderment. Like that of his client, his tone was decidedly cryptic. I later emailed him the relevant extract from *Six of the Best* covering my doubts about the ball's authenticity and suggested we should get together to discuss our next move. A face-to-face meeting at Shapero's bibliophilic base in London was now the most urgent item on the Operation Howzat? agenda.

During the first week of July, the investigation really started to pick up pace. From Alexander Clement, the saleroom director at Bonhams in Chester, came confirmation that he'd passed on my details to the ball's new owner so it was now a question of waiting to see if he would respond. The next day, Shapero rang me to discuss a meeting. He revealed that he'd again contacted his client who, Shapero emphasised, wanted me to continue with my search. I then asked a few more questions about the ball's last known whereabouts. At first, Shapero said it went missing about two or three years ago and was presumed lost. He then changed it to the owner "having some problems" and the ball being "stolen or lost." He later amended it to "I exported the ball to the owner but it never arrived. He was concerned but the ball wasn't insured and that was the end of it – until the proposed sale at Bonhams." Shapero also revealed that The Mystery Man lived on the Indian subcontinent – in either India or Pakistan. When I told him that I'd asked Bonhams to forward my contact details to the ball's consignor, he wanted me to give him the name and number of my contact in Chester – Alexander Clement – so that he, Shapero, as the known buyer, could demand the consignor's details. I declined and, on reflection, thought it would have been quite easy for him to ring Bonhams himself.

I remember Shapero becoming slightly annoyed when I remarked that I found everything a little confusing. He repeated that he'd bought the ball and sent it to the owner – which contradicted his earlier version in which he'd handed it over at a face-to-face meeting in London in 2006. Confusing? Not 'alf. More like completely baffling. I realised that everything had happened six years ago and, again, I understood his desire to protect his client's identity but, from what I could see, it was starting to muddy the waters a little too much. Surely, Shapero Rare Books kept a record of all their transactions? We provisionally arranged to meet at Shapero's offices to review my evidence the following week and I said I would confirm the time and date once I'd sorted out my travel arrangements.

When an email from someone called Ashish Singhal arrived in my inbox the very next day, I knew Operation Howzat? was really up and running. It was short but very sweet:

> Dear Mr. Lloyd ,
>
> Many congratulations on the success of your book " *Six of the Best*"
>
> Mr. Clement from bonhams mentioned that you want to contact me regarding Gary Sobers 'Six Sixes' ball . Please let us know how may i assist you .
>
> *Do not cry if the Sun sets at the end of the day, because the tears will not let you enjoy the beauty of the Stars.*

I wasn't to know it but this was the start of an exasperating exchange of emails with one of the most elusive people I have ever encountered in my whole career. The first thing that struck me was the way in which he signed off all his emails. I later discovered that the sunsets, tears and stars saying was the work of the Bengali philosopher and poet, Rabindranath Tagore, who, in 1913, had became the first non-European to win the Nobel Prize for Literature. He was also a prolific painter and songwriter who composed the Indian and Bangladesh national anthems. My reading of this particular saying is when you lose something, don't mourn for it too long. If you do, you will possibly lose more. Or perhaps put another way – don't become too depressed because tomorrow is another day. I was to be reminded of Tagore's sunsets, stars and tears maxim with every e-mail I received from Ashish Singhal and I was sometimes almost reduced to tears during the next six months as frustration became a frequent companion. Obtaining information from the ball owner was a little like getting burnt rice off the bottom of a saucepan – or scraping ice from a car windscreen with a credit card. Some of the sayings of the "Shakespeare of Bengal" have been described as banal – "Do not blame your food because you have no appetite" – but they have also been hailed as spiritual and mystical; Ashish Singhal's emails were simply mystifying. But, inspired by Tagore's advice to not dwell too long on despair, and with the help of Chris Davies, who'd spent some time in India researching the life of his great-grandfather, Eugen Sandow, I finally discovered more about Singhal's connection with the ball. I was also intrigued to come across another of Tagore's pithy sayings – "Either you have work or you have not. When you have to say 'let us do something', then begins mischief" – which appeared to be a variation on the proverbial theme of "the devil finds work for idle hands to do."

My strategy was straightforward: having tracked down the person who'd consigned the ball to Bonhams, I now wanted to persuade him to return it to Britain. Then, along with my evidence, I could take it to Christie's with Shapero, the man who'd originally bought it, and attempt to obtain a refund of the £26,400. I realised that the chances of the auction house co-operating were either very slim or non-existent – even with both Shapero and the ball on board – because their five-year 'bring back' condition of sale covering disputed or forged goods referred to by David Convery had already expired. From my earlier enquiries via the Metropolitan Police's Art and Antiques Unit and the Trading Standards Institute, I had discovered that an aggrieved party could pursue a charge of fraud by false representation under the 2006 Fraud Act, which had repealed the corresponding provisions of the 1968 Theft Act. I'd never intended to make any money out of the ball's return to Britain because, at the risk of sounding pious, it was all about truth and justice for me. I simply felt a wrong needed to be put right; the sale of the Duke sat uncomfortably within the spirit of cricket.

I was delighted to have made contact so quickly with the consignor and I immediately set about trying to find out more about Ashish Singhal. In my first email to him, I apologised for having caused the ball to be withdrawn by Bonhams and laid my cards on the table: I'd like to help him obtain some sort of financial re-dress, solve the mystery surrounding the sale and update *Six of the Best* following the extraordinary amount of interest shown in the Six Sixes story. So I asked him about his history and association with the ball. Simple questions like "where do you live, what do you do for a living?" and "where did you buy the ball?" Nothing too taxing and questions, to my mind, which required pretty straightforward answers. Singhal promised to help but, in the meantime, he asked me to share the evidence which cast doubts on his ball's authenticity. I politely repeated my request for information and wondered, after he'd used the word 'us' in one of his emails, if he was part of a syndicate who had bought the ball?

> There is no syndicate or Group , in Regular business communication we prefer use of words WE and US rather than I and ME . Now knowing your fascination with words , we shall be careful next time.

As I examined Singhal's emails, I became intrigued by what turned out to be an unusual and ultimately useful stylistic tic. His idiosyncratic punctuation meant that a comma or full stop was usually preceded by a space. I'd never come across anything like it before so, as Chris Davies and I continued to look into his background, Ashish Singhal acquired a nickname. After Bernard "The Book Man" Shapero and his anonymous client who I'd dubbed "The Mystery Man", the new ball owner making such distinctive use of the space bar on his computer's keyboard would henceforth be known as "The Space Man". My fascination with words was as nothing compared to my interest in Ashish Singhal – and "careful" neatly summed up his attitude to my enquiries. Apart from revealing that he was acting alone, he wasn't giving much away so I contacted Alexander Clement at Bonhams in an attempt to find out where Singhal lived. In my email, I said I suspected language difficulties meant something was being "lost in translation" via our correspondence and I wasn't sure if the ball had arrived with Singhal. Could he tell me when and where it had been sent to? But the man from Bonhams wasn't playing ball – he was, quite rightly, playing strictly by the rules governing customer confidentiality by merely confirming that the rejected item had been received by its owner. In my view, Bonhams had gone some way towards atoning for their initial rejection of my concerns about the ball's authenticity by forwarding my details to Singhal. I was grateful but I knew I'd be unlikely to receive any more help from them. Bonhams had set the ball rolling – it was now up to Operation Howzat? to make sure that it eventually came to rest at Christie's doorstep.

Questions, questions…
but not too many answers

I keep six honest serving-men
(They taught me all I knew);
Their names are What and Why and When
And How and Where and Who.

Rudyard Kipling, The Elephant's Child

"Who is your client?"

"I can't say."

"Where does he live and what does he do?"

"I can't say."

"What was your relationship with your client?"

"I don't want to talk about him."

"Was this the first time he'd asked you to bid for him?"

"No."

"Why didn't he want to bid directly with Christie's over the phone lines, or on the internet?"

"Convenience."

"Is bidding for an item on behalf of someone else something you've done before?"

"Yes, it's a common practice."

The first half dozen questions I put to Bernard Shapero at our meeting in London set the tone for a conversation which lasted quite long but yielded very little. To be honest, my expectations hadn't been great – mainly because of his extreme reluctance to reveal almost anything about his client during our phone conversations – but, putting my reservations to one side, I thought it was important to try to establish some form of working relationship with him by meeting face to face.

The plan was clear. I was hoping that in return for my showing him the evidence which proved the ball wasn't the genuine article, Shapero would tell me something about his involvement with its sale. I was relying on the principle of quid pro quo, or a favour for a favour or tit for tat – although I suspected, in this case, it would be more give than take. So I drew up a list of questions and by the time I'd finished, I realised I'd knocked up nearly a half-century's worth. I tried to trim them back but they all seemed pretty pertinent to me so there was no alternative but to go through them all – one by one.

With my bag bulging with documents, CDs and a DVD, I'd travelled to London by train for the 12.15 meeting and made my way from Kings Cross by tube and on foot to Shapero's headquarters in Mayfair. Having turned past the Hanover Square church on the corner, I noticed the Sotheby's flag fluttering on my right as I headed towards the impressive and imposing home of Shapero Rare Books. It was sandwiched between a more modern building and a much smaller men's designer clothes and shoes shop. Shapero was the first person I met as I walked through his front door. We shook hands, he asked me to wait until he'd finished dealing with another matter and, a couple of minutes later, I accompanied him to an upstairs room which was full, not surprisingly, of antiquarian books. They were packed wall to wall, in all shapes and sizes, on light blue shelving. I must admit to finding my new surroundings slightly intimidating and I momentarily began to realise how Andrew Hignell might have felt when he was invited to view the Six Sixes ball at Christie's six years earlier.

We settled ourselves around an enormous circular table in the middle of the room as Shapero engaged in some small talk, asking about my background. I explained that after a long career in news and current affairs, I was now specialising in sports reporting and writing books – *Six of the Best* being the latest. As I arranged my evidence on the table, Shapero got straight down to business.

"What are you hoping to get from this meeting?"

"My long-term aim is two-fold," I said. "I'd like to do the decent thing and help you get your client's money back and update my book by properly investigating the ball sale. You've told me that as far as Christie's are concerned, you are known as the buyer. If we are to work together, I need to be "in the know" so I'd be grateful if you could answer a few questions before I show you the evidence which might help you to retrieve your £26,400."

Shapero nodded and I turned to my clipboard of questions. I'd considered asking if it would be possible to record our conversation – I'd actually brought my dictaphone with me – but, in the end, I thought better of it. I would take a shorthand note instead. In the event, Shapero's answers were usually so brief that I was able to write them down in longhand. I soon discovered that, when he wanted to, Shapero could be a man of very few words. I'd typed up the list of questions beforehand and as I worked my way through it, I scribbled down his replies before moving on to the next one. When I returned home later that evening, I recalled a few other comments which I then included in a much fuller account of our meeting.

"How much research did you conduct into the ball's provenance?"

"None."

"You'd read the catalogue's lot notes?"

"Yes."

"Were you convinced it was the genuine article?"

"Yes."

"If you had any doubts, did the certificate of provenance signed by Sobers dispel them?"

"I had no doubts and even if I'd had any, I'd still have bid for the ball."

"In the auction world, how significant is a certificate of provenance?"

"It's a piece of very important evidence."

"What about the Christie's staff supervising the sale – David Convery, Max Dunbar & Rupert Neelands? Had you dealt with them before?"

"There wasn't much interaction with them. I had come across Rupert Neelands before but not the other two."

"You trusted them?"

"Yes."

"You and your client were happy that it was the Six Sixes ball?"

"Yes."

Along with truth and transparency, trust completes the triumvirate of guiding principles for the running of a successful auction house. Shapero had clearly trusted Christie's and I wanted him now to trust me but we appeared to be approaching the same subject from slightly different angles. While I felt he should be more forthcoming, his view seemed to be: "We are where we are – let's get to where we want to be as quickly as possible." My precise, painstaking questioning of him was an attempt to shed some light on his role in the purchase of the ball. My list of questions may have appeared a little perfunctory, even pedantic but, in my view, it was perfectly justified in the circumstances so I ploughed on.

"How did it work in practical terms – you went to the auction, you had contact with your client by telephone and you consulted him as the bidding went up and up?"

"Yes."

"What were his instructions to you before the auction?"

"My client was very keen to buy the ball but it wasn't a case of 'money no object'."

"Was there a limit beyond which he didn't want to go?"

"There was a figure but I can't remember what it was. The final price was obviously within that limit because we bought the ball."

"As the price kept going up, what were you thinking?"

"Nothing really much. Buying the ball was an interesting thing that happened to me on that day. Because of my line of business, I bid a lot at auctions. This was not a major thing in the big scheme of things."

"You didn't think it seemed a lot of money for just a cricket ball?"

"No. You have to realise that £26,400 – or just over $50,000 – is small beer when you consider that Christie's turn over nearly $4 billion a year. This is not big money for wealthy people at that end of the business."

"The reaction of your client as you informed him of the bidding?"

"None."

"How many other people were bidding in the room and were there other telephone bids coming in apart from yours?"

"I imagine so but I can't remember."

"Your final bid of £22,000 was accepted – your feelings then?"

"Good. I was pleased to have bought such an iconic item."

"What about your client?"

"Very pleased."

"Why was he so keen to own the ball?"

"I can't say why."

Shapero was back on familiar territory. I understood the importance of client confidentiality in certain business transactions but surely these rules could be bent just a little? The Book Man would only admit that The Mystery Man was "an existing customer" of his and said that he – Shapero – had an account with Christie's. He recalled paying for the ball and being paid for it, either by cheque or bank transfer, and picking it up from South Kensington sometime between the auction on 15th November and Christmas 2006. He then confirmed he'd also bought the G.G. Hearne bat for his client and, through the Bonhams website, I later discovered that, as well as W.G. Grace and other leading luminaries, the 1899 Australian touring team and the 1907 South Africans had also signed the bat. It had sold for £9,600 at Christie's in 2006 and for £4,625 at Bonhams in 2012. I realised I was being fed only crumbs by Shapero and I was still very hungry – especially to hear about the ball's post-auction movements.

"What happened to the ball after that?" I continued. "You've given me three versions since we began speaking on the phone. One, you met your client face to face in London and gave him the ball; two, it was sent to him and after two or three years, it then went missing or was stolen and three, that you exported it to him but it never arrived. You told me 'he was concerned but it wasn't insured and that was the end of it.' Which is the true version?"

"The second and third versions could be the same."

"No, they couldn't. The ball was either sent to him and arrived and was then lost or stolen or it didn't arrive – it couldn't be both."

"He used to come over to London occasionally. He says he never received the ball."

"Any idea who might have stolen the ball?"

"No."

"Has there been some sort of falling-out or dispute with one of your client's staff or a relative?"

"It's a complicated story that we can't go into at the moment."

At this stage, Shapero intimated that this wouldn't be our last meeting and he'd be able to tell me more during future ones. I looked down at my list of questions. Not too many to go. Almost there. Best just to keep going.

"What contact have you had with your client in the last six years?"

"Off and on."

"And in the last six months?"

"Not much."

"What was your reaction – and your client's reaction – to the news that the ball had been withdrawn by Bonhams?"

"We were surprised the ball was ever in Bonhams."

"Had your client in India heard about the ball's withdrawal?"

"No."

"What does your client want to do now?"

"Get his money back."

"On the phone, you've used the phrase 'I want my money back from Christie's' and 'my client wants his money back from Christie's'. Whose money is it you want to retrieve?"

"You're taking my comments out of context."

"I wrote down what you said to me on the phone. In the light of the ball's withdrawal, have you refunded £26,400 to your client because he bought a ball that wasn't genuine – and that's why you want your money back?"

"No."

"How desperate are you to get your money back?"

"Not desperate but very keen."

"Why don't you ring up Bonhams, explain your position as the buyer and ask them to put you in touch with the person who consigned the ball to their 29th May auction? Then you'd find out who the thief is."

"I'll get the ball rolling by ringing Bonhams – do you have a name?"

I then told Shapero that Alexander Clement was the saleroom director at Chester.

"If you want your money back, you're going to have to take the ball back to Christie's – how likely is that bearing in mind it's been stolen or lost?"

"We can't do anything without the ball."

We briefly discussed Christie's five-year 'bring back' condition of sale covering goods which buyers are unhappy with and Shapero repeated his belief that the return of the ball was paramount. He said that once it was back in Britain, via Bonhams, we could contact Christie's about a refund.

And that's where the formal part of our meeting ended. A complicated story had become…slightly less complicated. As you can imagine, I was doing my best to avoid venting my frustration at the majority of The Book Man's answers. For his part, Shapero, perhaps understandably, was beginning to become impatient and I realised he was reluctant to spend too much time examining my evidence. He was more talkative now and he seemed very keen to hear my reading of the situation covering the sale of the ball. But I wanted to go back to the source material – basically the Christie's lot notes – to show him how inaccurate they were. I insisted that we look at the evidence first so I gave him a copy and highlighted my three areas of concern: the make of the ball, the number of balls used in the over and how the writer of the notes, having admitted viewing video footage, had somehow not seen the first two balls being returned from outside the ground after the first two sixes. I then showed Shapero the 1968 Glamorgan newsletter confirming the ball as a Surridge and I was very surprised that he didn't ask to see the DVD of the event itself.

I then explained all the anecdotal evidence: my contact with Basharat Hassan via phone while I was writing *Six of the Best*, Peter Walker's briefing before the Six Sixes dinner in June 2008 and Hassan's reaction to the mention of his involvement after the book's publication. Finally, I told Shapero about the origins of the sale, including Jose Miller's desire to use the proceeds to help pay her medical bills (something I'd learned about since writing the book) and the part played by Hassan and Sobers.

I also told Shapero about David Convery's denial. We discussed who had benefited financially from the sale of the ball for the overall price of £26,400 and I suggested that Convery had perhaps been more interested in the kudos of selling the world's most famous cricket ball than the actual money it raised. I explained that Convery had left Christie's in 2007 and returned to Scotland to set up his own auction house and the ball sale would have been a big feather in his cap. Shapero said he thought Convery had denied any involvement because he was worried that his association with the ball would affect his reputation.

We then discussed how Bonhams would react to Shapero's claim that the ball didn't belong to the consignor. Shapero suggested the police should be alerted and although I didn't let on that I knew the identity of the new owner, I said I was pretty sure the ball had come to Bonhams from abroad because their catalogue had warned that import tax would have to be paid on both the bat and the ball. It seemed to me that if the theft had taken place in say India, it was unlikely that the British police would be able to follow up Shapero's complaint that the ball had been stolen from his client.

In light of Shapero's vast experience of auction houses, I asked him how he thought Christie's would respond. How would they react when presented with evidence which suggested that due diligence hadn't been carried out on the ball by their sporting memorabilia department and the ball sold had turned out not to be genuine? Shapero said he thought Christie's would throw some legal money at it, claim that Convery no longer worked for them and wouldn't refund the £26,400. He quoted the case of the Russian billionaire Viktor Vekselberg who, at that time, was suing Christie's after paying £1.7 million ($2.6 billion) for 'Odalisque', a painting of a nude said to be the work of Russian artist Boris Kustodiev but which Veksleberg claimed was a fake. The oil tycoon had initially voiced his concerns to Christie's in November 2006 – coincidentally the month they'd sold the Six Sixes ball – and had been reluctant to take legal action. He'd expected the matter to be settled through Christie's own dispute resolution procedure. The auction house stood by the attribution made before the sale. While admitting that two hugely different sums of money were involved in the two cases, I suggested that the status of both the ball and Sobers would surely be significant. Shapero disagreed. In short, he believed Christie's wouldn't be worried about the Six Sixes ball's dubious provenance.

I could sense that our meeting was drawing to a close and as I started to gather up my evidence, Shapero touched on an issue at the heart of my investigation. Was I, by dint of my revelations, prepared ultimately to besmirch Sobers' reputation as an iconic cricketer? I said I was – even though it would be a painful process because he'd been a hero of mine since I'd first seen him play for the West Indies at Trent Bridge in 1966. By signing the certificate of provenance, Sobers had given his word that the ball had been used in the famous over and although he had no connection with the Stock Exchange, I said I felt that their motto, "My Word is my Bond", also applied in this case. I then repeated my aims of solving the mystery of the ball's sale, possibly retrieving the money and updating my book. I handed Shapero some of my evidence and told him about the interest in the story from Tony Roe, a BBC producer/editor based in Nottingham, and *Wisden*, for whom I'd been asked to write an article. I said I felt it would be preferable if no contact were made with key players like Christie's until the commission of some kind of TV or radio programme had been confirmed. I'd drawn up a list of all the protagonists and because I'd probably have only one chance to question them, it would be best if they had no inkling that an approach was imminent. Shapero agreed and said he would contact Bonhams about the identity of the consignor – probably by the end of the week – in an attempt to locate the Duke ball.

As I was walking along Regent Street on my way back to Kings Cross, Chris Davies rang me on my mobile. It turned out that, unbeknown to me, he'd driven down from Lancaster to London – partly to sort out a couple of auction items and partly to discuss tactics with me. I had about an hour's wait before the next train so we met in a local pub where I showed him my list of questions and Shapero's replies. As I travelled home, Chris called in at Shapero Rare Books to discuss a possible deal involving Antarctica exploration books signed by his great-grandfather, Eugen Sandow. He felt it was important to put a face to a name and later told me that he'd got on well with Shapero, gaining a valuable insight into the way he liked to do business. Despite Shapero's initial recalcitrance, I felt my meeting with him had generally been worthwhile and I emailed him the next day to thank him for his time.

It was a strange position to find myself in: at one end of my investigation was the buyer of the ball, at the other its current owner. I was stuck in no man's land between two men who were reluctant to elaborate on their role in the journey of the Duke from South

Kensington to somewhere on the Indian subcontinent. Having made a start with Shapero, I now had a quiver full of questions to fire at Ashish Singhal and two days after my meeting in London, The Space Man started to take a few tentative steps in my direction. In my most recent email, I'd repeated my request for more information about his association with the ball and asked if he was based in India. At least his reply put that question to bed:

> Regarding my background , I am based out of India , Have done my Masters In International Business from one of the reputed B schools and belong to an Industrial house in india diversified into Automobile Engineering , Food Processing , Turnkey Electrification & Solar Energy Projects . I am an avid cricket fan and so is every Indian , as a interest I collect Memorabilia and other rare items of Historical significance .

Slowly but surely, progress was being made. Having received the most illuminating email from Singhal to date, I then asked him for the name of his company and referred again to my initial questions about his connection with the ball. As we waited for his reply, Chris and I made a concerted effort to find out more about him. The business networking website, LinkedIn, was a useful starting point but we knew we would have our work cut out because there were nearly 200 Ashish Singhals listed in India. The words 'needle' and 'haystack' came to mind more than once as we trawled the site trying to match up Singhal's description of his company with someone with the same name and a similar occupation. Among others, we came across a revenue specialist at Expedia, a senior test engineer with Hewitt, the head of privilege banking at the ICICI Bank and a cricket journalist. As Chris explored the industrial route, I decided to investigate the email trail so I typed in Singhal's address – Singhal_Ashish@hotmail.com – into my Google search engine. Up came a collectibles site where someone using the same name and email address had expressed an interest in buying an 1839 copper iridium coin in April 2012. The message, which claimed "we have licence to buy such products", contained two examples of Singhal's stylistic tic – a space preceding a comma and a full stop. This, it appeared to me, was our man, pursuing his hobby – or perhaps business – of collecting "rare items of interest". I later learned that the coins in question are magical, powerful and very useful for pulling up rice. Not a lot of people know that...

The following day, having not heard from Singhal for the best part of a week, I decided it was time to take off at least one of the gloves. As a result, my next email to him pulled very few punches. After questioning the validity of any future working relationship, I said his reluctance to provide information left me perplexed and I suggested that unless he could answer my enquiries, we ought to abandon the idea of joining forces.

In the meantime, Operation Howzat? was forging ahead on quite a few fronts. As well as searching for clues about the ball owner's identity, I was approaching broadcasting organisations about a possible television programme. This involved my contacting potential interested parties and then sending them a detailed proposal, provisionally titled Howzat? (A Load of Old Balls). Tony Roe, the editor of the BBC East Midlands current affairs programme, *Inside Out*, had been on board ever since I'd shown him my evidence at his Nottingham office but elsewhere there was little response – apart from a swift and polite emailed rejection of the idea by Channel 4's *Dispatches* programme. Despite owning the vital television footage, BBC Cymru Wales eventually made it clear they weren't interested.

All the while, I was continuing to surf the internet for information about the original sale of the ball and, in particular, David Convery's role in it. I couldn't believe he wasn't involved in some way – it kept niggling away at the back of my mind. Although details of the Duke ball lot had been easily accessible online, I'd searched in vain on the Christie's website for any other supporting evidence linking Convery to the auction. As I waited for Singhal to reply to my semi-ultimatum email, I embarked on yet another random, speculative trawl of the internet. I typed something along the lines of "David Convery Christie's auction Sobers Six Sixes ball" into Google and up popped a Christie's celebratory press release issued immediately after the 2006 sale. It revealed that, after the ball, the next two best sellers that day had been two copies of *Wisden* which went for £16,800 and £15,600 respectively as part of the total of £272,700 raised from the sale of 197 lots. Interesting, I thought, but not that interesting. Then I read on and underneath the table of items and prices, I found what

I was looking for. Howzat? Time, at least, to call the third umpire into action, to go upstairs and use DRS. Under the "comment" section of the press release, the associate director and head of the sporting memorabilia department was extensively quoted. According to Convery, "today's sale once again illustrated the continuing popularity of sporting memorabilia." He'd then described the ball as a "true relic of the sport" which was "subject to a fierce bidding battle that saw it eventually sell for £26,400 to a bidder in the room. The high price pays testament to Sobers' exceptional feat." That seemed to me like a first-hand account of one of the most important sales of his time at Christie's, something of which Convery, as head of department, would be enormously proud. So why was he being so coy on his website? I returned to the "About Us" section of Convery Auctions to check that the ball sale hadn't suddenly reappeared but there was no sign of it. Again, I couldn't understand why Convery was hiding such a significant part of his light under a bushel. It didn't make any sort of sense because surely someone in his position would have publicised the sale to the nth degree – along with all the shirts, balls and medals he'd auctioned during his career?

As Operation Howzat? continued – especially into Singhal's background - and I tried to interest broadcasters in a TV documentary about my investigation, I felt a little like a juggler trying to keep any number of balls in the air. I managed it most of the time but occasionally one would unavoidably slip out of my grasp and a setback would take the shine off a significant step forward. A high would be followed by a couple of lows – and sometimes vice versa – and I began to notice that, like wickets falling during an innings, meaningful moments in Operation Howzat? seemed to come in clusters. Three days after discovering the Christie's press release, another spot of detective work by Chris Davies produced some more information about the 2006 auction. By chance, he'd met an antiques dealer at a car boot sale near Lancaster and they'd started talking about the Duke ball. The dealer remembered the Christie's auction and later sent Chris a cutting of a report from the *Antiques Trade Gazette*. I then rang Alex Capon, the journalist who'd written the article in November 2006, and he emailed me a copy. Under the headline "Sobers signed sixer hit for £22,000", the report showed that the inaccurate Christie's lot notes had immediately become an integral and accepted part of the story. The article claimed that the cricket ball with its "splitting seam and scruff marks" was bowled for "the final four deliveries of the famous over." Nice alliteration – shame about the facts. The first two balls were "apparently only later returned to the umpires" and "this was the third ball used in the over." After it made its way to Trent Bridge, the ball was given to the secretary of the supporters' association and "apparently put on display at the ground's museum and later given to the next secretary who was the vendor." There seemed to be an excessive use of the word "apparently" in the report which then went on to reveal that the only doubts, apparently, in the minds of David Convery and Co were not about the ball's authenticity but its value:

> Estimated at £5000-8000, the auctioneers were unsure of how it would fare on the day, although they had received a commission bid sufficient for it to sell. Yet, proving that cricket enthusiasts will still turn out for the right object, four different parties competed for it in the room, pushing it up to a final price of £22,000.

After jokily acknowledging his mistake in using the word "scruff" instead of "scuff" in his article, Alex Capon explained that the overall figure had risen to £26,400 once the 20 per cent buyer's premium of £4,400 had been added on. Cricket lovers might well have been enthusiastic about genuine memorabilia from the game but I doubt if they would have bothered to turn out – let alone bid – had they known the ball was so patently the wrong object.

Later that evening, my email search threw up another piece of information which would help us to complete the identification of Ashish Singhal. I discovered that he'd been touting for work from a project and business developer working for two renewable energy companies in Africa, via the Global Village Energy Partnership's website. The GVEP is a non-profit organisation that works to increase access to modern energy and reduce poverty in developing countries. Singhal's description of his company matched the one he'd given me by email and again the message had clearly been written by The Space Man. I felt we were gradually edging closer to discovering his full identity and I emailed the Solar Power India website in an attempt to find out more about Singhal's businesses.

The next morning, I received a setback in the form of an email from Tony Roe at BBC East Midlands in Nottingham. He'd applied for some money from a special national fund for programmes which were likely to make an impact but he said the source had dried up because of the corporation-wide cutbacks. Although he was still committed to the idea, Tony had been told that an *Inside Out* half-hour documentary based solely on the ball mystery would break the format of the programme. "Frustration at this end," said his email. "I think I'm experiencing some of the walls you seem to have hit." Half an hour later, another email arrived in my inbox. Bonhams had been very good in helping me contact Ashish Singhal and although I'd feared it wouldn't be successful, I'd put in another request for more information about his whereabouts. Julian Roup, Bonhams director of press and marketing, summed up their position when he told me that "we cannot go beyond what we have already done. I wish you luck. It will all add to the colour of the book." Of that, I had no doubt and the kaleidoscopic cast of characters who had featured in the saga so far made me convinced that I'd be writing if not a bestseller then certainly a page-turner.

Later that morning, we had a stroke of luck when, after those two lows, along came an extremely big high. At the end of another extensive trawl of the internet, a new Mr Singhal popped up on my computer via LinkedIn – but this time with a slightly different Christian name. This one was Aashish rather than Ashish. I'd come across it before but ignored it because of the unusual spelling. Again, the extra 'a' didn't fill me with confidence but this time I decided to click on the name all the same. To both my surprise and delight, I discovered that this version of Mr Singhal appeared to be the one we'd been looking for. Despite the additional 'a', the LinkedIn entry revealed he was actually known as Ashish and he appeared to have quite a few fingers in quite a few pies. He was owner of Ashish Globotech and a natural mineral water company called Genius Aquatech "Kristal", executive director of AEW Infratech, which specialised in solar power and turnkey projects, and director of Faridabad Forgings, a petrochemical and automotive products company based in the industrial city of Faridabad. The entry revealed that he'd also obtained an MBA at the Symbiosis International University based in Pune. An adjoining photograph showed a man wearing glasses, probably in his late twenties or early thirties, dressed in jeans and a jacket standing alongside row upon row of solar panels. The spelling of his first name wasn't right but everything else seemed to fit. After ringing Chris Davies with the news, I clicked onto the Faridabad Forgings website. Two email addresses and three telephone numbers were listed and I immediately tried to make personal contact with this particular Ashish Singhal to confirm he was the owner of the Six Sixes ball. With India being five and a half hours ahead of us, I rang each of the numbers just before midday but a combination of background traffic noise and a rudimentary knowledge of English at the other end of a pretty crackly phone line meant I had difficulty in making myself clear. But during one of the very brief conversations, none of them lasted more than a couple of minutes, I did learn that Mr Singhal was away on business – something which tied in with an earlier email I'd received from him.

It was becoming more and more frustrating. The Space Man had still to reply to my last email in which I'd vented my displeasure at his reluctance to answer some simple questions. To be honest, I was starting to worry that I'd frightened him off. In my defence, I felt his attitude left me with no alternative but to express my concern and then make my own enquiries. For some inexplicable reason, he was being less than forthcoming – even secretive – about his background and connection with the ball. At that stage, we didn't know if he was Bernard Shapero's client or the 'thief' who had perhaps stolen the ball. Singhal had admitted he was a cricket fan but £26,400 seemed an awful lot of money for an individual to pay for a ball so we presumed he was also a successful businessman. Was he perhaps acting on behalf of a cricket museum or was he in some way connected with the rupee-rich Indian Premier League competition? We felt we needed to know more about him so Chris suggested going one stage further and injecting a dash of subterfuge into Operation Howzat? Why didn't he check out Singhal's business credentials by posing as a client? That way, I wouldn't be involved and, with Chris investigating under an alias and completely independently of me, we might be able to find out more about Singhal – without alerting him and thus putting him on edge. Through this approach, we felt we could confirm, once and for all, that he owned the ball – if only because his email-writing style would be a giveaway. I wouldn't normally have resorted to such a Baldrick-like cunning plan but, in this case, I felt the end justified the means so Chris sent a spoof email to the two addresses listed on the Faridabad Forgings website. He pretended to be someone developing a new film studio near London which he wanted to equip with a large number of solar panels. He said that after being given Singhal's details while working in Mumbai, he was now looking for information about his products and installation systems. "We have a skilled workforce here so it would just be a question of product price, build quality and shipping costs," his email read. "Costs are so high in the UK now." It sounded very authentic and professional so after forwarding me a draft copy, Chris pressed 'send' and we sat back and waited.

Later that afternoon, I emailed Carl Doran, an editor in Salford responsible for documentary commissioning in BBC Sport. I sent him the programme proposal and his encouraging reply said it sounded "very exciting if it is strong enough for a full doc." He suggested it would be best to discuss it in September because he'd be tied up with the Olympic torch relay and then the games themselves until then. No problem – I knew there was still a lot of digging to be done.

It was all quiet on the solar power front for a while but Chris and I weren't at all downhearted. Up until now, our Ashish Singhal hadn't been the quickest of emailers and we felt sure that we'd identified our man. The silence was par for the course. Five days later, my co-investigator received this reply:

DEAR CHRIS ,
OUR ENERGY GENERATION COMPANY IS "AEW INFRAT-
ECH" WHICH IS INVOLVED IN SOLAR BUSINESS. WE
DEVELOP MW SCALE SOLAR PV PROJECTS IN INDIA .
FOR CRITICAL INSTALLATIONS WE HAVE TECHNICAL JV
WITH SHARP CORPORATION JAPAN . I WOULD LIKE TO
UNDERSTAND MORE ABOUT YOUR PROJECT .
1) HOW MUCH AREA IS AVAILABLE

2) ROOF TOP INSTALLATION OR FREE FIELD INSTALLA-
TION
3) HOW MUCH POWER YOU ARE LOOKING TO GENER-
ATE
CAN YOU SHARE WITH ME SOME DRAWINGS SO THAT
WE CAN ADVISE YOU THE TYPE OF INSTALLATION AND
ALSO PROPERLY UTILISE THE AREA TO GENERATE
GREEN ENERGY FOR YOUR STUDIO.
FOR COMMUNICATION REGARDING SOLAR REQUEST
YOU TO C.C – EMAIL ADD ASHISH@AEWINFRA.COM

Thanking you
For Faridabad Forgings Pvt. Ltd.
 Ashish Singhal
MBA Int'l Business
Executive Director
 Direct: +91-9899622295, 9910062295 Fax: +91-129-4005573
VISIT US @ www.faridabadforgings.com

Howzat? The umpire's index finger was about to be raised. The
Space Man had landed. The reply contained four examples of his
unique writing style and we felt pretty sure that this particular Ashish
Singhal was indeed the owner of the ball. More importantly, we now
had two new direct phone numbers – in effect, a couple of hot lines
to the man himself. The next day, Chris sent Ashish a second
message to explain that he required a "medium scale rooftop installation" for his film studio and while his architect finalised the
drawings, he'd like details of previous schemes in which AEW
Infratech had been involved. Solar power had just provided an alternative source of energy for Operation Howzat? but there was no
sign of sunsets, tears or stars as a new dawn in the investigation was
about to break…

A passage to India

The items of Uncleared Cargo consist of Electronics, Computer Parts,
Medical/Surgical items, Paints, Plastics, Chemicals, Printed Matter, Spare Parts,
Machinery, Leather items, Telecommunications equipment/parts and Miscellaneous
import items. The auction of such items will be held on "as is, where is" basis.

Online e-Auction Catalogue, IGI Airport, New Delhi

We had been right to think that Operation Howzat? was on a roll.
Hot on the heels of identifying The Space Man, we almost immediately made another breakthrough – via a completely unexpected
source. Out of the blue, Bernard Shapero rang me the very next
day. Not only that, he rang me with some very pertinent information. Three weeks after our meeting in Mayfair, The Book Man
revealed that his client, The Mystery Man, had now explained what
had happened to the Six Sixes ball when it had left London.

According to Shapero, it had been sent to India and become
caught up in customs. Along with the antique bat, the Duke hadn't
made it out of the airport and was later sold in an unclaimed goods
auction for about £300. Apparently, his client – whom Shapero still
refused to identify – had later been offered the chance to buy back
the ball from a third party for $20,000 dollars – about £15,000 –
but he'd impolitely declined. Shapero explained that India was a very
bureaucratic country and his client was "continually having issues
with customs." After being told about the decision to auction the
bat and ball, he'd considered appealing but that would have meant
employing a lawyer and he'd been advised against it because of the
possible consequences for his business. Shapero said his client had
been asked the question: 'Do you really want to appeal when you
have so much material moving backwards and forwards through
customs?' The implication was that an appeal would have made The
Mystery Man's life difficult so he'd decided to let it drop. According
to Shapero, his client now felt it best to leave the matter alone to
avoid any further embarrassment.

I knew it wasn't the complete story but I felt I'd been given
enough information to fill in a few gaps and explain some of the
mystery surrounding Shapero's previous phone calls and our

meeting in London. I then asked him if Bonhams had been able to help identify the consignor of the ball to their sporting memorabilia auction in May. As I expected, they hadn't – once again, because of client confidentiality concerns.

In return for his surprising update, I decided that The Book Man should now be told about The Space Man. Without revealing my sources, I explained that I'd made email contact with Ashish Singhal and Shapero said he would mention the name to his client. He then suggested the three of us should work together to have the ball returned to Christie's in an attempt to retrieve the £26,400 – with me acting as broker. I said I'd be happy with that arrangement but explained that my direct line to Singhal had all but dried up. The Space Man was very reluctant to answer my questions about his connection with the ball. I decided not to mention Chris Davies' spoof solar energy email because Shapero didn't need to know how we'd managed to confirm Singhal's identity. Shapero suggested that I email Singhal to explain his plan. At this stage, there was no mention of splitting any possible refund and, to be honest, money wasn't on my mind. It never had been. All I'd ever wanted to do was to investigate the ball discrepancy. Anything I made out of Operation Howzat? would come through my writing. I began to realise that the unfolding story of the ball's passage to India meant that an updated re-print of *Six of the Best* was no longer viable. My next book would have to be a sequel instead. Journalist, broadcaster, author and now deal broker. Deal broker? I had a feeling that a whole new career was about to open up for me. As soon as I'd put down the phone to Shapero, I sent him my exchange of emails with Singhal and rang Chris with the latest news. How much did he know about airport auctions in India? Not a lot but, thanks to the internet, we knew we'd be able to find out something.

As we set about trying to track down the ball – and probably the bat – Chris ran into a few of the communication problems I'd already encountered with The Space Man. Having not heard from him for the best part of a week, he asked Singhal to ring because "we have moved forward with our project planning" for the studio with solar panels. Meanwhile, Chris continued to beaver away on his computer and quickly identified the importance of the 1962

Customs Act, as well as discovering that the Container Corporation of India and the Indira Gandhi International (IGI) Airport – or Delhi International Airport – in New Delhi both held online sales of uncleared cargo. His preliminary search of the lot list of an auction held in late March 2007 at the airport, more than three months after the Christie's sale, failed to throw up anything but we knew it was early days.

As usual, I was trying to keep several balls in the air. I wasn't having much luck in interesting a broadcaster in a documentary about the Six Sixes ball but Monday 6th August proved a significant date in Operation Howzat? A rejection from ITV's director of sport, Niall Sloane, prompted me to make a couple of crucial phone calls. I'd been at Sheffield University with Niall in the 1970s and then commentated on half a dozen football matches for *Match of the Day* when he was working on the BBC programme in the early 1990s. He didn't think my proposal was "one for us" although he could see there was a "potentially interesting tale" in it. I agreed to his forwarding my idea to ITV's current affairs team and then, on a whim, I decided to ring Bernard Shapero. It was time to take the bull – if not the ball – by the horns. The Book Man said he hadn't spoken to his client but repeated his plan for me to act as broker. Why didn't I email his details to Singhal and suggest that it would be "worth his while" and "financially advantageous" for him to speak to Shapero? I agreed but then, on a second whim, I decided to ring The Space Man rather than email him. Because Chris and I had been concentrating on our search for the bat and ball e-auction, we hadn't explored either of the two numbers unearthed by his spoof email to AEW Infratech. Why didn't I try one of them now?

I looked at my watch. It was almost three o'clock – that meant it was about half-past eight in India. I'd decided to record the conversation so after checking that my dictaphone was working properly, I dialled the first number. It just kept ringing out so I tried the second one – and unexpectedly hit the jackpot. Via a crackly phone line from Faridabad, I heard The Space Man's voice for the first time. After introducing myself and confirming that Singhal actually owned the ball, I explained that I was keen to sort out the matter we had discussed in our emails. My aim was to find out how he'd come by the ball, how much he'd paid for it and whether he was willing to return it to Britain. Having phoned Singhal on spec, I realised that I hadn't prepared any questions so I'd have to play it off the cuff, without the notes I usually had alongside my phone when making Operation Howzat? calls. When I mentioned the possibility of his getting some money back, Singhal made it clear that, at this point, he wasn't interested – "as I really do have a lot of regard for Sir Garfield Sobers." He went on to say it would be "a disgrace" to Sobers if we took the matter to court and questioned the ball's authenticity: it and the certificate were both signed by Sobers. I then cut to the chase by laying out two more indisputable facts of the matter:

"I can assure you that it is not the ball because it is the wrong make. The ball that was used in 1968 was made by Stuart Surridge and the ball that you have – you can see it – it's made by Duke & Son. It's the wrong make and also there was only one ball used in the over. According to the sale at Christie's in 2006, this was the third of three balls but I have BBC footage which shows that only one ball was used."

"Could it be a possibility that this was the ball that was used throughout the whole over?" said Singhal.

"No…because it's the wrong make. I have also spoken to Malcolm Nash, the bowler of the ball; he's willing to come over from America to Britain to support my case. He's very unhappy because he says 'I bowled only one ball in the over and it was a Stuart Surridge.' So I'm afraid that the ball you've got… "

"Is there any way in which we can get in touch with Sir Garfield Sobers himself and understand his point of view?"

"Yes, you can easily contact him. What I'd like to know is – are you able to tell me where you bought the ball? Where did you get the ball from Ashish? Who did you buy it from?"

"I bought it from one of my – somebody I know but I won't be able to disclose the name. But I have all the papers and everything is with me regarding the ball."

"How much did you pay for it – can you tell me that?"

"I paid a little premium over the price he bought it for. Not a lot of premium. I paid something 5-10 per cent premium over what he bought it for. He was the first owner."

"Where did your friend get the ball from?"

"The auction at Christie's."

"So what is your friend's name – can you tell me that?"

"That is something I will not be able to disclose at this stage but let me have a word with him. If he is comfortable, then I have no hesitation in disclosing his name to you."

So far, so not so good. Déjà vu. It was almost like having a telephone conversation with Bernard Shapero. What was it with these cricket ball people? The Space Man was behaving just like The Book Man. Ashish Singhal, in the manner of the known buyer at Christie's in 2006, was giving little or nothing away. I deliberately hadn't mentioned the airport auction because I didn't want Singhal to know that I knew about it. I preferred him to give me his version of events to see if it had anything in common with Shapero's account. I wondered if Singhal's "friend" was the person who'd bought the ball at the e-auction and then approached Shapero's anonymous client about buying it back? Or had Singhal been the online buyer? He obviously wasn't prepared to reveal the identity of his "friend" so I quickly moved on to my next question:

"Is there any chance that you would be willing to send the ball back to London so that it could be taken to Christie's and it could be explained to them that the ball is not *the* ball?"

"But will they be willing to refund the money?"

"Well…I'm hoping they will because my evidence is so conclusive. The other thing I'd like to do is put you in touch with a man who actually bought the ball for his client back in 2006. It's a man called Bernard Shapero, he's a London antique book dealer and he bought the ball and then sent it to India…"

"Yes…"

"…on behalf of his client. Have you heard of Mr Shapero before?"

"Yes…I know him."

"You know Bernard Shapero?"

"I don't know him personally but I know him."

"Well…he was the man who paid…"

"I know, I know…I know the complete background."

That was certainly more than I did. But at this stage, I felt that at least I was getting somewhere. Little by little, step by step. Quite how Singhal knew all about Shapero I wasn't sure but at least it was a point of reference – something to work from. I decided to bring The Space Man right up to date with my involvement with The Book Man and remind him of the strength of my evidence. He already knew that I'd persuaded Bonhams to withdraw the ball but it didn't hurt to tell him again.

"Mr Shapero is suggesting that the three of us, you, me and him – with my evidence – could actually take the ball back to Christie's and say to them: 'This ball is not the ball you said it was – and we have the evidence.' And I can tell you Ashish that I have conclusive evidence – because if I hadn't have had conclusive evidence, then Bonhams in Chester, where you consigned the ball for auction earlier this year, wouldn't have withdrawn it. They said to me: 'Mr Lloyd, your evidence is compelling and conclusive and we are withdrawing the ball from our auction.' "

"As far as I see it, this is a controversy," said Singhal. "There is an opinion that this is the ball which was used during that over and there is an opinion that this was the ball that was not used during that over."

"Well…all I can say to you Ashish is that there is an opinion that the ball is a fake and I have evidence which supports that. And there's very little evidence to support the view that that ball was used in the Six Sixes over."

"But what surprises me is then…how come Sir Garfield Sobers says that this is the ball? He must have gone through some evidence, he must have done some research into it?"

"Well… I think he did some research and I wouldn't like to cast any aspersions on him but the fact is that the incident happened – he signed that certificate of provenance that you have in 2006 and the incident took place 38 years before then. He hardly saw the ball and the ball that was returned to him by the little boy in the street – the actual ball that was hit out of the ground – was made by Stuart Surridge and not by Duke & Son. So, all I'm saying to you is – I'm not making any comment on Garry Sobers – the ball that you have, I'm afraid to say, is the wrong make and only one ball was used in the over – not three, which is what Christie's said in their lot notes. So the evidence is overwhelming and Garry Sobers has made a mistake. Now, I'd like to try and rectify that but I'm asking you: are you willing to send the ball back to this country so that I can take it…"

"I will definitely think it over – I will have to send the ball to you directly or to Christie's?"

"If you send it to me directly – and I'm happy to send you my postal address – I give you a guarantee that I will take it to Christie's. If you know Bernard Shapero, he is an honourable man. I have just spoken to him on the phone from London and he has suggested that I contact you and we see if we can get this sorted. Then there will be a chance of you getting a certain amount of your money back. That is the key point here."

What do they say? Once a legend, always a legend. Forty-four years after his most famous achievement and 38 years after he'd retired from cricket, the world's greatest all-rounder's reputation was beyond reproach. My conversation with Singhal had been punctuated by a series of almost disbelieving questions from him and although I was determined not to accuse Sobers of any wrongdoing, I had to make it clear that I felt he'd been caught up in some sort of mix-up. I repeated my offer to work in conjunction with The Space Man and The Book Man in an attempt to settle the authenticity question.

"Are you happy for me to send you some evidence via email?"

"Yes, please."

"And if you are happy with the evidence that I've sent you, then you'll send me the ball with the certificate and I will sort it out?"

"OK."

"I give you my word."

"OK. You do that."

"My word is my bond. If I say I'm going to sort something out, I will sort something out."

"Obviously I take your word and if something is coming from you, then I believe you."

"I will send you this information now and I would be grateful if you could wrap up the ball and send it to me with the certificate of provenance and I will get it sorted. I promise you."

"I will do that. Thank you."

I put down the phone with a huge sigh of relief. Not only had I spoken to the ball owner but I'd obtained an agreement in principle that, if my evidence was satisfactory, he would send the Duke ball back to Britain. It sounded too good to be true – and, deep down, I knew it was. I wasn't naïve enough to think that a deal had been done – simply because the brief mention of money had been so imprecise. I'd raised the subject of a possible refund from Christie's but that was all – no definite figures had been discussed because, at that stage, they simply couldn't be. If, as Singhal had claimed, he'd paid just over £26,400 for the ball, then it was obvious he wouldn't be prepared to send it to me without a guarantee of some sort of a financial return. He was a businessman and businessmen like to make a profit; I realised that the negotiations had barely begun. But I was pleased to have made contact with a key player in the Six Sixes ball saga. I immediately rang Chris Davies and then Shapero to tell them the good news.

Chris was delighted when I played him the Singhal interview down the phone and Shapero seemed pleased to hear the latest developments. When I told The Book Man that The Space Man had heard of him, he quoted the comment made by Kenneth Williams while playing Julius Caesar in *Carry On Cleo*: "Infamy! Infamy! They've all got it in for me!" I had to laugh – after all, it had been voted the funniest film one-liner in a 2007 Sky Movies Comedy poll – and I wondered again how Singhal knew about Shapero. Perhaps his name had appeared on some paperwork that had accompanied the bat and ball? Later that evening, I emailed Singhal a selection of my evidence – including newspaper cuttings, the 1968 Glamorgan newsletter which confirmed the real ball's make as a Surridge, and an extract from *Six of the Best* – and my postal address for him to send me the ball. To show willing, I'd also offered to send him a signed copy of *Six of the Best* and, having not heard anything for a couple of days, I later emailed to check if my original message had been received and to ask for his postal address.

I also emailed Andrew Hignell, Glamorgan's archivist, asking him again to confirm that the then Christie's head of sporting memorabilia, David Convery, was the man who he and his wife, Debra, had met when he'd gone to London to look at the ball in 2006. Back came another unsatisfactory reply:

> I'm still looking for my desk diary from 2006 which would confirm who we met. Will let you know the outcome when I unearth it.

Hignell had now produced an intriguing collection of reasons for not helping me out – including a file on the Six Sixes ball which contained no mention of any Christie's contacts, some deleted emails and a lost diary. I decided to look up the notes I'd made from my original interview with him while writing *Six of the Best* in 2008. They did the trick by refreshing my memories of the conversation and setting his current reluctance to answer such a simple question in fascinating context. He said he'd gone to Christie's in 2006 because they'd asked him to verify the details of the match, "to verify the circumstances". They'd shown him the ball, the signed certificate of provenance and the newspaper cutting about the Surridge ball being found by Richard Lewis in the street before it was returned to Garry Sobers. Hignell said he'd "looked at the make" and they'd wanted to know if the ball looked like a ball that could have been used at that time. He said he'd been "unable to say if the ball was or wasn't the ball used in the Six Sixes over." In other words, he'd not been able to give them a definitive answer. Hignell said he'd told Christie's about the reservations that ex-players such as Peter Walker and Malcolm Nash had voiced about the make of the ball because Glamorgan had only used Stuart Surridge balls and not Duke & Son in 1968.

When I'd told Hignell that his comments would be included in *Six of the Best*, he'd become very defensive and after a short, almost heated discussion, we'd agreed on a form of words with which he was content:

> Wynne-Thomas [Peter, the Nottinghamshire archivist] and his counterpart at Glamorgan, Dr. Andrew Hignell, discussed the intended sale on the telephone. Hignell travelled to London to verify the details of the match and was shown the ball.

I clearly remembered not being very happy about those two sentences. They were too stark, I'd wanted to shed more light on the

Christie's meeting and I couldn't understand why Hignell was so adamant that I couldn't go into any more detail. I'd agreed to his request because I wanted to include the verification section in the 'where are they now?' chapter. At that time, I hadn't realised how important Hignell's contribution would turn out to be. As I revisited the 2008 conversation, I wondered if he was in any way embarrassed by his specialist bit-part in the Christie's authentication process. He certainly seemed uncomfortable about it – otherwise, why did he appear to be so reluctant to discuss his role? My series of emails contained a perfectly reasonable question about his contact at Christie's so why was he being so uncooperative? It was yet another question to ponder as Operation Howzat? prepared to go subcontinental.

After being fired up by listening to the Singhal interview and then reading the transcript, Chris and I resumed our trawl for more information about the online airport auction. While he focused on finding the bat and ball on a lot list, I decided to follow the airport route – on the assumption that either Singhal or his "friend" had bought the ball at an e-auction held under the auspices of the nearest airport to Faridabad, the city where he worked. I'd discovered that Faridabad was served by the IGI Airport in New Delhi and that online auctions of unclaimed goods held there were run by an Ahmedabad firm called abcProcure, which described itself as "Asia's number 1 eProcurement solution provider." Acting on behalf of the Government of India, the company would arrange for items to be put on display in a conference room in the airport's cargo terminal before being sold online. I emailed abcProcure asking for their help and after explaining that I was writing a sequel to *Six of the Best*, I told them all I knew. Admittedly, they didn't have much to go on: a cricket bat and ball which had been sent to India from Britain sometime after Christmas 2006 and which, "for whatever reason," hadn't been collected by their owner. Did they have a record of the subsequent auction and contact details of the buyer? As I waited around for their reply, my phone rang. It was Chris:

"I've found it!"

"Found what?"

"The ball – and the bat. They were together."

"Where?"

"In a glass casket sold at an online auction at the IGI Airport in November 2009."

"Brilliant! Can you send me the details?"

When his email arrived a few moments later, it also contained two comments which perfectly summed up my mood: "Howzat?" and "mini-celebration?" Too right. In fact, make that a major celebration, I said rather rashly. Chris had done very well to find a cricket ball in a haystack or, as he succinctly put it later, a grain of truth in a bag of rice. I clicked onto the IGI Airport's website, located the auction catalogue for sale 192 before scrolling down to lot 112 (reference LKD401109) and finding the briefest of descriptions:

> SORVENIER CRICKET WOODEN BAT AND LEATHER
> BALL PACKED IN GLASS CASKET. SIGNED BY AND NAME
> OF 82 PLAYERS. WT = 36KG

So this is where the most famous ball in cricket had ended up: in an online airport auction of unclaimed goods, sandwiched between some bathroom fittings – including a deck mounted tub/shower set – and 50 Namda felted rugs. Along with the bat, it was one of 498 lots sold on Tuesday 17th and Wednesday 18th November 2009 – almost three years to the day since Bernard Shapero had bought it at Christie's in London. I scrolled back to the beginning of the catalogue in search of more details of the sale. Viewing had taken place at the airport the day before and the bat and ball had been included under "miscellaneous import items." Bidders were informed that the auction would take place on an "as is where is" basis – that is, on a "to be sold as seen" basis where an item is offered in its actual current condition. There is no warranty or guarantee and no possibility of bringing it back because it isn't perfect. "Where is" means that it's up to the buyer to remove the item from wherever it is currently stored at their own cost; delivery is not included in the deal. The Bonhams catalogue entry for the bat revealed that the "glass casket" was in fact a perspex display case with players' names inscribed on the inside of the case as well as on the bat.

The ball – along with the certificate of provenance – had presumably been put in the case for safe keeping when it had been sent to India. Whoever had bought lot 112 must have pinched themselves when they opened it up and found the accompanying certificate of provenance. This wasn't just any old cricket ball. Quite by chance, the buyer was apparently in possession of the one used in the game's most famous over; the signed certificate would have dispelled any doubts about its authenticity – if any had existed – but, in truth, the ball was a long way from being the genuine article. Then again, the online catalogue had also included probably the auction world's most well-known warning – "let the buyer beware."

I immediately emailed the details of the sale to abcProcure in the hope that the buyer could be identified while Chris, as was his wont, began to speculate on why the joint lot had become unclaimed cargo. Although the ball dated from the 1960s, the bat was allegedly more than 100 years old and, according to his research, it would probably have been classed as an antique by Indian customs and therefore subject to import duty of around 20 per cent. Perhaps such a not inconsiderable extra charge had led to the casket's extended stay at the IGI Airport? I joined in with some more general speculation: why had the ball been lying in the airport for nearly three years – if indeed it had been there for the whole time – and if it hadn't, precisely where had it been since being bought at Christie's and then sold in New Delhi? Why had The Mystery Man not simply gone along to the airport and picked up the bat and ball from customs?

Striking while the iron was very hot, I decided to follow up my emails to abcProcure with a phone call early the next morning. It wasn't a very good line – it seemed they never were to India – but I managed to talk to Vishal Dhori, one of the company's directors, about the ball buyer, the price he'd paid, the right of the airport to seize unclaimed goods and the right of the ball owner to appeal against a decision to consign an item to an online auction. Vishal promised that a member of his staff would try to find out who'd bought the ball at auction when they came back from their weekend break. About an hour after I'd put the phone down to Ahmedabad, The Space Man was back in touch:

Dear Mr. Grahame ,
Many thanks for the information , Very sorry for the delay in reply

due to lot of travelling . I am too occupied at this moment as we are finishing some time bound Solar Power Projects and there is lot of investment at stake . Will reply you in detail with my decision next week .

Thanks & Regards
Ashish Singhal

Do not cry if the Sun sets at the end of the day, because the tears will not let you enjoy the beauty of the Stars.

Singhal wasn't to know it but a lot of time and effort had already been invested via Operation Howzat? as we'd tracked the ball's journey from Britain to India. An hour after receiving Singhal's apology, and with the iron becoming even hotter, I made a series of short phone calls to the IGI Airport in a vain attempt to speak to someone about the online auction before deciding that an email would probably be the better option. I explained that I was trying to update *Six of the Best* and asked if I could be supplied with the name and contact details of both the person to whom the ball was sent in India and who ever had bought it at the airport e-auction. Not for the first time during Operation Howzat?, an important discovery had thrown up another set of intriguing questions – not least the one covering the identity of the New Delhi ball buyer. Who was it? My gut instinct told me it was Singhal because, true to form, he'd been more than a little secretive when we'd spoken on the phone three days earlier. He wouldn't tell me exactly how much he'd paid for the ball and preferred not to name the "friend" from whom he'd bought it. In terms of transparency, it was par for the course. As I waited for a message – or two – from India, I had a feeling that Rudyard Kipling's "six honest serving-men" were going to find themselves putting in a serious amount of overtime during the next few weeks.

An airport, an auction and
an art impresario

He did not know, but presently he would know.
Great is information, and she shall prevail.

E. M. Forster, *A Passage to India*

I didn't have to wait long to find out who had bought the Six Sixes ball from the e-auction. Although Vishal Dhori wasn't able to provide the name personally, he'd enlisted the help of abcProcure's deputy manager, Parin Desai, and just after 10 o'clock in the morning on Monday 13th August, another one of those short but very sweet emails arrived in my inbox:

> Dear Mr. Lloyd,
>
> Please find below given details for your ready reference.
>
> M/s. Ashish globotech
> Mr. Ashish Singhal
> Cell No. 0-9899622295
> Email – ashishglobotech@hotmail.com
>
> please revert back for any further clarifications.
>
> Regards,
> Parin Desai

Howzat? Up goes the dreaded finger again. Ashish Singhal, batting for Ashish Globotech – as opposed to Faridabad Forgings – was back in the pavilion after being comprehensively caught out. No need to go upstairs to the third umpire and the decision review system. Singhal had been induced to play a false shot and you could hear the snick all around the ground. It turned out that the "avid cricket fan", who claimed he'd bought the ball from an anonymous friend, clearly didn't know the meaning of the age-old adage "it's just not cricket." His version of events was neither right nor fair. It seemed the man with a Masters in Business also possessed a first-class degree in duplicity. Singhal had insisted that he'd paid a "little premium" over the Christie's price of £26,400 – or $50,000 – but he'd actually bought the ball for comparatively next to nothing at the e-auction – quite a tidy bit of business whichever way you looked at it. And, having picked it up for a knockdown price – about £300 according to Bernard Shapero – he'd then tried to sell it back to its original owner for something like £15,000. I already knew that Singhal was evasive and secretive but, in light of the abcProcure email, he'd now plumbed new depths. It not only revealed the bare-faced cheek of the man; it confirmed my suspicion that he was another person in the Six Sixes saga who was not averse to being economical with the facts.

Later that day, Shapero returned my call and I was able to update him on Operation Howzat? I explained that I'd emailed my evidence to Singhal who'd promised to let me know his decision about sending the ball back to Britain during the coming week. In return, The Book Man said The Mystery Man had told him that he didn't know The Space Man. Because I thought Singhal was in two minds about returning the ball, I suggested to Shapero that we should offer him some form of financial inducement. After all, Singhal had no guarantee that we would give him any money or send the ball back to India if, as was likely, our negotiations with Christie's failed.

"What do you want me to do Grahame?," asked Shapero.

"Are you prepared to put some money down as a sort of advance in lieu of receiving a refund from Christie's?"

When that idea went down like a lead balloon, I followed it up with another suggestion:

"Why don't we draw up a contract between the two of you to cover a split of any refund from Christie's?"

"As broker of any deal, you could do that."

"But shouldn't any contract come from Shapero Rare Books because your company, as the known buyer, actually bought the ball?"

"Look Grahame…I understood why this matter is very important to you but it's not to me. I'm too busy to get involved in drawing up a contract. Why not go for a three-way split of any refund – between Ashish Singhal, you and me?"

"I'm not interested in the money –"

"Well…give your share to charity!"

Shapero then suggested that, as a first step, I should email Singhal and ask him how much he'd be happy with if we took the ball to Christie's and somehow managed to obtain a full refund – would he be content with a third of the £26,400? Moving on to another important question, I asked Shapero why his client hadn't picked up the ball from the IGI Airport sometime in 2006 or 2007. He said he didn't think that mattered now.

I then mentioned the recent court ruling in the row between Christie's and Viktor Vekselberg. The Russian oligarch had sued the auction house after paying £1.7 million for 'Odalisque', a painting of a nude woman, because he'd maintained it wasn't by Boris Kustodiev. During the 20-day court case, lawyers acting for Christie's had claimed the painting had a "reliable provenance" and pointed out that it featured a distinctive chair known to have been owned by Kustodiev. In his written judgement, Judge Guy Newey cleared Christie's of negligence and misrepresentation but delivered this ruling: "I do not think certainty on the point is possible but my task is to determine authenticity on the balance of probabilities and the likelihood, in my view, is that 'Odalisque' is the work of someone other than Kustodiev." Consequently, Vekselberg's company, Aurora Fine Arts Investment, had the right to return it "and recover the money it paid." A spokesman for Christie's, who also had to pay around £1 million in costs, said the auction house was "surprised and disappointed" by the ruling. In his judgement, Newey also said that Kustodiev "is to Russians what Laurence Stephen Lowry is to the English, in terms of the affection in which he is held." As I pondered the revered position occupied by Garfield St Aubrun Sobers within the world of cricket, if not sport, I felt that, despite the vastly different amounts of money involved, a justifiable parallel could be drawn between the two cases.

"Isn't the Vekselberg verdict encouraging?" I asked Shapero.

"Yes", he replied, "we can give it a go."

We certainly could – and with that, we agreed that I would contact The Space Man with our financial proposition. At that stage, I decided not to tell Shapero that I knew Singhal had bought the ball at the e-auction. I thought it best to withhold that information for the time being. During my investigation, I'd often been kept in the dark by both the new ball owner and the known buyer so why shouldn't they occasionally be given a dose of their own medicine?

Singhal's disingenuousness was highlighted by the heartwarmingly honest attitude shown by abcProcure and IGI airport officials as Operation Howzat? now entered a crucial phase. After expressing my gratitude to Parin Desai, I immediately accepted his offer of further clarification by emailing him some follow-up questions. Eighteen hours later, I received this reply listing my enquiries and his answers:

> Are you able to tell me how much Mr Singhal paid for the ball? **–**
> **Due to NDA signed with the client we can not share information**
> Can you tell me when he collected the ball? **– details will be only
> with the bidder or IG**
> Do you know who the ball was sent to in India before it was seized
> by the disposal unit at the IGI Airport? Was there an address on the
> packaging or a note inside the casket which also contained the
> antique cricket bat? **– No Idea**
> Do you know why the ball was seized by the disposal unit at the
> airport? I understand it might have something to do with import
> duty. **– No idea we are just a service provider of e-Auction to
> IGI**
> Do you have the contact details of an official at the disposal unit at
> the airport who might be able to help me to discover the identity of
> the person for whom the ball was intended when it was sent to India
> from England? **– No**

Ah well. It was worth a try. The NDA – non-disclosure agreement – showed that abcProcure, like Bonhams and Bernard Shapero, placed great store by client confidentiality – and I understood why. The email meant that, for the moment at least, two questions remained unanswered: how much had Singhal paid for the ball and who was Shapero's mysterious client? When I told Chris Davies that The Space Man had bought the ball via the e-auction, he immediately set about trying to identify The Mystery Man – starting with his – the anonymous client's – working relationship with The Book Man. An early stab in the dark eventually proved pretty accurate – although not even Chris realised the importance of the person involved at that time. Among the initial list of runners and riders were the art auctioneers, Osian's, with offices in Mumbai and New Delhi, who had bought some photos of 19th century India from Shapero in 2005. Other names in the frame were the country's largest real estate developer, Kushal Pal Singh, the telecom mogul and philanthropist, Sunil Mittal, and India's most flamboyant businessman and chairman of United Breweries, the beer and spirits conglomerate, Vijay Mallya. Sometimes described as "India's Richard Branson", Mallya also owned a Formula 1 racing team and Kingfisher Airlines, which was later grounded because of debts and safety concerns. He had an impressive track record in terms of buying significant artefacts. He'd acquired the sword of 18th-century warrior king Tipu Sultan, which was seized by the British after a bloody war, and brought it back to India in 2004. Five years later, Mallya had bought five personal belongings of Mahatma Gandhi – including his iconic eyeglasses and a plate and bowl from which he'd eaten his last meal. Chris' money was on Mallya because he was also a huge cricket fan, having acquired a stake in the Royal Challengers Bangalore franchise in the Indian Premier League.

As Chris speculated, I opted to accumulate a few more facts. I decided to focus my attention on the IGI Airport at New Delhi by trying to speak to someone from the disposal unit where the ball had somehow ended up. After another flurry of confusing and confused phone calls, I began to make some progress when I spoke to Shrishti Choudhary, a software engineer at the airport, who supplied me with a more accurate telephone number and email address for the unit after I'd inadvertently rung her. Although it wasn't in her normal line of work, she said she'd be happy to make a few enquiries on my behalf if necessary because "ours is a cricket crazy nation." She also wished me all the best with this book and urged me to "stay blessed." I knew I would remain in that special state as long as I was dealing with such helpful people – and it was through Shrishti that I contacted Sushant Nigam, the general manager (cargo) at the airport. He was immediately on the case and during our subsequent exchange of emails, he told me that his 14-hour-a-day, seven-day-a-week job was his "passion." I understood what he meant when, less than 48 hours later, he came up with the vital information. The glass casket containing the bat and ball had been sent to Osian's Connoisseurs of Art in Mumbai aboard a Virgin Airways flight which had landed at the airport in June 2008 – 18 months after the sale at Christie's. When I mentioned the delay between the casket's purchase by Bernard Shapero and its dispatch, Nigam came back with more details:

> Osians Connoisseurs was the consignee, as per documents of the Airline, Virgin Atlantic, which had brought it to Delhi on their flight No. VS-300 on 3.6.2008. You may like to confirm the same from Virgin Atlantic in London. However, it was not cleared by the consignee for reasons best known to him only. Since it remained un-cleared / un-claimed for period beyond permissible limits, it was disposed of by the custodian after permission of Indian Customs under provisions of The Customs Act 1962. I hope it suffices for your purpose.

It certainly did. What a star Sushant Nigam was turning out to be! His first name meant 'calm' and 'satisfied': he'd been calm and I felt satisfied – very satisfied. I immediately began searching for more information about Osian's and, in particular, the company's founder, Neville Tuli. When I typed his name into Google, I was left in no doubt that he was a major player in the revitalised Indian arts scene – and, in particular, the auction world. As I looked at the collection of online photos and videos, I was immediately struck by Tuli's resemblance to the Pakistani cricketer-turned-politician, Imran Khan. Twelve years may have separated the two men in age – and they clearly operated in different spheres – but they seemed to have a lot in common: striking good looks, luxuriant black hair, a flamboyant if not foppish dress sense and a prominent public persona. And both appeared to court controversy. The headlines at the top of some of the stories which popped up through my Google search proved intriguing as I settled down to learn more about the man who, for some reason, had paid £26,400 for the world's most expensive cricket ball. One article in *Tehelka*, an Indian weekly newspaper specialising in public interest journalism, serious opinion and analysis, was both riveting and revealing. Under the headline, "The Mismanagement of Neville Tuli", I learned how he had been turned from "a gust of fresh air into a cautionary tale" by a recent financial crisis. Through such articles, I was able to build up a preliminary picture of probably India's best known art impresario – but without his help. At this stage, I didn't want to approach Tuli for fear of upsetting or even alienating Bernard Shapero who had assiduously protected his client's identity. I later supplemented my initial portrait with additional information supplied by the man himself after Shapero had finally admitted that Tuli was The Mystery Man.

Born in 1948 in London, Tuli was educated in Mumbai and then at Oxford University and the London School of Economics before returning to India in 1993 after 25 years in the West. He later revealed that while living in England, he'd become seriously addicted to gambling on horses and it soon became clear to me that risk-taking had always been a key component of his modus operandi. His subsequent career had been as chequered as the history of the Six Sixes ball which he bought at Christie's in 2006. A trained economist with no background in the arts, Tuli described himself as "a development theorist". When he arrived back in his homeland, he'd decided it was time to preserve and nurture India's artistic heritage. Initially, he'd helped to drive up the price of contemporary art through his determination to make Indian art more accessible and affordable to the emerging rich – rather than just the super rich. He travelled across the country meeting artists, taking in everything he saw as he visited hundreds of cities, towns, villages and monuments. He curated exhibitions and set up HEART, his charitable foundation for holistic education and art, which put him in touch with artists, dealers, galleries and collectors. He wanted to build an infrastructure for the Indian fine arts which didn't rely on government or corporate funding or private donations.

In 1997, Tuli published *The Flamed Mosaic*, a celebrated book about Indian contemporary art. It not only shone a light on certain forgotten artists but established Tuli as a serious player in the market. As well as promoting artists who he considered underrated, he bought up as many artworks as possible and raised the profile of obscure cinema memorabilia. He held the country's first independent auction without any assistance from organisations such as Sotheby's and Christie's. It established record prices for many artists and the catalogue also set new standards for documentation and design. At the turn of the 21st century, Tuli launched Osian's Connoisseurs of Art (OCA), which included India's first indigenous auction house, an archiving, research and documentation centre, a wealth management service and a film house. It wasn't long before OCA acquired a film festival, an art journal, a publishing and design house, the ownership of a football team and the sponsorship of a football tournament. Business was booming as hedge funds and private equity companies acquired stakes in Osian's – as did a well-known collection of entrepreneurs and industrialists. Equally high-profile individuals, such as Ashok Alexander, Melinda and Bill Gates Foundation's director, joined OCA's board.

By following his motto "materialism through creativity", Tuli became the new broom which swept though the notoriously sedate Indian art scene. As I read the online articles, it seemed to me that Tuli – which means "paintbrush" in Hindi and Bengali – was more of a broad brushstroke artist than a pointillist. I became aware of his sometimes unusual behaviour and purchases; he was a man prone to making grand gestures and quick decisions. People who worked for him talked of his incredible energy and passion – as well as his volatile temperament. He knew every employee in his offices – right down to the cleaners and drivers – and his outbursts of outrage were legendary as his exasperation at the slow pace of change often got the better of him. In pursuit of his grand vision, he started buying up 250,000 artefacts – such as Japanese Samurai masks and iconic posters of Marilyn Monroe, Alfred Hitchcock and Walt Disney – as he assembled the world's largest collection of film memorabilia from India, Hollywood, many Asian countries and much of Europe. A knowledgeable and passionate sportsman, Tuli had begun planning a series of cricket memorabilia events – including an exhibition and an auction – and the antique bat and the Six Sixes ball were just two of 600 rare items he would acquire from 2005 onwards.

The business and financial market news service, Bloomberg, reported that at a Sotheby's auction held in May 2006, Tuli "bought at least four contemporary works in an hour from his front-row seat…nodding continually until his rivals dropped out." One of the paintings, an untitled nude by the Indian artist, Francis Newton Souza, cost him £310,400 – almost double its estimate. Tuli maintained he was simply gathering art work for his proposed Osianama project, hailed as India's first integrated museum complex for film, arts and the environment. His critics accused him of indulging himself and, in the process, creating a false euphoria in the market. One particular comment by someone from whose firm Tuli had once bought art immediately struck a chord with me as I reflected on the fate of the Six Sixes ball: "He pays exorbitant rates for things he doesn't need to. He buys artwork and doesn't pick it up. With Neville, nothing makes sense."

But, for me at least, things were starting to make sense. I began to understand how the antique bat and ball had come to be bought for Tuli by Bernard Shapero via a mobile phone at Christie's in 2006. The estimates for both were between £5,000 and £8,000 and after paying £9,600 for the bat, Tuli would have been desperate to land the ball and complete the set. I started to imagine him listening intently down the phone as the price had gone through the roof. As the tension and the bidding intensified, Tuli had remained ice cool. He'd wanted the Duke and eventually he'd got it. Paying such an over-the-top price of £26,400 for a cricket ball didn't make much sense to me – until I discovered who'd actually bought it. It fitted neatly into Tuli's purchasing pattern, whether he was buying sporting memorabilia or fine arts.

His decision to launch Osian's Art Fund earlier in 2006 had been perfectly in keeping with the prevailing climate as India's economy continued to grow. Indian artists started to make headlines at global auctions and art funds began to woo investors – 656 of them buying units in the Osian's one. At first, it looked like being a roaring success with its value rising rapidly as the money was invested in the works of 146 artists, including Souza and "The Picasso of India", M. F. Husain. The fund was expected to generate 30-35 per cent returns as the good times kept on rolling and the bullish Tuli rode the wave to spectacular effect. But when the worldwide recession hit India in 2008, the art market was frozen and Osian's Art Fund collapsed because Tuli couldn't sell its stock and repay its investors at the end of its three-year term. His predictions had proved wide of the mark – especially when compared with returns from stocks and shares, real estate and gold – and Tuli was in trouble: the publishing house was shut down, the film festival left in limbo and prominent board members resigned from his company. To make matters worse, banks refused to lend him any money to tide him over his liquidity crisis. In short, Osian's went into freefall as Tuli's spending spree suddenly ground to a halt.

In hindsight, it would seem that Tuli had spread himself too thinly by initiating too many different ventures. Despite his good intentions – and he'd clearly rejuvenated a largely moribund Indian art market – Tuli had bitten off more than he could chew. He'd blamed his demise on the global downturn but his critics, annoyed by what they considered his arrogance, pointed to what they believed to be his reckless buying and hoarding of art work and the too hectic pace of expansion. They also criticised his flawed business model, in which each venture was intricately involved with the other and the auction house funded them all. It was a mistake Tuli later acknowledged: "In retrospect, I included too many diverse non-profit making activities, placing immense burden on the auction house. When the market melted, Osian's, having a huge debt, suffered the most." I could only assume that, as a result of his subsequent cash-flow problems, Tuli hadn't been able to pay the import duty on the bat and ball when they'd arrived at the IGI Airport in 2008. I couldn't contact him now but when the time was right, I'd be looking for an answer to the one outstanding question: just why had the Duke remained locked in customs for 18 months?

As I continued my research into his life and times, it became clear that Tuli was nothing if not a survivor. He may have been down – in that he was still struggling to pay back the art fund investors – but he certainly wasn't out. In fact, he was on his way back. Osian's stopped subsidising his other projects and reverted to being an auction house and Tuli returned to his artistic roots. After lying low for more than a year after the art fund collapse in June 2010, he'd re-surfaced as a speaker at a couple of conferences before announcing Osian's Creative Bengal Series auction which featured the works of the Tagore trio (Abanindranath, Gaganendranath and Rabindranath) the latter being the cultural all-rounder so admired by The Space Man, Ashish Singhal. Nearly half the 130 lots remained unsold and the auction raised only two-thirds of its target but Tuli insisted that "given the economic situation, it was a success." Similar auctions followed during the next six months with the proceeds helping to pay off the art fund investors.

After a two-year sabbatical, the Cinefan Film Festival returned in the summer of 2012 to showcase Indian, Asian and Arab cinema. It included an auction of Indian film memorabilia to mark the 100th anniversary of the country's cinema industry which produced record receipts after 86 per cent of the lots had been sold. "The auction emphatically indicated that an enormous potential exists for developing the market for Indian cinema memorabilia and that the film fraternity now feels a sense of respect for its cinematic heritage," declared a typically ebullient Tuli. "Hereafter no one will dismiss these items as *raddi* (junk). They are collectibles and they have significant financial value." I read with interest that one of the lots sold had been a cricket bat used in *Lagaan: Once Upon a Time in India,* an epic musical drama film about the payment of land tax under British rule which had a cricket match as its centrepiece. The charismatic and inspirational art impresario had now learned that another of his highly rated collectibles – not a Bollywood bat but the Six Sixes ball – had acquired a less than significant financial value: the famous Duke had become nothing more than an infamous piece of junk.

When I resumed my search for the price paid for the ball by its new owner, my contact at the IGI Airport's disposal unit, Sushant Nigam, revealed his cricketing credentials. He was a fan but his heavy work schedule meant he wasn't able to devote much time to the game. But he said he was happy to be "able to contribute to some interesting facts being recorded in an international book." I couldn't have been happier with his contribution. In further emails, Sushant explained that an item "becomes ripe for disposal if it remains unclaimed/uncleared 30 days after its landing at the destination airport." He then said the bat and ball had been bought at the online auction in November 2009 for about 72,000 Indian rupees. I quickly calculated that, via the then exchange rates, Ashish Singhal had paid about £940 for the casket's contents – a long way from the "little premium" over £26,400 he'd claimed to have spent on the ball alone.

With another two major questions answered, Operation Howzat? was making real headway. We knew how much the ball's new owner had paid for it and Neville Tuli had been identified as The Mystery Man. I realised that I now needed to switch from journalist to broker mode. The moment had arrived to bring The Space Man back down to earth.

Spinning with The Space Man

Start out with an ideal and end up with a deal.

Karl Albrecht

During my 30-career as a freelance broadcaster and journalist, I've been involved in quite a few discussions about money. It's not always easy putting a price on your own worth but it's an occupational hazard which I've usually found enjoyable and rewarding. Sometimes the fees are fixed through a trades union; sometimes you have to play it by ear and fight for a figure without fear or favour. I've occasionally negotiated on behalf of other people – like the chairmen of half a dozen of the most successful League of Wales football clubs in the 1990s. Having qualified to play in European competitions, they wanted someone in the broadcasting business to help maximise their subsequent TV rights income and I found myself representing their teams in talks with a number of companies – first via phone and fax and then in a grand hotel in Geneva. But nothing – and I mean nothing – had prepared me for my role as broker in the Six Sixes ball saga. Trying to thrash out a deal between The Book Man and The Space Man would have tested the patience of Job. At times, Singhal's approach was so convoluted that I felt I was losing the will to live.

As I opened negotiations with him over the safe return of the Duke ball to Britain, I knew the truth – but not quite the final truth – about his association with the ball. He wasn't aware that I'd found out about the airport e-auction and I'd decided that I wouldn't lay some of my other cards on the table either – like Bernard Shapero's suggested three-way split of any refund – until I had a clearer idea of The Space Man's demands. It was important to test the water so my opening gambit was intentionally on the low side, in expectation that, having claimed to have paid just over £26,400 for the ball, Singhal would be coming to the table with a figure from the higher end of the scale. It might have seemed naïve, and it probably was, but based on the assumption that the ball had actually cost him somewhere between £300 and £400, I felt that a profit of about 25 per cent – or £100 – would represent a fair return on his investment. I knew it was a ridiculously small offer but I thought I'd start at the bottom and work my way up. In my first email, I explained that I'd been commissioned to write an article for *Wisden* about the Six Sixes ball and strongly hinted that I knew more about the method by which Singhal had acquired it than he thought I did:

> I would like to avoid having to write a more negative account involving mysterious buyers and bidders at real and online auctions so I would be grateful if you could send me the ball in order that I can facilitate a mutually beneficial outcome. I have also spoken to Bernard Shapero, who bought the ball from Christie's in 2006 for his client in India. He has asked me to ask you how much money you would be prepared to accept – if we were able to negotiate a refund from Christie's on the grounds of the ball's false provenance? I realise that as a businessman, you are looking to make a profit on your investment so would you be happy with a sum to cover your total purchase price plus, say, 25 per cent of that amount?

I said I couldn't be more specific because Singhal hadn't told me how many Indian rupees he'd paid for the ball. I suggested that if we could agree an acceptable figure, I would draw up a contract guaranteeing him that sum if a refund were to be obtained from Christie's. I reiterated my view that, in light of my evidence, his ball was essentially worthless and mentioned that the Vekselberg – Christie's court case might help to produce what I called "a positive result for all parties concerned." I also asked if he could now tell me from whom he'd bought the ball and reply to me promptly because of the pressing deadline for my *Wisden* article.

The Space Man hadn't exactly endeared himself to me by declining to divulge the truth about his purchase of the ball and he hardly helped himself as the negotiations continued. When his next email landed in my inbox, Abraham Lincoln's quote that "knavery and flattery are blood relations" immediately came to mind. After updating me on his solar energy projects, Singhal quickly turned his attention to my writing skills – despite never having read any of my work:

> The amount of Research you do and your use of proper and powerful words is indeed very impressive.There is no doubt about the fact that you are a very fine writer and a distinguished Journalist . I

> Respect your concern and the amount of time you are spending to
> bring this issue to conclusion .

It proved to be the first half of the classic 'nice 'n nasty' negotiating
technique: butter 'em up and then hit 'em with an outrageous
demand. With the compliments out of the way, Singhal got right
down to business:

> I personally feel that court matters and litigation takes lot of time to
> settle the issue I really do not even wish to be part of it and would
> like if it is settled in some other way , whichever way possible .
> Generally there should be a expectation of profit on any investment
> , and any piece of art or collectible appreciates in its value over time .
> But We are not looking at making any profit on this investment and
> in fact willing to settle the same at even less then what i have pur-
> chased it for . The ball was sold at $50,000 at auction in Christies in
> 2006 , i propose to sell the same at 40% less at $30,000 on outright
> basis . Hope you will understand my concern and will find my offer
> to be very reasonable.

I must admit that "reasonable" wasn't the first word which came to
mind as I read this email; quite the opposite in fact. After reaching
for my calculator, I quickly checked the figures; 40 per cent of
$50,000 was indeed $20,000 so Singhal was offering to sell the ball
for $30,000 – about £19,000 according to the exchange rate con-
version site I quickly found online. Was he really expecting Shapero
to take the ball back to Christie's and then see most of the £26,400
disappear to India? It seemed like he was. I picked up my calculator
again: £19,000 – or nearly three quarters of a full refund – was a
long way from the third which Shapero was happy for Singhal to
have under any agreement I might broker. My first impression of
The Space Man was confirmed by this email: he was clearly living
in his own little world – perhaps on a space station? – or even on
another planet. "Unreasonable" and "unrealistic" were the two
descriptions of his offer which I included in my reply as I took him
to task for his duplicitous behaviour. I didn't pull any punches but
I had to be careful not to alienate him completely.

I described his response to my 25 per cent suggestion as "disrespectful" and then explained that, because of his evasive attitude,
I'd been forced to make my own enquiries into his background. I

then revealed that I knew the full extent of his association with the ball – including his negotiations with Neville Tuli about its possible re-sale. Inevitably, some of my financial accusations were complete shots in the dark because I couldn't be 100 per cent sure of the precise amount of money he'd paid or requested for the ball but I felt they were necessary to flush him out, to find out more about his involvement. The thrust of my email was unequivocal: you've been less than forthcoming from the outset and you've not told me the truth. One financial fact of which I was certain was his offer to sell the ball for $30,000. I poured scorn on his claim to have paid "a little premium" on top of the $50,000 it had fetched in 2006 and explained that if Shapero and I were somehow able to secure a full refund from Christie's and then agreed to Singhal's suggestion, only just under a quarter of the price paid for the ball in 2006 would be left. "Speaking in my role as broker between yourself and Mr Shapero," I said, "I know that he would not entertain such a dis-proportionate division of any reimbursement."

I agreed with Singhal's claim that "any piece of art or collectible appreciates in value over time" but only if it was the genuine article – like the antique bat which he'd bought with the ball in the e-auction job lot. I reminded him that his ball wasn't the one bowled in the over and that balls signed by Sobers were ten a penny on web-sites like ebay. I then felt I had no alternative but to lay it on the line, not for the first time or the last:

> You have to accept that your ball is virtually worthless. It has been withdrawn from sale by the world's leading auction house because of doubts about its authenticity and, thanks to the internet, that fact is now very well-known.

> Nobody in their right mind would buy your ball as the one used in the Six Sixes over – even with the certificate of provenance. The only way you will be able to realise a significant return on your ball is by allowing me to take it to Christie's – along with the certificate of provenance and my mountain of evidence – in an attempt to gain a refund.

I pointed out that even if the ball were genuine, it would be unlikely to hold its price because of the worldwide recession. He should remember that the antique bat which he'd sold through Bonhams for £4,625 in 2012 had fetched £9,600 at Christie's back in 2006. I then decided to exert some rather unsubtle pressure by explaining that his behaviour would inevitably produce a negative account of the story for my article in *Wisden* and my sequel to *Six of the Best*:

> During my career, I have developed a range of contacts throughout the world – including some journalists in Mumbai who work for, among other papers, the *India Daily Post*, the *Pakistan Observer* and the *Lahore Times*. They have keenly followed the ball story and would undoubtedly be very interested in your involvement – bearing in your mind your high profile in the Indian business community through your various family companies such as Faridabad Forgings, Ashish Globtech, Genius Aquatech "Kristal" and AEW Infratech. I'm not sure how your approach to Mr Tuli or your attempt to use the Six Sixes ball to obtain $30,000 from me – tarnishing the name of Sir Garfield Sobers in the process – will be viewed in India.

I then suggested to Singhal that he might like to reconsider his position. I said I was prepared to forgive and overlook his "indiscretion" and repeated my offer to cover the price he'd paid for the ball plus 25 per cent – but only if we were successful in gaining a refund from Christie's. I said I was open to negotiation and encouraged him to take the opportunity of realising some sort of return on his investment as well as playing a "fascinating role in resolving one of cricket's greatest mysteries." As an alternative, I suggested that we could agree on a percentage of whatever final amount might be obtained in a refund. I stressed to Singhal that I would be taking my evidence to Christie's – with or without his ball – because of the suspicious circumstances surrounding the sale in 2006. I had no interest in buying the ball – especially as it hadn't been used in the famous over.

Three days later, Singhal emailed me in an attempt to clarify his involvement with the Duke. My problem was that his habit of being economical with the facts meant I had to take his various assertions with a very large pinch of salt. He rightly stressed that he was the "only legal owner" before pointing out that it was me who had made initial contact with him and he was "least interested." He then claimed that he'd never spoken to Neville Tuli but that a representative of the art impresario had rung two or three times in 2009 in an attempt to buy back the ball. Singhal had asked him for about

$20,000 and was offered $8,000 which he rejected. Singhal recalled his experience with Bonhams – "we never thought there will be any problem auctioning it" – before revealing a little more about his business operations and stating a viewpoint which never wavered: he just couldn't accept that his prized possession was not the actual ball:

> As far as we are concerned, The ball is genuine as auctioned by Christies, If not then they are liable to take it back and we shall follow up with them when I have time. As informed to you earlier I am too busy with My Solar Energy Projects as they are time bound. The cost of 10 MW project which I am developing presently is 20 Million US$ (Rs.100 Cr Appx) hope you will understand how much significance $30,000 or the Monetary value of this ball hold for me.

Singhal then denied offering to sell the ball for $30,000 – "the balance would be $20,000" – before suggesting Shapero should make a "genuine and reasonable" offer for it. He attacked me for trying to contact him by "sending fake email" – the Chris Davies enquiry about solar power for his fictitious studio – and eventually making a "desperate" phone call after I'd provided him with my evidence and CV to prove that I was genuine.

> I acknowledge the effort made by you but as a business man why will I hand over the ball and certificate to you without knowing the complete deal and how I am part of it .

Singhal went on to, justifiably, criticise me for mentioning my range of media contacts and the possible impact a negative article about his behaviour might have on his operations:

> Our business house is more than 50 years old if you think your article will affect any of my business than you are mistaken. Whatever i have built for myself is what i have done in my last 10 years in business after education without help of my family . I am a self made man and such kind of articles doesn't affect any of our businesses and we do not get involved for such small issues in court. We believe in maintaining cordial relations. You are free to write whatever the truth is and do not try to blackmail us by mentioning that you can write negative about us.

Fair play, it was an understandable response. But again, given Singhal's deceit from day one, I believed that adopting a slightly underhand approach was occasionally justified. My tactics had at least fired up The Space Man and brought him to the negotiating table. After making it clear that he didn't have to sell the ball – "it will not make any difference to me. I will be happy to keep it in my office" – he repeated his willingness to consider a "reasonable" offer. As I re-read this long and rambling email again, I came across a phrase to which I repeatedly returned during our discussions:

> I have no grudges against you that because of your evidence The ball could not be auctioned . The ball was purchased because it was auctioned by Christies and carried certificate of provenance by Sir Garfield Sobers himself but Whatever the truth is must prevail and we all should be happy to abide by it.

What an interesting observation: "whatever the truth is must prevail and we should all be happy to abide by it." I took a deep breath and read it again. This was a statement from a man who had shown little respect for the facts and it left me bemused, bothered and not a little bewildered. But, having exchanged opening salvos, I realised it was time to initiate a truce in an attempt to secure a more equitable split of any refund which might be obtained from Christie's somewhere down the line. In my reply, I apologised for having to make certain assumptions but explained that "trying to find out the facts" had been very difficult after being given only one side of the story from Shapero. I said that if we were going to arrive at the truth, Singhal had to accept two things: the ball was not the genuine article and any attempt to gain financial redress from Christie's would have to involve Shapero as the man who'd actually bought it in 2006. I explained that Malcolm Nash was so keen to resolve the matter that he was prepared to fly over from America to sort it out. Would an email from the man who'd bowled the ball help to convince Singhal that it wasn't the one used at St Helen's in 1968? I repeated my offer to agree a split and draw up a contract for the safe return of the ball to Britain – and then back to India if no refund were obtained from Christie's. It was fine by me if he didn't want to sell the ball: it would simply gather dust in his office. But I urged him to put himself in Shapero's position, even though I realised it was highly unlikely that Singhal would agree to such a low return on his online investment:

After spending $50,000 on a ball which turns out not to be genuine, why should he share the proceeds of any refund with someone who paid about $474 – or £300 – for it at an e-auction? Whether you like it or not, the ball you own is not genuine and it is unreasonable for Mr Shapero to have to pay more money in an attempt to obtain some financial redress and to right a wrong.

I emphasised that as I was investigating one controversial sale, I was reluctant to become involved in what would, in effect, be another because Singhal "would be making a lot of money out of a ball that is not genuine." I suggested that he would do well to lower his expectations and I then came up with a possible solution. I knew that the souvenir Surridge ball, given to the schoolboy, Richard Lewis, for returning the actual ball to St Helen's two days after the over, had just been consigned to Hansons, an auction house based at Etwall in Derbyshire. Because of this ball's connections with the game but not with the over, a reserve price of £1,000 had been placed on it. If a refund were obtained from Christie's, I promised Singhal that Shapero would pay him, as the owner of the disputed Duke ball, a similar sum – about $1,582. While I knew this was a long way short of his original offer of £19,000, or even Shapero's suggested £8,800, I felt that any movement towards a mutually acceptable figure had to be gradual. Although I'd never played poker, I was determined not to show my hand too early. Based on the figure I believed that Singhal had paid – somewhere between £300 and £400 – I felt that £1,000 wasn't a bad return for a ball which had not been bowled in the Six Sixes over and I described my offer as "both genuine and reasonable." I explained my growing exasperation at having to act as broker – "I have wasted far too much time on this matter" – and suggested it might be better if Singhal dealt directly with Shapero rather than with me. I said I wanted to resolve the matter "amicably and swiftly" and asked him to reply within 48 hours, otherwise I would assume our correspondence was over. Progress was undoubtedly being made but it was painfully slow and time-consuming so I felt it was important to include a deadline in a bid to inject some urgency into the situation. But given The Space Man's track record during our tortuous talks, I wouldn't be holding my breath.

Deal or no deal?

My father said: 'You must never try to make all the money that's in a deal.
Let the other fellow make some money too, because if you have a reputation
for always making all the money, you won't have many deals.'

J. Paul Getty

"So what do you want to do Grahame?"

It was classic Bernard Shapero: straight to the point, no messing around with any small talk or preamble; as usual, he was cutting to the chase. I'd barely begun briefing him on developments from India when he interrupted me with one of his trademark questions. Ten days after making my £1,000 offer to the legal owner of the ball, I was suddenly aware that the known buyer was becoming impatient.

"What do *you* want to do?" I replied.

"I don't want to do anything," Shapero began. "He's not interested in accepting the fact that the ball isn't genuine. He doesn't want to know – 'none are so deaf as those who don't want to hear.' He's not interested."

As I prepared to respond, Shapero started to warm to his theme by hinting that we were facing a classic clash of cultures. I didn't know for sure but I wondered if his judgement had been formed through his business dealings with India and negotiations he'd had with clients there over the years. Shapero said it would be fine if we were dealing with someone in this country who would accept the facts but Singhal was living in India and clearly wouldn't.

"Get the ball back and we'll go to Christie's," Shapero said. "Without the body, there's no crime."

When I mentioned my improved offer to Singhal and suggested that I might be prepared to send a bank transfer of £1,000 to India, Shapero said he didn't think it would work. The Book Man's message was clear: forget it, you've no chance. He described my negotiating approach as a "mad idea" and repeated his offer of a three-way split of £8,800 each. As I struggled to recover from this withering but, to my mind, unwarranted attack on my tactics, I at least managed to explain the £1,000 figure – the equivalent to the reserve price put on Richard Lewis' Surridge ball at the Hansons auction later in October – but Shapero didn't want to hear about the ins and outs of the offer. I then mentioned my unease about being involved in a second possible sale of a ball that wasn't genuine. All along, I'd simply been searching for the truth and while investigating one dubious deal, I didn't want to play a key part in another: I knew the ball was the wrong make. It was a case, I told Shapero, of putting principles before profits – and of making sure that he didn't become a victim for the second time.

"If I compromise this principle," I explained, "and we agree to pay Singhal nearly £9,000 for a fake ball, then I could be accused of hypocrisy. I also don't like the idea of you being hit by a double whammy – in 2006 when you bought the ball at Christie's and again in 2012."

"A third of £26,400 would mean a payment of about £9,000", said Shapero. "It would be money I didn't have before. I've got nothing now so anything I got would be good."

"I've obviously been arguing your case too strongly in my negotiations with Singhal…"

"Offer him the three-way split I've suggested. Singhal should be paid for the ball, you should be paid for all the work you've put in and I should be paid because I was the original buyer. If you don't want your third, then you could give some of it to him and me or to charity."

"I don't want to give him anything but a fair price for a ball that is virtually worthless."

I then let it be known that I felt too many people involved in my investigation had been less than forthcoming about the facts when talking to me. I told Shapero that, as my research into Singhal's involvement with the ball had continued, I'd come across certain information which needed to be explored and explained. We were back on familiar conversational territory as Shapero continued to shield his client.

"Why was the ball not sent to India until June 2008?" I said. "Why was there an 18-month delay after the Christie's sale in 2006?"

"I can't remember."

"Why did your client not pick up the bat and ball from the IGI

Airport at New Delhi?"

"No idea."

"Did it have something to do with import tax?"

"It could have."

Shapero then launched another attack on what he called the "back story" or "the add-on" to the main story of the goings-on at Christie's. He dismissed all my questions about the ball's movements in India as irrelevant – saying it had been sent there and it was now owned by an Indian businessman. According to The Book Man, all of what he called the "in-between stuff" was incidental; it was a strange story but not relevant.

"The minutiae are not important enough," Shapero declared. "Just concentrate on the main story – the sale at Christie's. How was Sobers involved and what happened to the money?"

Shapero wouldn't be the last person to ask me about Sobers' role in the sale of the ball. I had no idea about that – or how the £26,400 had been distributed. It was obviously a question I would have to ask Sobers towards the end of Operation Howzat? All I knew for sure was that he had signed the certificate of provenance through his agent Basharat Hassan – and that was about it. Shapero re-iterated that he wasn't prepared to go to Christie's without the ball and again repeated his three-way split offer. I'd wanted to ask him if he was prepared to deal with The Space Man himself but I didn't get the chance. As I put down the phone, my immediate assessment of Shapero's attitude was pretty depressing: one of indifference combined with outright scorn for my naïveté. Maybe he had a point. It was a very long way from £19,000 to £1,000 but Singhal had to face facts – his ball had not been bowled by Malcolm Nash in 1968. He'd paid peanuts for it but he was treating it like a Samundari Khazana Curry – a mix of caviar, sea snails, a whole lobster and edible gold. The most expensive curry in the world had been created in Mumbai to coincide with the DVD launch of the Oscar-winning film, *Slumdog Millionaire*. I didn't know whether Singhal's successful business empire meant he could afford this Indian delicacy but I felt I just couldn't be party to a deal enabling him to dine out on the proceeds of a highly contentious sale of a cricketing, rather than a seafood treasure.

After a gap of ten days, The Space Man emailed to explain his delay in responding. He'd been in a "remote place with low net connectivity" but he would be in touch after the weekend. For once, he was as good as his word. Towards the end of another misguided, misinformed, confusing and confused email, I learned that my seemingly naïve negotiating stance had paid off. Singhal explained that Shapero/Tuli had lost ownership of the ball when the airport duties weren't paid before insisting that "even if this ball was genuine after losing ownership he would have got nothing. He cannot make all the money now in a property which does not belong to him whether it be genuine or fake." I was saddened – not to say frustrated – to realise that at the heart of Singhal's flawed reasoning lay his refusal to accept that the ball was not the real deal. In quoting distinguished auctioneers such as Sotheby's, Bonhams and Graham Budd – who worked closely with Sotheby's – The Space Man preferred to reflect on what might have been as opposed to what was. He may have thought he'd bought the most famous ball in the history of cricket but, in fact, he now owned a nigh-on worthless impostor; his ball had not been used in the Six Sixes over. It appeared that he simply couldn't come to terms with the fact that an object he'd expected to make money out of had turned out to be worthless:

> If this ball was genuine i would have sucessfully auctioned it at Bonhams or Sothebys , in fact Grahame Budd auctions was ready to auction it initially when i contacted them after purchase of the ball but at that point of time i felt like keeping the ball to myself and later then sent it to bonhams. Had this ball be genuine i would have sold it for anything more than £20,000 – £25,000 as this was the Reserve Price and considering the popularity of This ball and The over you can well imagine how much it could have gone for .

Indeed I could but, unfortunately for Singhal, the ball wasn't genuine and thus Bonhams' reserve price was irrelevant. In the wake of the price fetched at Christie's in 2006, the figure confidently quoted in the Bonhams catalogue may have been justified, but it meant nothing because the ball was the wrong make and had subsequently been withdrawn from their sporting memorabilia sale. As he yearned for a possibility in the past and ignored a certainty in the present, Singhal's vision of the future was, once again, sadly delusional. He quoted the outcome of the Vekselberg's-Christie's court case when the judge had ruled that the Russian oligarch was entitled to recover the £1.7 million he'd paid for a disputed painting and around £1 million in costs. According to The Space Man, Shapero would be entitled to some compensation as well as the original £26,400 he'd paid for the ball. The fact that the Veksleberg decision was settled in court as opposed to the Christie's internal disputes procedure appeared not to have registered with Singhal. It was another example of his illogical approach to our negotiations but, as I read on, I realised that, at last, he had started to smell the coffee:

> In the current situation i propose of selling the ball to him at 50% at £13,200 and he can further claim £26,400 along with compensation charges. This way he is able to recover 50% of his money as well as compensation from the christies which could also be sizeable . This is too small a amount for christies to settle in order to safeguard there reputation. Regarding making Profit , We are in business to make money sometimes it may be huge profit and at time there is huge loss as well . In this you may consider i will make lot of money but in my opinion i have lost lot of money which i could have earned had there be no controversary surrounding it .

Although I was delighted to have beaten Singhal down from an outrageous demand of almost 75 per cent of any possible full refund, I thought I shouldn't leave it there. It didn't seem right to quit while I was, marginally, ahead. Having reduced his cut by 25 per cent so easily, I felt it was worth having another go – so I used his comment about the need for "the truth to prevail" as the centrepiece of my next email. I said I felt obliged to correct one or two of his observations because he didn't seem to "quite understand the current situation." I explained that Shapero wasn't concerned with making money but with recovering some – or perhaps all – of his original outlay; this was money he had genuinely, and through no fault of his own, lost. Surely, I suggested, that was something Singhal would do in the same position? After quoting his truth comment in full, I then told him a few home truths. The ball was the wrong make, he – unlike Shapero or Tuli – hadn't lost any actual money after buying the bat and ball but a potential amount; it was his bad luck that the ball wasn't genuine – unlike the bat he'd bought at the airport e-auction which was, I observed, an asset that he had "liquidated very handsomely."

From the outset, I'd been aware that the chances of gaining any sort of refund from Christie's were always going to be slim – even with the ball – because the auction house's five-year 'bring back' condition of sale had already expired. The question of compensation – on top of any refund – had never entered my head but, for some reason, Singhal considered it important, so I tried to put him straight:

> Mr Shapero will not be claiming any compensation charges from anyone. As I have explained to you several times, this matter will not be settled in court but through the Christie's internal disputes procedure. If you send me the ball, we will take it, the certificate of provenance and my evidence to the auction house and attempt to gain a full refund for Mr Shapero – the man who, on behalf of Mr Tuli, actually paid £26,400.

As I had insisted from the start, I told Singhal there was no guarantee of Christie's refunding any money but I felt he needed to know that we remained hopeful. I made it clear that his offer of £13,200 was unreasonable and would not be entertained by Shapero. I then decided to introduce Singhal's burgeoning solar energy business into the negotiations – in an attempt to bring down his asking price for the ball to below 50 per cent:

> Ashish...in your last email you said "the cost of 10 MW project which I am developing presently is 20 Million US$ (Rs.100 Cr Appx) hope you will understand how much significance $30,000 or the Monetary value of this ball hold for me."
> If that is the case, if the monetary value of the ball means so little to you - bearing in mind the millions of dollars involved in your solar energy projects – then why are you making such an unfair request for £13,200? What does it matter to you how much you receive for the ball – £100, £1,000, £3,000 or £13,200? In that email, you seemed to be suggesting that the money is not important to you – if so, why are we involved in these difficult negotiations? Why is there no simple solution to this matter when the facts are so very clear?

In conclusion, I made two suggestions: Singhal should deal directly with Shapero in future and also show our email correspondence to a trusted friend who could "fully understand the meaning of my words" because I feared that something essential was being "lost in translation." I revealed that I had already consulted a colleague [Chris Davies] to confirm my interpretation of Singhal's emails. Before we could abide by the truth, I said, we had to understand and accept the truth. Something in my email obviously touched a nerve because, untrue to form, Singhal replied just over 12 hours later. It appeared that he, too, wanted to clarify a few points. He repeated that Tuli, having failed to pay the customs duties on the ball at New Delhi airport, had known that it would be auctioned as a result but had done nothing and he queried my estimate of £300 that he – Singhal – had paid for the ball:

> any how it really does not matter how much i purchased for but the thing is how much i am willing to sell. i could have bought a piece of property for $2 10 years back and now if i wish to sell it for $50 , its entirely my choice .

Singhal said he wasn't going to gift the ball to Shapero and "neither am I inclined to any charity in this case." He reiterated that he would only accept a 50-50 split and would not "settle for peanuts." He said it would be unfair when "somebody is going to recover $50,000 dollars on it". I couldn't disagree with some of his comments but I'd felt it had been worth having another crack at reducing the percentage split. But, as I scrolled down the email, my heart sank when I read Singhal's closing remark:

> It really does not matter to me and the Simple solution to the matter is let me be happy with the ball & ill try to sort out the issue myself when i want to .

My first thought was that I'd blown it – well and truly. Maybe Shapero had been right: my negotiating technique had been a "mad idea" and perhaps I should have quit while I was ahead, having brought down Singhal's demand from three-quarters to a half. I discussed the developments with Chris Davies on the telephone and decided to take at least one step backwards. I needed some time to reflect.

Three hours later, I received an email from Sushant Nigam, from the New Delhi Airport's disposal unit, enquiring about the book.

'Don't ask!' was my first thought but I simply explained that I was gradually making progress. I reassured him that his help had been crucial and that, as a result, he'd be given a credit when the book was finally published. Sushant's reply brought a smile to my face at a particularly trying moment:

> Thanks a lot for information and lots of thanks for acknowledging my little help. I appreciate. I appreciate more of your efforts in exploring factual information and capturing such historic moment in print. Wow. Best of luck and good wishes for your book.

Wow! What a timely email. We were both fully paid-up members of the Mutual Appreciation Society – even though Sushant had no idea exactly just how much effort I was expending in "exploring factual information" as I tried to capture the historic moment and its amazing aftermath in print. I felt I needed all the good luck that was going. As I reflected on Singhal's most recent email, I realised it was time to eat some humble pie – as opposed to a plate of Samundari Khazana Curry. Twenty four hours later, I emailed The Space Man to acknowledge the validity of some of his points. I said we knew that without him as the legal owner returning the ball to Britain, Shapero would have little chance of gaining any sort of refund from Christie's. Likewise, Singhal must accept that without Shapero and my evidence, there would be no chance of him making any money because Shapero, and not Singhal, was the known buyer of the ball. I said that, on reflection, the 50-50 offer was acceptable but I felt it was important to be clear about the terms and conditions of any agreement:

> Please understand that this does not mean that you are selling the ball to Mr Shapero for 50% of £26,400. It means that if, after you have returned the ball and certificate of provenance to Britain, a full refund of £26,400 is gained, then Mr Shapero will pay you £13,200. If he negotiates a lower figure with Christie's, he will pay you half of that sum – whatever it is. No advance deposit will be paid and any agreement between you and Mr Shapero will be totally dependant on him securing some sort of refund on the grounds of the ball's false authenticity.

I said that if we could proceed on this basis, I would draw up a contract which would include a clause covering the safe return of the ball and certificate to India in the event of a refund not being obtained from Christie's. I suggested that, once the contract had been signed, Singhal should name a trusted third party he knew in Britain to whom the ball could be sent and said I looked forward to hearing from him. It was then a case of just sitting, fingers crossed, and waiting for the next email to arrive from India. Just over 24 hours later, this one pinged into my inbox:

> Dear Mr Grahame,
> Please send us draft copy of contract , we shall get it checked by our corporate lawyer.

Result! Or Deal! J. Paul Getty – or rather his father – was right. I had let the other fellow make some money too – just not quite as much as he'd been hoping for. I felt totally elated by Singhal's email because, despite that 11th hour blip, I'd managed to pull it off. You win some, you lose some: my attempt to reduce his split from 75 per cent had been successful but he wouldn't budge from 50 per cent. The deal, if not yet done, had at least been set in motion. The Space Man had been brought down to earth; away from the atmosphere, he no longer had his head in the clouds. In the spirit of compromise, both of us had given ground – me more than him to be fair – but I realised that he held all the cards in the shape of the ball. And in light of his previous email, I felt I had, in hackneyed sports writers' parlance, snatched victory from the jaws of apparent defeat. I now had to sell the deal to Shapero: it was clear that something would have to be sacrificed. I rang him at his office in Mayfair and after a quick exchange of pleasantries, I came, in true Shapero-style, straight to the point:

"I've got your third for you – £8,800 – are you happy with that?"
"Yes. Good."

"This is the deal. Ashish Singhal came back to me. He dropped his demand for about 75 per cent of a possible full refund to 50 per cent – that's £13,200 instead of about £19,000. He wouldn't accept a third share, he insisted on half but I'll take a hit on my third if it helps us to get the ball back."

"Good."

"Just to make it clear – you will receive your original third – £8,800 – and I will receive the remaining £4,400 from your half of the £26,400?

"Yes."

As I'd already explained to Shapero, I'd not been looking to make anything at all from brokering any deal. From the start of Operation Howzat?, I'd only been interested in finding out the truth and I still had certain moral reservations about being involved in another deal involving the Six Sixes ball. But needs must: what was my long-term aim? It was to right the initial wrong and, as Shapero had repeatedly stressed, the return of the ball was paramount. Negotiations with Singhal had stalled and the deadlock needed to be broken – otherwise there would have been no deal. After weighing up all the options, I'd felt there'd been no alternative but to sacrifice my principles for the profits which might be accrued by The Book Man and The Space Man. Anyway, it was all completely hypothetical because, at this stage, I knew there was no guarantee at all that Christie's would play ball – even with the disputed Duke back in Britain. Shapero's initial warning that the auction house would throw some legal money at the case, claim that Convery no longer worked for them and refuse to refund the £26,400 was never far from my thoughts. Nevertheless, and it may have been naïve of me, I felt we had to at least try so I agreed to draw up a contract between the two parties. Shapero and I then discussed the independent person in Britain to whom the ball could be sent by Singhal. Shapero said he didn't know my suggestion, the auctioneer Charles Hanson, but he thought that Singhal would probably have an associate in London who could act as temporary keeper of the ball and the certificate of provenance. He repeated that he wouldn't be paying Singhal any money until the ball had been taken to Christie's: he would give him half of whatever money was received although he emphasised that any refund was, at this stage, a long way off.

Drawing on my limited experience of negotiating with TV rights companies and previous employers, I drafted a five-clause contract between Ashish Singhal, ("The Owner") of Faridabad Forgings, India, and Bernard Shapero, ("The Known Buyer") of Shapero Rare Books of London, England. It was pretty simple but then so was its subject matter. After emailing it to Mayfair for The Book Man's approval – which arrived almost immediately – I forwarded it to The Space Man. I suggested that if Singhal found the contract acceptable, then signed copies could be faxed back and forth to avoid postal delays and the ball and certificate could then be sent to Britain. It all sounded very straightforward and I was encouraged by a reply revealing that Singhal had instructed his lawyer to draft a "legal triparty agreement." He said he would forward it for our approval as soon as he received it.

As I waited for Singhal's interpretation of a rudimentary contract, I realised I now had to return to my day job, to writing of a very different kind. I needed to concentrate more on this book and a press release to publicise the sale of the 'other' Six Sixes Surridge ball – given to Richard Lewis by Glamorgan in return for his finding and bringing back the actual ball used in Swansea in 1968. I'd offered to help Hansons the auctioneers after Lewis had consigned his ball to their autumn fine art and antiques sale scheduled for late October. Almost by accident, I'd now become a world authority on the Six Sixes and I wanted to make sure the Surridge ball didn't suffer the same fate as the much more famous Duke through an over-zealous, not to say opportunistic lot-note writer. Little was I to know that a combination of fabrication and wishful thinking would result in the spinning of another web of half-truths and intrigue around a second perfectly innocent cricket ball.

A matter of fact

Never let the facts get in the way of a good story.

Mark Twain

The Duke and the 'other' Surridge did have one thing in common: neither of them was the actual ball hit for Six Sixes by Garry Sobers in the famous over at St Helen's in Swansea in 1968. Richard Lewis's souvenir ball was closer to the real thing than the Duke but I didn't want the Surridge connection to confuse the situation when it featured in any publicity ahead of the Hansons' sale. It was not the Six Sixes ball. There could be no fudging of the issue or hedging of any bets. The Lewis ball's provenance was 100 per cent accurate: it was a Surridge but it wasn't the original ball bowled by Malcolm Nash.

As I began writing the press release for Hansons, I realised I would have to go back to basics when explaining its significance – not only in the interests of brevity and clarity but because accuracy was at the heart of an often complex story. As a result, it took me some time to produce a form of words with which I was completely happy and which wouldn't land me in any legal trouble further down the line. As well as some invaluable input from Chris Davies, I also received sound advice from a trusted and experienced broadcast journalist friend and colleague, Dave Simmonds. He rightly emphasised some pitfalls I'd have to avoid when describing the mystery of the Six Sixes ball's sale. As I put together the press release, Dave suggested I should continue along the route I'd been following while writing *Six of the Best*, the *Wisden* article and this book: "I think all you can do is present the evidence and let people decide for themselves."

When I rang Richard Lewis for some quotes for the press release, he repeated his view that the publicity generated by the Duke's withdrawal from the Bonhams sale provided him with the perfect opportunity to sell his ball. He felt it was now time to move on. I was curious to know how he'd be spending the proceeds of the sale. Apparently, he'd be taking a holiday which he would "always associate with those splendid memories of 1968." I then settled down to write the press release and after the headline, "New signed Sobers

'Six Sixes' match ball up for sale", the opening sentence was pretty straightforward:

> A cricket ball which may have been used during the famous Six Sixes match at Swansea in 1968 is being put up for auction later this month – amid continuing speculation about the authenticity of the ball allegedly hit over the boundary by Garry Sobers.

That introduction was important for two reasons: to emphasise the second Surridge ball's slightly tenuous connection with the match and to publicise the fact that the Duke ball dispute was still going strong. After leaving room for a couple of comments from Charles Hanson, the manager of the auction house who regularly appears on BBC One's *Bargain Hunt* and *Antiques Roadtrip* programmes, I ended the release by outlining my doubts about the Duke ball's provenance and re-stating the Surridge's connection to the Six Sixes match. There was nothing too complicated or controversial about the opening sentence – or so I thought until I received a phone call from Richard Lewis, then viewed the draft version produced by Hansons and later surfed the internet to find out how the story had been reported around the world. Lewis rang to voice his concern and then emailed me the Hansons' re-written press release. As a journalist, I've never been averse to accentuating the positive when trying to sell a story but you have to draw the line somewhere. Like Lewis, I was concerned when I read that, according to Hansons, his ball had "probably" been used in the Six Sixes match. I was even unhappier to discover that the link with the Duke ball controversy had been removed from the opening paragraph altogether. What had happened to the ongoing, topical news angle? As I read on, I found one or two other disturbing inaccuracies and alterations – a la Christie's 2006 lot notes. What was it with these auction houses? Why couldn't they just stick to the facts?

I agreed with Lewis that the Hansons version was far too definite about his ball's association with the Six Sixes match and, conse-quently, the truth was in danger of being distorted. But it soon transpired that Lewis wasn't at all worried by the omission of the continuing Duke ball controversy in the press release's introduction. In fact, he was pretty pleased about it: he didn't want to give the

A MATTER OF FACT

impression that aspersions were being cast on Sobers' character or intentions by the sale of the souvenir ball being linked to the Duke dispute. He wasn't very keen either on any mention being made of the certificate of provenance that Sobers had signed – even though it was a key part of the whole story. I politely explained to Lewis that I'd be looking to have the two-ball link restored to the opening paragraph because, without the Sobers connection, news organisations would be far less interested in running the story and therefore Hansons would receive far less publicity. More media coverage before the auction would produce more interest on the day and probably a higher price for Lewis's prized possession so it made sound financial sense all round for the link between the balls to be established in the press release's introduction. After assuring Lewis that I'd sort out all the amendments, I contacted Charles Hanson, who apologised for the inappropriate tweaking. Then, with the help of Rachael Morley from their publicity department, I put the original press release back together. A couple of days later, Lewis made another attempt to remove the Sobers references but I told him it was too late for any more changes.

On the day I received the final version of the correct press release, Ashish Singhal emailed his response to a query about the contract covering the Duke ball's return to Britain. He apologised for the three-week delay – he'd been very busy – and then claimed he and his lawyer would finalise it as soon as possible before they made a firm commitment about sending back the ball:

> In the meanwhile i suggest you to proceed ahead with resolving the issue with christies and i assure you that the ball when required will be sent to you along with all the documents within 24 hours . Fedex Express courier only takes max 24 hours for destination delivery in U.K . Request you to keep me in loop in all your correspondence with Christies.

My reply was a mixture of explanation and exasperation as, once again, I found myself having to regurgitate the facts of the matter. For some reason, The Space Man seemed incapable of comprehending the situation facing Shapero as the buyer of the ball in 2006:

> I'm afraid I cannot go ahead with resolving the issue with Christie's

117

until I have the ball in my possession. I'm sure you are aware of the legal saying "no body, no crime" – in this case, it is "no ball, no money" or "no ball, no progress". I can assure you that Christie's will not consider refunding any money to Mr Shapero without seeing the ball so I cannot approach Christie's unless I have it. When it is with me, we will then take it and my evidence to Christie's in an attempt to obtain a refund.

I really couldn't have made it any clearer: keep your side of the deal we've just struck and I'll get the ball rolling. I then drew up a list of suggested news and cricket media contacts around the world for Rachael Morley to send the press release to – and sat back and waited.

The coverage of the Surridge ball's impending sale ranged from the sublime to the ridiculous. The story was very well reported by Robin Turner in the *Western Mail*, the national newspaper of Wales, which, because the Six Sixes had been hit in Swansea, had always taken a keen interest in the event. Under the headline, "The strange tale of Sir Garry Sobers, the Six Sixes and the signed ball", the article focused on the human interest angle of the "excited" and "honest" Richard Lewis, whose souvenir thank-you present had now had a price guide of £1,000-£1,500 placed on it by Hansons. The story included the paper's original report of the event and the photograph of Lewis returning the actual ball to Sobers at St Helen's in 1968 so it more than ticked all my boxes. The *Nottingham Evening Post*'s account, written by Dominic Howell, kept the pot boiling nicely with the headline "Notts cricket legend Gary Sobers' finest hour sets off another cash chase" and it contained my observation that the ball was "a memento from that game which we can rely upon."

The Cricketworld website used a verbatim version of the press release – plus a photograph of the ball – but a three-paragraph story in the *Daily Express* stating that "a cricket ball used in a match where West Indies legend Gary Sobers hit Six Sixes in one over is to go on sale" appeared to be the source of erroneous reports found on a number of other websites – notably in India and the West Indies – as the facts were either misconstrued or misinterpreted. The *Express* version was quoted by, among others, Yahoo! News India, while cricketcountry.com, a website for Indian cricket enthusiasts, went even further by describing the 'other' Surridge as "the ball that was smashed for Six Sixes by Garry Sobers." Other news outlets produced garbled versions of the story but, in general, I was pleased with the coverage generated by the press release. The origins of the maxim "there's no such thing as bad publicity" are unclear, although it's often associated with Phineas T. Barnum, the 19th century American showman and circus owner. Personally, I prefer either Oscar Wilde's variation on the theme that "the only thing worse than being talked about is not being talked about" or the adapted proverb found in the *Atlanta Constitution* newspaper, nearly 100 years ago, that "all publicity is good if it is intelligent." Although some of the coverage of the ball's sale left me frustrated, I was delighted that the impending auction was being talked about. In truth, the inaccurate reports simply added to the mystery surrounding the original sale of the Duke ball at Christie's in 2006.

As the story started to travel, I was rung up by Clive Ellis, a fellow freelance journalist and author who lived in London. He'd got my number from the Hansons' press release and immediately revealed that he was more interested in what had happened at Christie's in 2006. He explained that he'd been sports news editor at the *Daily Telegraph* until 2001 when he'd left to go freelance. The paper had given him work for four or five years and then it had dried up. I later discovered that he'd written books about Fanny Craddock, C.B. Fry, Kent cricket and British Olympians and, like me, had set up his own publishing company.

When I asked if our conversation was going to be 'on' or 'off the record', Ellis replied 'off.' By that, I assumed that nothing I said during the course of it would be attributed to me or used by him. In other words, it would act as background information to help his understanding of the story and, on that basis, I said I was prepared to answer his questions. Very early on in the conversation, I used a phrase along the lines of "the situation is very delicate at the moment" for the first but definitely not the last time. I quoted my prepared response to any questions about the latest Six Sixes situation: i.e. I was still trying to locate the ball withdrawn by Bonhams in May – which I believed was somewhere in India – and I was still convinced it wasn't genuine because of its make and the number of balls bowled in the over. After that, I was happy to let Ellis explain what he knew about the Six Sixes ball mystery – and he certainly seemed to have done his homework. It was a strange conversation; he quoted internet articles from the *Nottingham Evening Post* about *Six of the Best* and he appeared to be pretty clued up – so much so that it almost felt as if I was having a conversation with or even interviewing myself. I explained that I wouldn't be providing any details of my investigation; it was something I'd been working on non-stop for six months and my enquiries were now at an advanced stage.

The wide-ranging discussion lasted for about 45 minutes and covered subjects like 2012 being the year the truth came out about Hillsborough, Lance Armstrong and Jimmy Savile and the aura surrounding Sobers as the game's greatest cricketer. Towards the end of the conversation, Ellis mentioned Bernard Shapero and the £26,400 he'd paid for the ball in 2006. He said that if he were Shapero, he'd be taking the matter up with Christie's because the ball was obviously worthless. At this point, I first confirmed that our conversation was 'off the record' and then assured Ellis that I was already on the case; I had reached the crucial point he'd just mentioned in my investigation. Again, I didn't go into details but I politely asked him to back off because my enquiries had entered a "very delicate stage." I didn't want anyone queering my pitch and I'd be grateful if he didn't pursue the story any further for the moment.

I presumed that Ellis had understood the message but my suspicions were aroused later that evening when he sent me an email thanking me for my time. He described my investigation as "intriguing stuff" and then asked if I knew the whereabouts of the actual ball bowled in the over. This seemed a strange interpretation of my entreaty to end his enquiries but I expressed my view that the ball had disappeared during the re-development of Trent Bridge. I deliberately ended my reply with the phrase "thank you for your interest and your co-operation." I wanted to make sure he was in no doubt that I'd asked him to exit stage left.

Three days later, I unexpectedly heard from Julian Roup, the director of press and marketing at Bonhams. He'd copied me into an email he'd just sent to Clive Ellis following an inquiry about the vendor who'd consigned the ball to Bonhams for their sporting memorabilia sale in May 2012:

> Your summary is pretty much on the button. It is indeed a tangled web. I suggest you contact the author Grahame Lloyd cc'd above, who has written about this subject extensively and is really very well briefed.

To slightly paraphrase Victor Meldrew's most famous expression, I couldn't believe it. Just what was Ellis playing at? If a fellow freelance asks you to back off, surely you do the decent thing and withdraw gracefully? For whatever reason, it appeared that he'd done precisely the opposite and actually ramped up his own investigation behind my back. When I rang him to protest about his behaviour, we had a mainly heated discussion and he eventually apologised. I said I was very disappointed and felt it was disrespectful of him to have ignored my request. Ellis maintained that I hadn't told him anything about my enquiries and that, anyway, he had "no intention of writing about this story" or "putting anything in a paper." I explained that I felt any more digging by him at this point would endanger my whole investigation – I didn't want to alert Christie's to the fact that the Six Sixes ball controversy was back on a journalist's agenda until Operation Howzat? was nearer its conclusion. While I was on the phone to Ellis, The Space Man emailed me in response to another reminder about the contract. He said he would sort out the final draft and try to send it to me within three days.

As a way of keeping Ellis in the loop, I suggested that, sometime in the future, it might be possible for us to meet and for me to reveal more details of my investigation. He said he wouldn't be attending the Hansons sale in Derbyshire during the following week and then admitted that he'd also contacted Christie's as well as Bonhams as part of his enquiries. As my heart sank, my blood pressure rose. I hit the roof – expressing my amazement at his decision to continue with his investigation, especially after I'd helped him and then respectfully asked him to back off. He tried to bluster his way out of it but I was having none of it. I said I'd made the position crystal clear once he'd mentioned Shapero buying the ball at Christie's during our first con-versation. I asked Ellis to forward me his email to Matthew Paton in the Christie's press office and when I read his detailed – and very well articulated – list of observations to Paton, I was even more displeased. I rang Ellis again to vent my spleen and during a much briefer conversation, I remember asking him this question:

"What do you think is the result I'm working towards with this story? What's the end game of my enquiries?"

Ellis paused for a minute and then said: "You're looking for truth and justice."

"Got it in one," I replied, "and you have put that search in jeopardy by contacting Christie's. You've alerted them – and given them time to prepare a defence against the allegations and evidence which I've spent the last six months accumulating."

I emphasised that although I obviously couldn't tell him what to do, I'd be grateful (again) if he would withdraw and let me finish my investigation. If he didn't, I said, there was no way I would share any information with him in the future. Both of us preferred not to re-visit the arguments so the conversation ended with his agreeing to forward any reply from Christie's – which he later did. As expected, Paton had refused to comment, pointed Ellis in the direction of the lot notes and emphasised the importance of the signed certificate of provenance and the role of the two cricket club archivists in preparing the catalogue entry. Ellis said he wasn't sure if Paton's reply "helps or hinders." My final email to Ellis was polite and suitably short. I hoped he would respond positively this time but I did wonder if I'd heard the last of him. I then texted Bernard Shapero in New York with the contract news from India and advised him not to talk to Ellis if he happened to ring before we spoke at the end of the month.

Looking back, I think I slightly over-reacted to Ellis's approach to both Bonhams and Christie's. In retrospect, his behaviour probably helped more than hindered my investigation because it confirmed my view that the auction house's longstanding stance on the Duke ball probably hadn't changed: the certificate of provenance was paramount and the archivists had played a key role in the verification process. In truth, I sympathised with Ellis because I recognised myself in him. He was a journalist after my own heart. I understood completely when he'd said during out first conversation that he'd felt like a detective while making his own enquiries into the story. Just by reading the lot notes and the publicity surrounding the launch of *Six of the Best*, Ellis had clearly smelt a rat and now, quite understandably, wanted to track down the source of the smell.

It was becoming clear that most radio and TV programme commissioners weren't interested in the story while some friends and relatives weren't afraid, I hope semi-jokingly, to describe me as a bar-room bore after they'd quite innocently asked me for a progress précis. But the fact that many close acquaintances were genuinely intrigued by this tallest of tall tales did wonders for my spirits. OK, I would have to reluctantly accept that the Six Sixes ball mystery wouldn't make a broadcast documentary but I was now both heartened and reassured that a completely independent journalist so obviously shared my enthusiasm for the subject. Sadly for Clive Ellis, one rival had already stolen my thunder – when the *Times* broke the story of the ball's withdrawal by Bonhams – and I wasn't prepared to let it happen again. All the skills and experience I'd acquired during 40 years in journalism – through being inquisitive and fascinated by people's behaviour – were being called upon as Operation Howazt? proceeded, step by step, continent by continent and from one auction house to another to another. My approach to writing books, based on note-taking during and immediately after interviews even if they were being recorded, had always been unashamedly forensic; attention to detail and persistent and pertinent questioning produced results and I was still looking for many more answers. It was unfortunate for Clive Ellis but he would just have to curb his enthusiasm. Despite his growing knowledge of the case, I knew all the key cards remained in my hand: it was now just a matter of how – and when – I decided to play them.

After ensuring the accuracy of the 'other' Surridge press release and sidelining Richard Lewis's reservations about its references to Sobers and the Duke ball controversy, I thought I was duty bound to make sure that Hansons didn't emulate Christie's by producing some inaccurate lot notes. I realised that cataloguing nearly 1,000 items for their two-day autumn auction was a huge and time-consuming operation for their staff but the description of this ball – given its history within the wider Six Sixes ball authenticity story –

had to be 100 per cent correct. I'd been very critical of the Duke ball's dubious depiction in the Christie's catalogue so I just couldn't be involved in helping to sell something which wasn't genuine. And as Hansons prepared for their first online auction, the last thing they needed was to be accused of providing misleading descriptions of goods. Sadly, their catalogue lot notes appeared to have been written by someone with little knowledge of cricket who'd had a conversation with Richard Lewis. The main cause for concern was another misunderstanding about the likelihood of the ball being involved in the Six Sixes match. Fortunately, an amendment was handed out on the day of the auction to rectify the mistake: the ball had "possibly" rather than "probably" been used during the game. I also suggested that the online version of the catalogue should be altered and to make absolutely sure that nobody was in any doubt, Charles Hanson allowed me to produce a statement about the Surridge ball's authenticity to be read out just before the lot came up for sale.

A week before the auction, and nearly three months after my previous enquiry to Glamorgan's archivist and scorer, Andrew Hignell, I made another attempt by email to discover the name of the person he'd met at Christie's before the Duke ball was sold:

> As Richard Lewis's ball is about to go under the hammer, I wonder if you've been able to confirm the question I asked in my last email to you – that David Convery was your contact at Christie's in South Kensington when you went to look at the 'ball' in 2006?

Again, it was a perfectly simple question which should have elicited a perfectly simple answer but I wasn't surprised when Hignell declined to reply. Why, I wondered again, was the curator of the Museum of Welsh Cricket refusing to help? It was all very strange, especially as the full Hansons press release about the impending sale – including my observation that the Duke sold by Christie's wasn't the real ball – had been posted on the Glamorgan website.

As the date of the auction approached, I was becoming increasingly worried. I now had a more than passing personal interest in the sale of Richard Lewis's ball after being told that Hansons had received pre-event enquiries from India and the Cricket Legends of Barbados Museum in the West Indies. The museum's general manager, Michael Lucas, had declared in an email to Hansons that he would be "thrilled to take part in the auction." It might sound far-fetched but our recent lack of contact with Ashish Singhal in India had made Chris Davies and I wonder if he was cooking up a cunning plan to buy the ball. Having acquired the Duke via an e-auction held on behalf of New Delhi Airport in 2009, would he now try to snap up Richard Lewis' ball online and then swap it for the one which had pride of place in his Faridabad Forgings office? Given The Space Man's track record, neither of us was prepared to put it past him. We knew that the signed certificate of provenance which accompanied the Duke made no mention of the ball's manufacturer because it stated only that "this signed cricket ball was bowled during the over in which I [Sobers] hit Six Sixes off Malcolm Nash." As a result, we were worried that the Lewis ball could easily be passed off as the actual Surridge ball used in the over – with the imposter then being discarded. Even so, I politely declined Chris's invitation to contribute to the cost of buying the ball being sold by Hansons. He may not have been deterred by their guide price but I was – and I preferred to let the fates decide. Que sera, sera and all that.

On the day of the auction at their saleroom in the village of Etwall in Derbyshire, it was a question of killing time – for me, for Chris and for Tony Roe, the editor of the BBC East Midlands current affairs programme, *Inside Out*, who was filming the ball sale for possible use in a future series. We all arrived separately and I introduced myself to Charles Hanson and then Rachael Morley who were, understandably, very busy with the auction. It began just after half-past ten and because the ball was listed as lot 369, we were advised that it wouldn't be on sale until after lunch – on the basis that an average of 100 items would be sold every hour. As it happened, the availability of online bids for the first time at Hansons meant the whole process took longer and the ball didn't come up until just before four o'clock. We kicked our heels, drank coffee, had lunch and then just waited. Tony had already obtained a few shots of the ball beforehand and he now busied himself with general views of the saleroom. As I wandered around taking a cursory interest in the auction, I managed to sell a couple of copies of *Six of the Best* to

Charlie Ross, the other auctioneer alongside Charles Hanson, so the omens were good. There'd been some interest in the ball's sale from BBC Radio Derby and after I'd explained the auction timetable to their reporter on the phone, he'd started to watch proceedings online. Just after lunch, Richard Lewis and a friend arrived. Having only communicated with him via phone and email until then, it was good to finally meet him. He graciously thanked me for all my help and then went to sit in the front row of the saleroom.

I noticed that the ball had been placed in the auction's collectors' section which included sporting and autographed items and vintage cars. Lot 365 was a signed photograph of Neil Armstrong, a slightly more famous space man than Ashish Singhal, Lot 370 consisted of a rare set of five convict letters sent from Freemantle prison in Western Australia by a Derbyshire man and lot 371 – to be sold the following day – was a 1964 A series 1 E-type Jaguar car. Just before lot 369 came up, I was heartened to hear from Charles Hanson of interest from two telephone bidders in England but none via the internet. For all we knew, these people could have been representing interested parties from abroad so I was still on tenterhooks but at least an online bid from Singhal had been ruled out.

With a crack of his gavel, Charlie Ross, another regular on the current plethora of TV auction programmes, got things underway by reading out my prepared statement confirming the ball's history and authenticity. He made it clear that it definitely wasn't the one hit for six sixes by Garry Sobers and said that although Hansons didn't know if it had been used in the match, it might have been. I had to laugh when, before opening the bidding at £550, Ross ironically became a victim of the Six Sixes Curse of the Inaccurate:

"Those of you that remember, the first five sixes went whistling over the boundary, the sixth was caught and the poor chap fell over the boundary so, of course, it counted for six."

Not exactly. After a telephone bidder had pushed up the price to £750, Chris Davies pointed out the mistake from his seat in the middle of the audience during a brief discussion with the man at the lectern.

"It wasn't the sixth ball," then explained the slightly embarrassed auctioneer. "It was the fourth ball that was caught on the boundary.

Thank you so much sir. No, no, I need putting right on this. History has a habit of playing tricks doesn't it?"

Indeed it does. And Ross wasn't alone in needing to brush up on his facts. Having worked so closely with me on the Six Sixes ball mystery, I suppose Chris really should have known better but, to be fair, I wasn't sure either for a moment. For the record, it was the fifth ball that Roger Davis caught just before falling over the St Helen's boundary back in 1968.

"I have £750 on the telephone," continued Ross. "£750. £800… would you like on that telephone? No. £750 is the latest bid. £800 I am now bid. £800, £850, £900? Were you there sir?"

"No," said Chris, "but I do know about it."

"Yes. £900?"

"Am I fighting against India here?"

"I can't honestly tell you whether you're fighting against India. You might well be! It might be Bombay – or Mumbai should I say? £850 the bid's here. £900? No."

As one telephone bidder dropped out, the chances of the ball disappearing to India or somewhere else overseas via a phone line were immediately halved. They disappeared altogether when the price reached £950 and the other interested party hung up. It was now a straight fight between Chris and someone "in the back." We had no idea about the other bidder's plans for the ball should he be successful so a final destination of India still couldn't be discounted. The tension was palpable because I knew Chris had imposed a bid limit of somewhere around the four-figure mark. It was crunch time. I looked across at my fellow Operation Howzat? investigator: he had decided to go for it. Up went his hand before Ross, as all good auctioneers are required to do, acknowledged his interest and then tried to tease some more money out of Chris's rival.

"The bid is now in the front of the room at £1,000, I will take £50 – in the back. You're both out on the telephones but you're there at the back. £1,000 I'm bid here. £1,050? No. £1,000 I am bid – £1,050 your last chance. Then I'm going to sell this ball for exactly £1,000. £1,000 for the first time – your last chance in the back – £1,000 for the second time and £1,000 for the third and last time. All done? Sold! Yours sir – thank you very much."

When the hammer came down, I must admit to heaving a huge sigh of relief. My attempt to bring the Duke back to Blighty could continue – safe in the knowledge that a genuine Surridge ball wouldn't be joining it in India. Richard Lewis was another grateful member of the audience.

"I'd like to say 'thank you' to my uncle who suggested that I go looking for the last six," he said afterwards, "and 'thank you' particularly to my mother who then suggested that the ball wasn't really mine to keep and that I should return it. She said it belonged to the occasion and particularly to Sobers. Two days later I did return it and Glamorgan gave me the thank-you ball which Sobers signed.

"The memory is still vivid, resonating down over the decades, of Sobers, no helmet, smashing the ball to all parts of the ground and of me being its proud possessor for two days. I'm particularly fond of the artist, Nicholas Poussin, and so hopefully, with the money, I'll be able to get to a few more continental museums to see his work."

The Surridge ball, along with two photos of Richard Lewis and Garry Sobers in 1968 and 2008, was immediately taken to Chris Davies' home in Lancaster. As a cricket enthusiast, he was delighted to have bought it – and not broken the bank in the process.

"As a 14-year old", he explained, "I watched the 1968 footage on *Sunday Grandstand* the following day. Back then, I was an avid cricket follower, I was always reading *Wisden* and Sobers was one of my heroes. Why did I buy the ball? Well, words that spring to mind are truth, integrity and historical accuracy but the ball is also a beautiful object in itself.

"Its background is quite clearly one of the most fascinating and mysterious sports stories I've ever heard. There can be no doubt about the authenticity of this ball so it actually represents firm ground in an otherwise marshy and murky territory.

"Apart from that, it's a good investment. Bearing in mind the iconic stature of the Six Sixes over in Swansea, I'm sure it's going to stand the test of time. The ball is – and does – exactly what it says on the tin: it's 100 per cent correct and has a totally verifiable provenance."

The part-time antiques collector was to be proved right about the worth of his acquisition. The Cricket Legends of Barbados Museum

Sobersmania hits Newark as the West Indian legend transforms
Nottinghamshire's fortunes from 1968

The setting for the historic over which put St Helen's
in Swansea on the cricketing map

The Six Sixes...one after the other (from top, left to right)

Jose Miller (above, left) at the 1975 retirement party of the Nottinghamshire Supporters' Association's secretary, John Gough (third from left). When she succeeded him, he gave her the ball that he'd been given by Garry Sobers

...and right, with NSA chairman Eddie Marshall at The Tavern pub at Trent Bridge. The ball was wrongly said to have been kept behind the bar in the lounge named after him

Jose Miller's make-up drawer, where the ball remained for 31 years…

…wrapped in a piece of Nottingham lace until ill-health forced her to sell it

A trip down memory lane (1)
May 2006…(left to right) former Glamorgan batsman Roger Davis, who
'caught' the fifth six, Garry Sobers and ex-Glamorgan all-rounder Peter Walker
at St Helen's when Sobers admitted that just one ball was used in the over

A trip down memory lane (2)
November 2006…the South Kensington saleroom in London where Christie's
claimed the Duke ball was the last of three bowled to Sobers

The former agent and county team-mate of Garry Sobers, Basharat Hassan. He arranged for Sobers to sign the certificate of provenance at a Nottingham hotel before the ball was taken to Christie's by Jose Miller

The curator of the Museum of Welsh Cricket, Andrew Hignell, (right), at a meeting of Chesterfield Cricket Society in 2008. The Glamorgan archivist viewed the ball before it went under the hammer

Nottinghamshire's archivist, Peter Wynne-Thomas, with a scorebook and his treasured typewriter in the Trent Bridge library

The Mayfair headquarters of Shapero Rare Books, run by Bernard Shapero, the man on the mobile who successfully bid for the ball at Christie's and later played a prominent part in Operation Howzat?

A Mumbai sale held by Osian's, the auction house which galvanised the Indian arts scene before being hit by the worldwide economic downturn

Osian's founder and chairman, Neville Tuli, who bought the Duke ball for £26,400 at Christie's for a sporting memorabilia collection

I Sir Garfield Sobers, confirm that this signed cricket ball was bowled during the over, in which I hit six sixes off Malcolm Nash in the County Championship Match at the St Helens Ground Swansea in 1968 between Glamorgan & Nottinghamshire.

sir garfield sobers.

An antique bat, the Duke ball and its certificate of provenance which spent 18 months in this display case at the IGI Airport in New Delhi (below) because Neville Tuli's financial problems meant he couldn't afford to pay the statutory import duty

GLAMORGAN
CRICKET NEWS
Glamorgan County Cricket Club Members Newsletter
No. 11
December, 1968

Richard Lewis returns "the" ball to Sobers

A World Record clutch of Sixes

The official Score Book of Sunday September 1st, 1968, records Garfield Sobers romantic innings of 76 runs in thirty-five batting minutes, the twenty-minute tea interval which intervened did not count, made 4,4,1,4,6,4,1,1,1,2,1,1,1,4,4,1,6,6,6,6,6. The last historic over was bowled by Malcolm Nash and it contained a world record of sixes and inevitably a world record of the most runs off a six ball over. One towering six finished half way up the Members' Enclosure, another hit the "Cricketers" Hotel, another went over the wall north of the Score Board, another bounced into the concrete bank south of the Score Board and was then flung back by a Mr. Richard Lewis of Pontardawe, who returned it to the Club the following day and as a result appeared on television. Glamorgan presented this ball, which was made at the firm of Stuart Surridge the former Surrey Captain, to Nottinghamshire to reside in a place of honour in their Sporting Museum.

The fifth six was controversial. It was caught chest high by Roger Davis on the edge of the deep long off boundary, but as he held the ball part of him fell back over the line. After various consultations it was decided by a recently introduced law which states that if part of the person catching crosses the line it is a boundary and this catch constituted a six.

Malcolm Nash of course, received just about as much publicity as the great Sobers although of a somewhat different flavour. He finally announced to his team mates who had been ribbing him about going into the record books for all time, that he would one day write a book about the incident, whereon a wag in the ranks asked "What are you going to call it — Gone with the wind?"

The 1968 Glamorgan
members newsletter
confirming that the Six
Sixes ball was made by
Stuart Surridge – and not,
as the Christie's lot notes
stated, by Duke & Son

Garry Sobers and Richard Lewis meet at a special anniversary dinner
40 years after the schoolboy – now a semi-retired teacher –
found the battered ball in a Swansea street

It cost £26k but is this the real six sixes ball?

40 years on, new book raises doubts

Mystery of Sir Garry's 'sixes' ball

SIX OF THE BEST: The ball Sobers hit into the record books

Hold the front page…*Six of the Best* ignites a new authenticity row as the *Nottingham Evening Post* poses the crucial question in 2008

Bowler says 'six sixes' ball is a wrong 'un

It was a Surridge not a Duke insists ex-Glamorgan player

From America with anger…the bowler on the receiving end, Malcolm Nash, vents his spleen over the infamous ball a month later

The Duke ball's current owner, businessman Ashish Singhal,
with his wife Nandini…and some of his solar panels

After being consigned by Ashish Singhal to Bonhams in Chester in May 2012, the ball is immediately withdrawn because of "compelling and conclusive" evidence unearthed during Operation Howzat?

Disputed ball is dropped

By Dominic Howell

A CRICKET ball which was supposedly hit for six sixes in one over by Notts cricket legend Sir Garry Sobers has been withdrawn from sale by auctioneers amid claims it's not genuine.

Evidence brought to the attention of the auctioneers, Bonhams, by a journalist and author Grahame Lloyd has caused the ball to be withdrawn from sale "for further research".

The ball was allegedly smashed for six sixes during a match between Notts and Glamorgan at Swansea on August 31, 1968.

When it was put up for sale at Christie's in 2006 an unknown buyer from overseas bought the ball for £26,400.

The person who sold it was 65-year-old Josie Miller, of West Bridgford, who was the Notts Supporters' Association secretary for 12 years.

She said: "It was the genuine ball. End of story.

"And Garry Sobers himself signed a letter to that effect, he saw the ball and agreed it was the genuine thing.

"Garry had no problem with me having the ball.

"These accusations are a mark against my character."

But it was Mr Lloyd's book Six of the Best: Cricket's Most Famous Over, published two years after the 2006 sale, which cast doubt on the ball's authenticity.

Mr Lloyd, of Lincoln, said he doubted the ball was genuine.

He said Glamorgan always used a Stuart Surridge ball in their matches.

The one that was sold was made by Duke & Son.

Bonhams was unaware of the controversy when it accepted the ball for an auction of sports memorabilia in Chester on May 29.

The ball was entered in the auction with an estimated price of £20,000 to £25,000.

Mr Lloyd said: "I first became concerned after one of the Glamorgan players who took part in the match gave me some old photos from the 1960s.

"When I opened the envelope I found the 1968 club newsletter which stated that the ball was made at the firm of Stuart Surridge.

"I then contacted some other former Glamorgan players, including Malcolm Nash.

"He confirmed that the county had only used Surridge balls at the time. They all insisted that only one ball was used in the over. When I first spoke to Alexander Clement, Bonhams saleroom director at Chester, on the phone about 10 days ago, he said he was extremely grateful that I had contacted them.

"I travelled to Chester and we spent more than an hour examining a range of documents, listening to radio interviews with key people, in particular Malcolm Nash, and watching the BBC Wales footage of the event.

"He told me that Bonhams would be withdrawing the ball

Mighty blow: Garry Sobers in action. Above left: The ball which was due to be auctioned at Bonhams.

from sale."

Julian Roup, a spokesman for Bonhams, confirmed the lot had been pulled for further research. He said: "An auction house has to have the history and provenance right.

"In this case the provenance has been questioned quite seriously and once that happens the automatic response is to withdraw."

Among those who do not believe the ball is genuine is Malcolm Nash - the man who was bowling against Sir Garry.

He said: "We used Stuart Surridge balls and we used them in that game; the answer is simple."

In the wake of the Duke's withdrawal, Richard Lewis (top left) puts the 'other' Surridge ball up for sale. BBC East Midlands TV producer Tony Roe (top right) films the Derbyshire auction and part-time antiques collector Chris Davies (bottom left) stumps up £1,000 to keep the ball in Britain

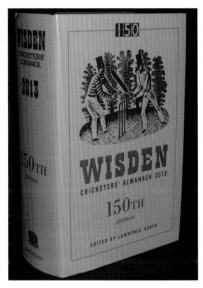

An article about Operation Howzat? for *Wisden* bites the dust… but editor Lawrence Booth agrees to courier the Duke ball back from India after England's Test series win in December 2012

Shipping on the Hooghly River at Calcutta…one of 25 photographs owned by Ashish Singhal which led to negotiations to bring the disputed ball home to Britain finally being aborted

Don't look back…ex-Christie's specialists David Convery (left) and Max Dunbar who are both strangely shy about discussing their part in the sale of the world's most expensive cricket ball in 2006

'I was there'…the Nottinghamshire non-striking batsman, John Parkin, is adamant that only one ball was used in the over bowled to his superstar skipper at St Helen's in 1968

Still unhappy after all these years… having inadvertently helped to make history, Malcolm Nash wants the record to be set straight once and for all later contacted Hansons and offered to buy the ball from Chris for £1,500. Although he declined the chance to make an instant 50 per cent profit, he subsequently accepted a substantially improved offer of £3,000. Like the proverbial Canadian Mountie, the museum's general manager, Michael Lucas, had got his man – or, in this case, his ball – as Chris found out through a touching exchange of emails when its safe passage to the West Indies High Commission in London and then on to Barbados was being arranged. Lucas explained that he'd only recently started working for the museum and securing the ball was a considerable coup for him:

> Please understand that this ball does mean quite a lot to us and being a HUGE cricket fan, having it in Barbados also means a lot to me personally. I wasn't quite good enough to do it on the field of cricket but leading the administration of this company now is literally a dream come true. If that ball were to slip through our grasp now after initially thinking it was gone for good after the auction, I would literally be in tears. Chris, thank you for your continuing desire to ensure that the ball and its effects get to their rightful home in Barbados.

When I heard that Chris's package had been received by the High Commission's officials and they were "enthralled by its contents", I was chuffed about a job well done. Although I didn't think that Barbados was the ball's rightful home – surely it should have been in Swansea? – I was delighted that at least one chapter of the Six Sixes ball saga had been successfully concluded. Everyone was happy with the outcome – Richard Lewis, Chris Davies, Charles Hanson, Michael Lucas and me – but I feared that a similarly satisfactory solution to two crucial questions would prove far more elusive. Was The Space Man going to keep his word and send the Duke ball back to Britain and would we eventually be able to right the wrong? Buoyed by the Hansons sale and Tony Roe's support, I made contact again with Carl Doran, from the BBC's TV documentary department in Salford, but it appeared that a programme about the Six Sixes ball story, despite the enthusiastic response it had received from nearly everyone I met, was unlikely to be made. It was time for the focus of Operation Howzat? – not to mention that of cricket lovers around the world – to switch back to the subcontinent.

The duel for the crown

It's our only hope. The truth is the only guide. If you are led by a lie,
of course you're going to fall off the planet.

Alice Walker

On the day Chris Davies ensured that the 'other' Surridge ball
wouldn't be following the Duke to India, Captain Cook and his team
of intrepid travellers were beginning their preparation for England's
first full winter tour of that cricket-mad country for four years. As
the hammer came down at the Etwall auction, the squad were relax-
ing at the end of the first of a three-day training session at the
International Cricket Council's Global Cricket Academy in Dubai.
From there, they would travel to India for three first-class matches
ahead of the four-Test series, two Twenty20s and four one-day
internationals.

In announcing the tour itinerary in May 2012, the England and
Wales Cricket Board's managing director, Hugh Morris, had said he
was sure that "fans in both countries will be eagerly anticipating an
exciting series of contests in all three formats of the game." At the
time, everyone was hoping England would go to the subcontinent
with their No 1 Test ranking intact but, along with the series against
South Africa, it had disappeared during a summer of discontent both
on and off the pitch. Now though, on the eve of the Indian tour,
everything in the English garden was, if not rosy, then certainly
showing healthy signs of recovery. In the aftermath of the "Textgate"
affair, star batsman Kevin Pietersen had undergone a successful
period of reintegration and the squad was united – even though
nobody really expected that, under new skipper Alastair Cook,
England could secure a first series win in India for almost 28 years.

With the Test match part of the tour rapidly approaching, I was
one of those eager fans referred to by Hugh Morris. I couldn't wait
for the series to begin in Ahmedabad – so much so that I was
inspired to re-ignite a fourth format of the fierce rivalry between the
two countries as part of Operation Howzat? It had been simmering
for six months and there was now every chance that it would soon

boil over. I'd decided that The Battle for the Ball between me The Broker and The Space Man had to be settled – one way or the other. Either Ashish Singhal would return the contract and then the Duke as agreed or he would tell the truth which, I strongly suspected, meant admitting that he wouldn't be sending me either of them.

As I'd already told him, I'd begun to tire of our seemingly never-ending negotiations. I was now busy writing my *Wisden* article and this book as Operation Howzat? moved towards its denouement when my evidence would be put to the nine people who were directly or indirectly involved with the 2006 sale. I simply didn't have time for any more talking. I thought I'd set up a deal which I now wanted to conclude it but it was clear that The Space Man was still in orbit. Unlike Glamorgan's archivist, Andrew Hignell, who at least had finally told me that he was still looking for his file of Christie's notes and contact details, Singhal had stopped replying to my emails. In early November, I took off the gloves again in an attempt to force the issue; did we have a deal or not?:

> I know you are very busy but I hope you can find the time to answer a simple question: do you have any intention of returning your ball to Britain? I need to ask you this question because I feel we are nearing the end of our relationship. Since making contact with you four months ago, I have done my best to broker a deal between you and Mr Shapero covering the safe return of the ball – showing a great deal of respect, perseverance and patience in the process – but I now feel powerless to take the negotiations any further.

After noting that he'd not replied to my last three emails, I said I was confused by the mixed messages being sent about the draft agreement and the return of the ball. Why we were bothering to draw up a contract if he was happy to send me the ball and the certificate of provenance within 24 hours? Why couldn't he just put the ball in the post so I could take it to Christie's with Bernard Shapero? It didn't make sense and The Broker had had enough. I repeated the message that without the ball, there would be no chance of a refund:

> I would be grateful if you could let me know your answer as soon as possible. It's time to draw a line under this matter and resolve the really important business – revealing the truth about the highly dubious sale of the ball in 2006.

Once again, I wasn't about to hold my breath in anticipation of a prompt reply. It was time to leave The Space Man and catch up with The Book Man. The day after an England XI had completed a hat-trick of drawn warm-up matches against Haryana at Ahmedabad in mid-November, I rang Bernard Shapero to update him on developments.

"I'm afraid I've hit a bit of a stumbling block with Ashish Singhal in India."

"What's the problem?"

"Well…you remember that I agreed a 50-50 split if we managed to get any sort of refund from Christie's and I sent him the contract that you'd approved?"

"Yes."

"Well…I'd heard nothing for about a month so I chivvied him along with a few emails and about three weeks ago, he said he hoped to send the draft soon. But nothing arrived so I emailed him again and asked him if he had any intention of sending the ball to Britain. There's been no response at all – he's gone to ground."

Unusually for him, Shapero seemed to have time to listen so I then explained Clive Ellis's interest in the story in more detail. I said I hoped I'd persuaded him to back off and when Shapero revealed that he'd not heard from Ellis, I felt it was safe to assume that the newshound had aborted his hunt. I mentioned my *Wisden* article, the book and my vain attempts to interest a broadcaster in the story and we discussed The Space Man's seemingly contradictory attitude towards returning the contract and the ball. Shapero acknowledged Singhal's promise to send back the ball within 24 hours and said again that a trip to Christie's without it was a non-starter: no ball, no refund – or even a chance of a refund.

"What about the idea of him sending the ball to one of his business associates in London or to an independent third party?," he asked.

"I've already mentioned that to him in an earlier email," I replied, "but he's not responded. Have you any other suggestions?"

"Go there."

"Pardon?"

"Go there. To India."

"It's funny you should say that because I see actually travelling there to collect the ball as a last resort."

"Say you're planning to go to India on some other business and suggest meeting up so he can give you the ball and the certificate."

"Well…or I could just make a flying visit to New Delhi airport to collect the ball. I'm quite happy to go out there but the big question is, Bernard – would you be willing to pay my air fare?"

"Let's see what develops," replied The Book Man and I agreed to float the idea with The Space Man and get back to him. I immediately emailed Singhal to ask for a progress report and then sent Andrew Hignell a photo of David Convery via email to try to jog his memory:

Morning Andrew
Is this the man you saw when you went up to Christie's in 2006?

Hignell's responses were becoming more and more like Singhal's. Not for the first time, "answer came there none" – as Tweedledee and Tweedledum declared in a poem in Lewis Carroll's *Through the Looking Glass (And what Alice found there)* when all the oysters had been eaten by the walrus and the carpenter.

After another week of silence from the subcontinent, I decided to ring The Space Man at his home. As I'd done in August, I felt I needed to make telephonic rather than electronic contact with the elusive Indian. He'd revealed in one of his earliest emails that he was a cricket fan. With India on the brink of beating England on the last day of the first Test, I reckoned it would be an ideal time to ring him. A comprehensive home victory looked on the cards so I was confident that he'd be in a good mood and perhaps more inclined to seal the deal. But I was disappointed to discover that, as well as not answering my emails, Singhal had now forgotten who I was:

"Is that Ashish?
"Yes."
"It's Grahame Lloyd here – about the Six Sixes ball."
"Yes."
"How are you?"
"Who's phoning?"

"How are you? Are you well?"

"Yes. I am good. Who are you?"

"My name is Grahame Lloyd. I've been emailing you over the Six Sixes ball but you haven't replied to my last few emails so I wondered if everything is alright?"

"Oh. Mr Lloyd?"

"Mr Lloyd. Mr Grahame."

"Yes…everything is fine. We actually have had the Diwali festival."

"That's right. It's just finished hasn't it?"

"Yes. It started on 13th November."

"Yes. I thought I would leave it until the festival was over – and also until after your win over England in the first Test!"

"Yes."

After my half-hearted attempt at light-hearted banter had died such a miserable death, I quickly cut to the chase. I said I wanted to conclude the matter and Singhal immediately assured me that we would "close it this week" and he would "reply to my email tomorrow." Once again, he repeated his assurance that, because of his experience of dealing with auction houses, he could quickly dispatch the ball to Britain:

"I have been sending valuables very regularly to Christie's, Bonhams and Sotheby's and it doesn't take more than 24 hours."

"I appreciate that but I'm not going to go to Christie's until I have the ball."

"I understand."

"And I have spoken to Mr Shapero…"

"Do I understand…in your first round of discussions with Christie's, will you carry the ball along with you?"

"Yes, I would like to take the ball along with me. I would like to say…"

"Is it necessary?"

"Yes."

"I don't think they will be interested in looking at the ball. They already know that the ball is in our ownership."

"No. I must disagree with you Ashish. If we do not have the ball, Mr Shapero says he cannot take this matter any further because they will want to see the ball that they sold. We must have the ball."

"I understand."

But I really don't think that Singhal did understand – ever. Neither the fact that his ball wasn't genuine nor that it had to be returned to Christie's if we were to have any chance of securing a refund. Most importantly, he didn't understand the importance of the ball to my attempt to reveal the truth about its sale. Before the phone call ended, The Space Man confirmed his intention to reply in one or two days – "within this week for sure" – but, par for the course, I then heard absolutely nothing.

Around this time, I was looking for appropriate chapter titles and epigraphs to use in this book. Schoolboy memories of E. M. Forster's *A Passage to India* came flooding back to me and I suspected that the novel, set against the backdrop of the British Raj and the Indian independence movement of the 1920s, would feature in one or other category because of the Duke ball's journey from South Kensington to Faridabad. I remembered that the book begins and ends with a question: is it possible for the Indians and the English to be friends? By the final page, the answer seems to be in the negative – at least for the moment. Although I wanted to be friends with Ashish Singhal, I was finding his attitude more and more perplexing and exasperating. Why did he keep saying he'd do something and then not do it? Why was he prevaricating over the draft contract but at the same time insisting that the ball could be returned to Britain within 24 hours? I just couldn't comprehend his contradictory, even contrary approach. But when I typed the title of Forster's book into Google and started to surf around the plethora of literary criticism websites, it all became clear – or at least a whole lot clearer.

My search threw up a long list of quotations which examined the relationship between England and India – often through the novel's two main characters, Cyril Fielding and Dr. Aziz. My light-bulb moment arrived when I discovered a passage about a tea party at Fielding's house which illustrates Aziz's tendency to embroider his conversation in order to impress and then retain the interest of his English lady friends. He says the water which he and Mrs Moore had observed at the mosque runs, via "a skilful arrangement of the Emperors," into the tank in the front of Fielding's house. Forster then makes this observation:

> He was wrong about the water which no Emperor, however skilful,
> can cause to gravitate uphill......Fielding did not even want to pull
> him up; he had dulled his craving for verbal truth and cared chiefly
> for truth of mood.

I discovered that the contrast between these two types of truth was
the subject of much website analysis – including this remark in the
literary study section of sparknotes.com:

> Forster shows that Indians value the emotion and purpose behind a
> statement more than the literal words being stated. Indeed, we see
> that Aziz often tells lies — or, at least, lies by English standards —
> that are nonetheless truthful to Aziz himself because they reflect his
> desire to be hospitable, or because they serve to keep a conversation
> progressing smoothly.

Howzat? The umpire's index finger was starting to twitch. For Aziz
read Ashish. The Space Man was telling me what he knew I wanted
to hear about the ball in order to be hospitable and to keep a conversation – or specifically, in our case, negotiations – progressing
smoothly. Nearly 90 years after Forster had highlighted this national
characteristic in *A Passage to India*, it seemed that an Indian still
always wants to please the person he's talking to. By preferring the
"truth of mood" rather than "verbal truth," Singhal was quite happy
to tell me he would send the contract and the ball – even though he
knew, deep down, that he wouldn't. I might feel he was telling lies
but he considered his attitude to be welcoming and generous, and
nevertheless truthful. A quick review of our negotiations so far
seemed to bear out my new-found theory – time after time, The
Space Man had promised much but actually delivered precious little.

So much for the diagnosis of the problem; the prognosis was
much less promising. In the absence of a quick fix, and in despera-
tion, I decided to try a more conciliatory, inclusive and, frankly,
off-the-wall approach. Almost from the outset of our correspondence, I'd known that Singhal loved both cricket and the work of
Rabindranath Tagore, the Bengali poet, painter and cultural icon. I
was unlikely to forget the Tagore saying with which The Space Man
always ended his emails; in fact, it was beginning to become ingrained

in my memory: "Do not cry if the Sun sets at the end of the day, because the tears will not let you enjoy the beauty of the Stars."

So, I reasoned to myself, why didn't I appeal to Singhal through two of his passions – cricket and poetry – in an attempt to overcome the latest obstacle? The second Test had just got underway at the Wankhede Stadium in Mumbai where Ravi Shastri had become the second man after Sobers to hit six sixes off a six-ball over while playing for Bombay against Baroda in 1985. This surely could be interpreted as a sign, an omen, a portent? Just as Shastri had emulated Sobers – and, in the process, scored an unbeaten double hundred – could I make another significant, if less spectacular breakthrough? As I say, I was becoming desperate. I decided to switch tack by coming up with a slightly skewed take on the current India versus England rivalry. Weren't Singhal and I actually on the same side and not in opposition? Weren't we working as a team – using the sword of truth and the shield of fair play to try to right a wrong which had implicated cricket's greatest all-rounder, Sir Garfield Sobers? I've always written song lyrics and poems – mainly about football – and although cricket was virgin territory for me, I thought I'd see what I could come up with. Within an hour, the deed was done and I emailed Singhal:

> As well as being a journalist, I'm an occasional poet – although I'm no Rabindranath Tagore. While listening to the cricket on the BBC today, I was inspired to pen a few lines about our current position.
>
> **A Winning Partnership**
> India and England may be rivals at cricket
> But Ashish and Grahame are together at the wicket.
> Building an innings to win us the game
> Not for a fortune but perhaps a little fame.
> Ashish owns the ball, Grahame has the proof
> Ashish wants a profit, Grahame seeks the truth.
> We've worked well so far; it's a promising stand
> There are runs on the board and wickets in hand;
> Let's write the last chapter of the Six Sixes tale
> The result's in no doubt: and the truth must prevail.
>
> And, as you said in one of your emails, "we should all be happy to abide by that."

All right – don't laugh. I'm not an idiot. I realised full well that my pithy ditty would never win me, Tagore-like, the Nobel Prize for Literature – or even the Costa Poetry Award. But I felt that the poem, dogged and bordering on doggerel, neatly summed up the situation in which we now found ourselves. I hoped it might touch a nerve and prick Singhal's conscience. While I'd been racking my brains to think of a way to break the deadlock, I'd found time to submit a proposal to BBC Radio Wales for a programme on the ongoing Six Sixes ball mystery. I was hoping that an hour-long documentary I'd made for them on the famous over itself four years earlier would stand me in good stead. As I waited in vain to hear from Singhal, I made another fruitless attempt to persuade Andrew Hignell to co-operate by sending him the photo of the proprietor of Convery Auctions again:

> My investigation into the Six Sixes ball business is approaching a
> very vital stage. I would be grateful for your help. It's a simple question: please can you tell me if this is the person who you met when
> you went to Christie's to look at the ball in 2006?

Once again, Hignell declined to reply. No matter. After producing the poem and the programme proposal, I felt I was on a creative roll. The day after England had beaten India by 10 wickets in the second Test to square the series, I experienced a truly Eureka moment. Like Archimedes, I was lying in the bath one morning, contemplating my navel, the Singhal impasse and the meaning of life in general, when the idea came to me: why didn't I ask Lawrence Booth, the editor of *Wisden*, to courier the Duke ball back to Britain? All of a sudden, it seemed so obvious. Lawrence's credentials were impeccable: he was a respected journalist, he was covering the England tour of India and he was an independent third party – although he did have a certain vested interest in the Six Sixes controversy because the return of the ball would hopefully be featuring in my article. In my Operation Howzat? update, I told Lawrence about The Space Man's cold feet – which I felt might be connected with Sobers' reputation – and the sale of the 'other' Surridge ball. I then turned to the idea of my going to India to collect the Duke:

> I haven't discussed that possibility with Singhal – in my view it's a

last resort – but I'm wondering if you might be able to meet him and
collect the ball sometime between now and 23rd December?
I think your position as editor of *Wisden* would be very helpful.
Would you be willing to act as courier if Singhal brought the ball to
you – at your hotel or at a ground where England are playing?

Given Lawrence's workload, I suspected that the other option of
him travelling to pick up the ball from Singhal during a break in his
work schedule wasn't a realistic runner and so it proved. He was far
too busy covering the cricket to be jetting around India on the whim
of a frankly unreliable local businessman but he was prepared to
have the ball delivered to one of his two hotels or any of the two
remaining Test venues in Kolkata and Nagpur. Lawrence said he'd
enjoyed the latest version of my article and asked when I'd be able
to finish it. I immediately emailed Singhal and after providing a brief
potted history of our frustrating four months of correspondence,
I went on the attack again:

I now find myself in a very difficult and hugely embarrassing position as far as Mr Shapero is concerned. I assured him that the deal
was done but I am now being forced to confess to him that I have
no idea what is happening. Although I negotiated the 50-50 split
with you in good faith, you refuse to reply to my emails and, more
importantly, you decline to honour your side of our agreement.

I then gave The Space Man two choices: I could travel to India to
collect the ball myself or an independent third party would act as
courier. I didn't reveal that it was Lawrence Booth; I said simply that
this "trusted and distinguished member of the international cricket
fraternity" would be willing to take possession of the ball and certificate of provenance at his hotel and bring it back to Britain. I
reminded Singhal of his comment that "whatever the truth is must
prevail and we should all be happy to abide by it":

The truth is that your ball is not genuine, we have agreed a deal
which will help prove it and although Mr Shapero wants to keep his
side of the bargain, you seem strangely reluctant to do the same.
What is the problem? Why is this matter proving so difficult to
resolve? Please tell me.

As I waited for Singhal's response, I emailed Lawrence again. I wanted to explain my difficult dilemma – in terms of making a TV or radio documentary whilst also writing the *Wisden* article – and the subsequent timetable I was working to. The article needed to be written and approved by the latter part of February so Lawrence was obviously keen to have it sooner rather than later. But I felt that the nine people involved in the Christie's sale should be presented with my evidence at the same time and in a single hit. To me, it was important to adopt an all-inclusive, one-stop approach on behalf of *Wisden*, this book and a possible broadcasting organisation, which I was still hoping might eventually come on board. I said I was also worried that the people at the heart of the matter could depict the sale of the Duke ball as an "unfortunate coming together of circumstances and slight misunderstandings" which would then render each party only moderately responsible. I also explained to Lawrence that I was still waiting to hear from The Space Man about my courier plan. Privately, I felt I was doing my utmost to accommodate his infuriating equivocation but it was becoming more and more difficult. Lawrence didn't seem too worried about the return of the ball and his next email dealt mainly with the importance of giving the right of reply to everyone involved in the Christie's sale:

> As for the ball, it would obviously be great to have it, not least so we could use a photo in the piece. But I'm relaxed about what its absence would mean for the article…I think it's best to get a piece to me by the end of the year, and we can tweak it later if necessary.

I might have had found dealing with one particular Indian immensely frustrating but England's cricketers had cracked it when up against a team of them. After losing the first Test so miserably in Ahmedabad, they had re-grouped and re-thought their strategy. They'd realised that batting long and not giving away their wickets cheaply would then enable their superior bowlers to show their worth. Their 10-wicket win in Mumbai was followed by another thumping defeat of the Indians – this time by seven wickets – in Kolkata. On the last day, just after England had survived an early batting collapse to reach their victory target of 41, I decided to ring The Space Man. He wanted to postpone any conversation about the ball's return until the next day but I insisted that we talk about it there and then. After confirming he'd received the email containing my two suggestions, I told him that Lawrence Booth was the independent third party who was prepared to courier the ball to Britain. During a short discussion, I emphasised Lawrence's standing in the cricket world and said I was enlisting his help to prove that my intentions were honourable. Singhal said he or one of his representatives would be willing to take the ball to a Nagpur hotel or send it to me in Britain. I stressed that I didn't want to involve such a distinguished editor as Lawrence in the whole process unless the ball was definitely going to be delivered to his hotel. I also emphasised the urgency of the situation because of Lawrence's return to Britain in eight days time. Although The Space Man assured me that he would reply soon, he remained silent for the best part of another week – apparently because of business commitments.

As I waited for his response, I learned that BBC Radio Wales had rejected my programme idea. The decision was disappointing but not entirely unexpected. The day after the fourth and final Test began in Nagpur, Singhal's next email arrived in my inbox. After politely declining Lawrence's services as a courier, Singhal made another confused comment about the importance of the ball to any refund attempt – as well as another offer:

> The ball will be handed over to the christies only when they agree to refund the amount , they do not require the ball to check its authenticity . They know what they have auctioned and to whom they have auctioned . I request you to ask Mr. Shapero to at least Write or approach christies with your bundle of evidence and when the need be i will either courier or come myself personally with THE BALL . In case you need it Urgently than i propose to sell the ball to Mr. Shapero at £10,000 , and he can do whatever he wishes . If he and you is so confident then he might as well get to realise £26,400 plus compensation from the christies . Else i have a scheduled business trip to UK in March and i can bring the ball along with me and we all can go to christies to conclude the matter.

Out of left field or what? Where on earth had that come from? I must admit I was now at the end of my tether. The twin olive branch of my poem and the courier offer had patently failed and just as England and India's cricketers had resumed their rivalry in

Nagpur, hostilities in The Battle for the Ball seemed to have begun again. I had no idea what had prompted The Space Man to mention the Christie's refund process or to reduce his asking price for the ball from £13,200 to £10,000 or to offer to involve himself personally in its return to Britain. I'd always tried to remain positive about any refund from Christie's but neither Bernard Shapero nor I had ever been that confident of success and compensation had never been mentioned. We both realised that, given the amount of time that had passed since the sale, a successful approach to Christie's was a very long shot but, with the ball in our possession, it would at least be worth pursuing. Putting my incomprehension and exasperation to one side, I met the current challenge posed by The Space Man head-on. I felt as if I was talking to a child when I tried to explain why the ball had to come with me to Christie's:

> If you buy an item of clothing at a shop – say a silk shirt – and when you take it home, you find that one of the sleeves is torn, what do you do? You have to return the shirt to the shop to show them that they have sold you faulty goods. Without the shirt, the shop will not give you – or even consider giving you – a refund. They need to see the damaged item for themselves.
> The same principle applies when returning items to Christie's on grounds of authenticity.

On The Book Man's behalf, I declined Singhal's offer to sell Shapero the Duke for £10,000 because, as I'd repeatedly told him, there was no guarantee of any refund from Christie's. I then explained that sorting out the matter via a personal visit by him in March would be too late for my *Wisden* article. I gave Singhal my address and crossed my fingers. On the very next day, which immediately made me suspicious, he replied with yet another obstacle in the form of yet another offer. It was one I felt sure Shapero would have to refuse and it marked a turning point in our negotiations:

> I understand your concern but before i courier the ball to you , i require your assistance . I have some very rare vintage Photographs . Earlier i had planned to send them for auction but that will take some time and also we shall have to pay 20% commision for the same . Mr. Shapero will be aware about the photographs as it was purchased by me from the same auction . All the proceeds which i

will receive from sale of these will be for charity . We have trust
which Runs School and College for Education of Underprivilidged
Girl child . We are doing some Expansion there and thought this
money could also be helpful . It is a noble cause and if you can talk
to Mr. Shapero of his interest in buying this at genuine market price
then i shall be really greatfull.

There then followed a list of 25 photos of a range of people and
places – including the ruling Princes of India, the Trimurti
Elephanta Caves, the Palitana Temples and Rampart Row in
Mumbai. There was no doubt about it: The Space Man had well and
truly departed this planet. As I said to Chris Davies when I forwarded the email to him, "you just couldn't make it up. This truly is
the story that keeps on giving." The message seemed pretty clear to
me: if Shapero didn't buy the photos, then Singhal wouldn't send
the ball. Just as I'd been thinking that The Space Man's exhaustive
supply of excuses for being evasive and equivocal had dried up, he'd
suddenly produced one to trump the lot. Not only that, he'd quite
cynically played the sympathy card by introducing the word 'charity.'
Having agreed that it did indeed seem like a "very noble cause," I
asked for more details of the organisation involved so that The
Book Man would be aware of the full picture when I put the proposition to him. I told Singhal that, until now, I'd known nothing about
the photos and, to my mind, they should be kept separate from the
negotiations involving the ball. I stressed that I had no power, influ-
ence or control over Shapero: I was merely The Broker. The Space
Man appeared keen to conclude the deal – or rather off-load the
photos – because he replied almost immediately with details of the
charity and some pdf attachments of the goods for sale:

It is a family owned Non Profit Trust named after my Great
GrandMother "Yashoda Devi Memorial Trust" it is managed and
funded by our family only and Runs schools and colleges for education of girls . A certain percentage of profit from our business
operations are transferred to this trust every year . However we are
not asking Mr. Shapero for any charity , we are asking him to buy the
Photographs which is his business the proceeds which i will get from
the sale of my property (photographs) will be transferred to the trust.

As England's cricketers wrapped up their first series win in India for almost 28 years, I felt I was about to lose The Battle for the Ball. After last-day centuries by both Ian Bell and Jonathan Trott had sealed a draw in the final game at Nagpur, the Test part of the tour was over – and so, virtually, was my attempt to have the Duke returned to Britain. Singhal's procrastination suggested there would always be another hurdle to jump and I was on the verge of giving up. When I rang Shapero, I explained that I was very unhappy about The Space Man's decision to move the goalposts at this late stage of the negotiations but it wasn't my call. I offered to forward the relevant email and photos details but The Book Man said I should ask Singhal just two questions: "What have the photos got to do with the ball?" and "How much money do you want for the photos?" The almost frantic exchange of emails continued:

> Please tell Mr. Shapero that Photos have nothing to do with the Ball , I do not know the value of the photographs , Mr. Shapero is in this business and selling vintage photographs on his website , so he must know the value of the same .

It seemed to me that Singhal wanted Shapero to make him a serious offer on the basis of a few images of some old photographs. I knew it wasn't going to happen but I forwarded the email to London and then rang Shapero to discuss our next move the next day. His response was perfectly understandable. The Book Man's approach to the photographs was the same as his attitude to any antiquarian items he came across:

"I need to see them before I can make an offer on these types of things. Ask him to send them with the ball and the certificate and if we can't agree a price, I'll put them into auction on his behalf."

That seemed pretty reasonable to me and I relayed the message back to The Space Man – along with a simple request of my own:

> As I have provided you with my assistance in approaching Mr Shapero about the photographs, I hope you will now send me your ball as agreed – whether or not you wish to send the photos to Mr Shapero.

Surprise, surprise – the flurry of emails from India suddenly ended. I sent another one two days later asking if our deal had been given the green light. No reply. I had a feeling the end game was approaching and, after waiting another 24 hours, I decided to hasten its arrival. After discussing the latest impasse with Shapero on the phone, I emailed Singhal. I pulled no punches this time. After a brief comment about his refusal to reply to my emails, I vented my spleen about his behaviour over the last six months:

> Throughout all our discussions, I have acted in good faith – working on the understanding that in business, a deal is a deal.
>
> I have enlisted the support of one of the world's most distinguished cricket journalists, the editor of *Wisden*, Lawrence Booth, and have even offered to fly to India myself to collect your ball. Now it seems that a deal is not a deal – and I feel very disappointed and let down. You say you understand my concern and my eagerness to conclude the matter but I'm afraid I don't think you do.
>
> Time – and my patience – has run out. I sadly have to tell you that if your ball and the certificate of provenance have not arrived at my home in Lincoln by 31st December 2012, our correspondence will be at an end. I will no longer act as broker between you and Mr Shapero.
>
> We have a saying in Britain – "actions speak louder than words". The time for talking is over. Action is needed now. It is up to you, Ashish. I have to move on. I have no more time to waste.

It may have been a little melodramatic but it was also very therapeutic. I could feel all my pent-up frustration being released as I carefully composed that email – in fact, I think I quite enjoyed writing it. But would the ultimatum work? I doubted it but if the ball didn't arrive by the end of the year, I could at least draw a line under the negotiations and move on to the final chapters of this book. As Christmas approached and I heard nothing from Singhal, I stepped up my recording of the ups and downs of Operation Howzat? having mentally written off the possibility of the ball being returned. Then out of the blue, The Space Man responded:

> I apologise for not being able to answer your emails , I am out of India on vacation with Family and will be back on 2nd January 2013 . I assume you , Mr. Shapero & Christies will also be on Christmas & New Year Holidays . You will only be able to take the Ball to Christies in New Year .
>
> Wish you Merry Christmas & Happy New Year 2013 !!

And the same to you. Singhal always seemed to have an answer but I wasn't quite sure what he was saying this time. Was this yet another trick to tease me or simply his latest plan to please me or would he be sending the ball after the festivities were over? I had no idea but, given my personal experience of his negotiating style, I didn't expect the Duke to be returned any time soon.

A new year meant a new start with a new set of resolutions. I made a couple: one, not to contact Singhal unless he significantly tried to break the impasse or I came across another realistic solution to the stalemate and two, to bring the Six Sixes ball mystery to some sort of conclusion. I'd spent almost nine months gathering all my evidence; it now had to be put to The Gang of Nine. I drew up a list of the people who, in some way, had been connected with the ball's sale – from the woman who'd originally consigned it to Christie's to the man who'd consistently batted away questions about its ambiguous authenticity on behalf of the auction house since 2006. For the moment, the Duke would have to be left lying in some foreign land; it was time to uncover a few home truths.

Play up! play up!
and play the game!

The psychology of the game is accurately condensed in far less than a chapter – in fact, in those few words, "That is not cricket." The brightest gem ever worn by any pursuit: in constant use on the platform, in the pulpit, Parliament and the Press, to dub something as being not fair, not honourable, not noble. What a tribute for a game to have won, but what responsibility on those who play and manage it!

Lord Harris, A Few Short Runs

It wasn't the best of starts to 2013 but at least I now knew where I stood. Having re-established contact with Carl Doran, a commissioning editor in the sports department at the BBC in Salford, I soon realised that the chances of a programme about the Six Sixes ball story being made were very slim. He said there was no money available and members of his department were busy producing documentaries about Mohammad Ali and Andy Murray. But he suggested I should contact Richard Burgess, the BBC's head of sports news who might be interested in running a piece. I immediately did so but, after being told that my email message would be considered by Burgess when he returned from holiday, I heard nothing and decided it was time to move on and concentrate on my *Wisden* article.

Throughout Operation Howzat?, Lawrence Booth had been both enthusiastic and supportive – witness his willingness to act as ball courier in India – and I realised I needed to approach the story's denouement on behalf of *Wisden* as quickly as possible. Any broadcast interest – perhaps from Tony Roe at the BBC in Nottingham – might follow when the full picture emerged a little later down the line. I rang Lawrence to discuss developments and then drafted a copy of the letter I proposed to send to the nine people on my list: the ball seller, Jose Miller, Garry Sobers and his agent, Basharat Hassan, the two cricket club archivists, Glamorgan's Andrew Hignell and Nottinghamshire's Peter Wynne-Thomas, two ex-Christie's specialists, David Convery and Max Dunbar, the auction house's current director of sale, Rupert Neelands and its head of communications, Matthew Paton. Lawrence turned down my suggestion of using *Wisden*-headed notepaper for fear of scaring off any of those involved but he asked if it was worth pointing out that "the recipient of each letter plays a part in the story as you're going to be telling it in *Wisden*? If you don't say that, they may think they can just avoid involvement by keeping their head down." I was more than happy to oblige by tweaking my original version:

> I have been commissioned to write an article for the 150th edition of *Wisden* about the controversial sale of the cricket ball allegedly used in the over when Sir Garfield Sobers hit Malcolm Nash for six successive sixes at Swansea in 1968.
>
> After extensive research over a number of years, I have uncovered evidence which strongly suggests that a fraudulent act took place before the ball was sold for £26,400 at Christie's in London on 15th November 2006.
>
> You may know that the same Duke & Son "Special County" ball was withdrawn from an auction by Bonhams in Chester in May last year because of what the auctioneers called my "compelling and conclusive" material.

The same letter was sent to each person but every version had a slightly different final paragraph which mentioned their individual roles in the sale. I explained that I would be ringing in the next couple of days to discuss their involvement as I prepared "to tell the Six Sixes ball story in its entirety in *Wisden*." I had postal addresses for everyone apart from Sobers and Miller. A swift surf of the internet located one in the West Indies for Sobers but there were two possible addresses for Miller – both in the West Bridgford area of Nottingham. I was pretty sure which of them was correct but I needed to make sure before posting the letter. I understood that Miller lived with her sister and a visit to Rushcliffe Borough Council's offices, not far from their home, provided confirmation of their address via the electoral register. All the letters were sent by recorded delivery and I checked on their progress through the Royal Mail's 'track and trace' service. One went to Sobers at his home in Wildey, not far from Bridgetown, the capital of Barbados, and I posted another to him via Hassan's address in Nottingham – in case the original's journey to the West Indies proved lengthy or troublesome. One by one, the letters arrived in places like London, Cardiff and Blackburn near Edinburgh – apart from, initially, those sent to Hassan, Sobers, Wynne-Thomas and Dunbar which, for reasons I never discovered, somehow went astray. So I hand-delivered three new copies to addresses in Nottingham on my way back from a football match in Derby and Chris Davies dropped off Dunbar's letter at the Manchester Jewish Museum when heading from Lancaster to the Midlands. As soon as I'd confirmed that the letters had been signed for or accepted, I emailed a copy to each recipient to make sure they knew I was on the case; that there was no chance, as Lawrence had put it, of them keeping their heads down.

The next question involved the order of questioning. It made sense to start at the beginning with Miller but I wasn't sure about the rest of the runners and riders. Sobers and Hassan were obviously key players and I suspected that Christie's would be my last port of call as I looked for an official concluding comment but it wasn't clear where Convery and his former colleagues fitted into the timetable. I supposed it depended on the responses I received to the letters. As I sat down at my computer to draw up a list of questions for each person, I realised that some of them would never be asked. For various reasons, I sensed that not everyone would be prepared to speak to me but I went through the pre-interview process all the same. In the event, Convery was the first to reply – via email almost immediately after receiving my letter requesting an interview:

As I have previously commented on this matter. Yes I was the head of sporting memorabilia at the time the ball was sold. However, I was involved in another private matter at that time and had no involvement in the sale of the ball. My former colleague took charge of that auction and he is no longer in the auction world. Sorry but I can't add anything more.

I was sorry too because I had quite a few questions to ask him. From his reply, I deduced that, because Rupert Neelands was still employed by Christie's, Convery was implicitly implicating Max Dunbar in the sale. A couple of days later, I emailed Convery to ask if I would be right to assume that Dunbar was his "former colleague." If so, did Dunbar write the lot notes for the ball or were they the handiwork of Neelands, the third listed specialist involved in the sporting memorabilia auction? Twenty minutes later, back came this short but revealing reply:

Max and Rupert would have catalogued that sale.

Howzat? It looked pretty plumb to me. Convery was officially passing the buck. Nothing to do with me, guv. The blame game had begun. He had no knowledge of the ball's auction but he knew a man – or two – who did. Later that day, I received a predictable yet faintly promising reply from Matthew Paton, Christie's head of communications:

Dear Mr. Lloyd,
Many thanks for your letter and email. I'm afraid we no longer offer auctions of Sporting Memorabilia and the department no longer exists at Christie's. As such, it is difficult for us to add any comment. Having said that, do let me know if you have any specific questions. In case it is helpful, I attach a link to the cataloguing for the lot in question when it was offered at Christie's. It was sold with a certificate of provenance signed by Sir Garfield Sobers. We also thanked the archivists at Glamorgan County Cricket Club and Nottinghamshire County Cricket Club for their help in preparing the catalogue entry.

Having read Paton's regular responses to any enquiry about the ball's authenticity since its sale in 2006, this was par for the course for Christie's. His reply broadly echoed the one he'd given freelance journalist Clive Ellis in the previous October – with the signed certificate and provenance and the contributions of the two archivists again being highlighted. Although I failed to see why the absence of sporting memorabilia auctions or the closure of that particular department posed a problem for Christie's, at least that remark was new. And, as I mentioned to Lawrence Booth, the willingness to answer "specific questions" was an improvement on the usual "no comment." Lawrence agreed that I should ring Neelands and then Paton in light of the Christie's email.

My conversation with Neelands at his office in London was short and to the point: he couldn't speak to me because I was a journalist so he referred me to Paton. He said it was company policy for all press enquiries to go through the communications director so I left a message on Paton's voicemail and waited for him to return my call. He did so the next day and immediately apologised for the delay in getting back to me: he'd been busy compiling a press release about Christie's annual results. Under the headline "Christie's attracts new collectors as global appeal for art continues to grow in 2012", I read all about the record figures. Annual sales totalled nearly £4 billion – up 10 per cent on 2011 – 19 per cent of all registered bids at Christie's global auctions were placed by new clients and the average number of registered bidders per auction had risen by more than half in the last decade. Business was indeed booming at Christie's – especially at the South Kensington saleroom, which offers works of art from under £1,000 and had recorded its highest ever total for the third consecutive year. As I read that Mark Rothko's 'Orange, Red, Yellow' had fetched a world record price for any contemporary work of art at auction when it was sold for £53,867,150 in New York in May 2012, I couldn't help but think of the sale of the world's most expensive cricket ball for £26,400 at South Kensington in November 2006. Small beer in comparison perhaps but it had still been sold by the world's leading auction house which, according to the press release, was "a name and place that speaks of extraordinary art, unparalleled service and expertise, as well as international glamour." I just hoped that the "unparalleled service and expertise" would be at the forefront of my impending discussions over the Duke ball.

During the course of the subsequent circular and wide-ranging conversation with Matthew Paton, I asked him for a meeting to discuss my evidence at least three times. It became clear that he was very reluctant to agree to my request. He repeated his email comment about the sporting memorabilia department and its former auctions which I immediately dismissed as irrelevant. The ball had been sold at an auction held in the South Kensington saleroom more than six years ago; that was a fact, period, but not, because of the continuing controversy, end of story. I said it didn't matter whether the department existed now – or whether such sales were still held. But, countered Paton, two of the people possibly involved – Convery and

Dunbar – were now ex-Christie's employees.

"But," I replied, "one of the three people involved in the sale was Rupert Neelands and he still works for Christie's."

"He works in the books department."

"He has many titles – director, head of sale, books specialist, senior specialist and auctioneer and he was named as specialist in the catalogue for the sporting memorabilia auction when the ball was sold in 2006."

My knowledge of Neelands's impressive multi-tasking didn't cut much ice with Paton – neither did my suggestion of a meeting to consider my evidence. He asked if my material could be reviewed via email and I explained that because a key part of it consisted of a DVD of the Six Sixes TV footage and CDs containing interviews with ex-Glamorgan players, I felt the evidence should be seen and heard with me in attendance to explain it.

Paton said it would be a waste of my time to travel up to London with my evidence.

"Who would look at it?," he said.

"How about Rupert Neelands or you or someone in a position of authority?"

Paton refused to entertain such an idea. Throughout the conversation, I stressed that "some honest answers were needed to some honest questions" and I said I wanted to give the nine people involved in the ball's sale the right of reply. When I mentioned that I'd contacted the Metropolitan Police's Art and Antiques Unit while exploring the 1968 Theft Act and 2006 Fraud Act, Paton reacted by saying that lawyers would be involved in dealing with what he called "my grand accusation." I immediately corrected him by stressing that I wasn't accusing anybody of anything and repeated my view that my evidence strongly suggested that a fraudulent act had taken place before the ball was sold in 2006.

"I fail to understand why you won't see me," I said, "especially after Bonhams agreed to – and then withdrew the ball because of what they called my 'compelling and conclusive' evidence."

"That was before they were going to sell it," replied Paton. "We would have done if someone had doubted its authenticity before the sale."

"Someone did – the former Glamorgan players who, when they were spoken to by Christie's, explained that they used only Surridge rather than Duke balls at the time. There was also some disquiet in the saleroom on the day."

When Paton asked me specifically about my evidence, I explained that the ball was the wrong make and only one was used in the over – not three as per the Christie's lot notes.

"Those were two fundamental errors and there's a lot of other overwhelming and damning evidence which I think you ought to see. I'm trying to help you here. When you see my material, you'll understand why I feel you ought to look at it."

Towards the end of our discussion, I brought up my most recent correspondence with David Convery, Christie's former head of sporting memorabilia who'd denied being involved with the Six Sixes ball sale.

"He says he had nothing to do with it and according to him – and I quote from his email – 'Max and Rupert would have catalogued that sale.'"

At this point, Paton paused for thought and his attitude altered quite noticeably. He said Convery's comment could change the situation and he would ask Neelands if he'd written the lot notes. I asked him to also enquire about the ball's consignor. Although Jose Miller's name had been in the public domain for more than six years, I thought this question might help me to discover who had provided Christie's with the erroneous information in the notes: in other words, had someone else, apart from Miller and the two county archivists, been involved in the verification process? I then asked Paton if I should contact Bernard Shapero, who, having bought the ball from Christie's in 2006, was now a very dissatisfied Christie's customer. Paton suggested I should wait until he'd spoken to Neelands before contacting the known buyer.

As I put down the phone and started to collate my notes of the conversation, my general feeling was that Paton hadn't taken me or my evidence very seriously. He'd argued that the sale had taken place six years ago, it had involved two people who no longer worked for Christie's and it wasn't worth him now sparing me an hour of his time to view my evidence. When I'd heard nothing for four days, I decided to record my disquiet about his attitude in an email to him. I said I thought Christie's had "a corporate responsibility to explain the process by which the ball was sold and to try to clear up some alarming discrepancies" and I repeated my observations about Neelands' role in the sale:

> You said I should let you know if I had any specific questions. Apart from "when can I come to London to show you my evidence"?", I asked two particular ones:
> 1 Who consigned the ball to Christie's in 2006 and, in doing so, claimed it was used in the Six Sixes over?
> 2 Did Rupert Neelands write the catalogue lot notes for the ball and if he didn't, who did?
> It is now four days since I posed those two questions and I'm at a loss to understand why you haven't provided me with any answers. Bearing in mind Christie's reputation as the world's leading auction house and Sir Garfield Sobers' standing as cricket's greatest ever all-rounder, I was hoping you would be able to help me sort out this controversy as soon as possible.
> As I explained on the phone, I'm in the process of finishing my article for Wisden and I would appreciate a prompt reply to this email. If one is not forthcoming, I'm afraid I will have no alternative but to seek answers to these two questions – and quite a few more – from alternative sources within the auction house world.

With that final remark, I was deliberately preparing the ground for a possible repetition of the tactic I'd used nine months earlier in Operation Howzat? When Bonhams had initially been less than helpful, I'd been forced to go above the heads of the saleroom staff at Chester and involve the top brass in London. It had worked then so, I reasoned, why shouldn't it work again with Christie's? It all depended on Paton's response to my email.

As I waited for his reply, the post arrived. Inside an envelope addressed to me, I found the two letters I'd sent to Garry Sobers via Basharat Hassan's address in Nottingham – one by recorded delivery, the other by hand. Both were unopened. I presumed they'd been returned to me by Hassan but there was no note with them. I must admit that my first thought was, wrongly as it turned out, that Hassan was trying to distance himself from Sobers, the man who'd actually signed the certificate of provenance. A little later, the phone rang. It was Hassan. He was not a happy bunny. As he started to speak, I was reminded of his phone calls to me in 2008. I'd actually been expecting him to ring – in fact, I'd even prepared for his call by making a few notes on a piece of paper – and I immediately told him that I was recording the conversation.

Hassan came straight to the point: he wanted to meet me "face to face" because such a meeting would be "easier" for me. He explained that he'd sent back the two letters because he was no longer Sobers' agent and he had never opened his mail. He'd just been helping him "as a friend" for about four years by organising occasional events for him when Sobers visited Britain in the summer. I apologised for sending the Sobers letters to Hassan's address but, because of his association with the former West Indies captain, I'd felt it had been the best thing to do. I explained that I'd also written to his former client at his home in Barbados.

Having dealt with the letters, we turned to more important matters. Hassan admitted that, as Sobers' agent at the time, he'd been involved in the certificate of provenance being signed. He'd told Jose Miller that Sobers was staying at the Beeches Hotel in Nottingham in the summer of 2006 and then attended the subsequent meeting. He said the ball had been produced by Miller and Sobers had asked her if it was the one he'd given to John Gough, her predecessor as secretary of the Nottinghamshire Supporters' Association, in 1968. She'd confirmed that it was and after inspecting it, Sobers had asked if the certificate could be slightly altered because he wasn't happy with the description of the ball's seam. Hassan denied taking the ball to Christie's in London, saying he'd only been there once – in 2000 when Sobers had sold the Six Sixes bat and the one used to hit his record Test score of 365 via the Christie's saleroom in Melbourne in Australia.

"I've got to speak to Garry," I said, "because his name, his reputation is being besmirched."

"I don't know why you want to write the article," replied Hassan. "I don't know where you're going with this article. I don't know what you're trying to do Grahame.

"I'm trying to get to the truth, Basher."

"The truth is that ball was there from Miss Miller which Sir Garry gave to Mr Gough and that's the ball she brought. I know what she said to Sir Garry."

"Basher…the ball that was used in the Six Sixes over was made by Stuart Surridge – that ball is made by Duke & Son. It cannot be the ball."

"I don't know about that."

"That ball is not the ball that was used the Six Sixes over. You know that and I know that."

"I don't know – I couldn't tell you that."

When I returned to the possibility of speaking to Sobers, Hassan agreed to try to set up an interview with him in the West Indies. Ten minutes later, he'd supplied me with the number. Hassan's insistence that I rang Sobers straightaway rather caught me on the hop because I hadn't yet prepared for that particular interview. I quickly scribbled down a few questions on a piece of paper and dialled the number. In many ways, this interview with Sobers was the most important one of the lot in that, through it, I was hoping to be able to clear his name once and for all. I just couldn't believe that such a cricketing colossus could have been involved in anything irregular. This was the first opportunity I'd had to speak to Sobers about his association with the sale and I was keen to hear his side of the story in full – as opposed to the often truncated versions found in various newspaper reports over the last seven years.

The rambling and often repetitive interview lasted the best part of 40 minutes and largely consisted of Sobers protesting his innocence. At times, it seemed his answers had been pre-recorded on some sort of loop – so adamant was he about putting the record straight and so similar were his replies as he recalled his connection with the ball. After introducing myself, I explained that I was writing an article for *Wisden* and a book on the "Six Sixes ball business" and I'd be recording our conversation. I told him about my evidence which had led to the ball being withdrawn by Bonhams in May 2012. Almost at once, Sobers was on the front foot:

"Before you go any further, let me tell you what I know about the ball. A few years ago, Basher came to me and said that this lady had this ball which I had given to John Gough who was a member at the Notts Cricket Club. I knew him very well and I remember giving him the ball when I hit the Six Sixes because there was no memorabilia in those days. It didn't matter – you just gave whatever you had away.

"But did you remember the make of the ball that was returned?"

"I can't remember that. It was 1968 so when it came up how would I ever remember that? I mean, as far as I was concerned, I hit the ball for six sixes and that was it. A ball was presented to me, I didn't look at the name of it and even if I did, I wouldn't remember what the name of it was – impossible! Because as far as I was concerned, I had given it to this chap John Gough and it came up about – what? six years ago it came to me when this girl said he had given this ball to her. And I remember giving him the ball and that was nearly 40 years earlier. How am I meant to remember?"

"I understand that Sir Garfield but you signed a certificate of provenance stating that this was the ball that was used in the over."

"I signed it because the girl brought the ball to me and said that this is the ball John Gough had given her. I remember giving it to him, I didn't think the girl was a liar. She brought it to me because she needed money and she was very sick. I was told that was the ball that John Gough had given her so who am I to say that he didn't?"

And those few questions and answers, in a nutshell, encapsulated the Sobers version of events – an account which was repeated more than once during the course of our conversation. When I pressed him again about his decision to sign the certificate of provenance, he said that, at the time, he'd thought he was "doing a good service for the lady who needed money" and he'd only signed it "because of my feeling that that was the ball." He recalled a conversation he'd had with Miller at the Nottingham hotel:

"I asked her: 'you're sure this is the ball that Mr Gough has given to you that I had hit for the Six Sixes?'

"'Yes', she said. 'He gave me this ball and he said to me: 'This is the ball that Sir Garry hit for the Six Sixes and I am going to give it to you.'"

When I explained to Sobers that the BBC TV footage confirmed that Malcolm Nash had bowled only one ball in the over but Christie's had maintained that three were used, Sobers made his position clear:

"I don't know anything about that. I don't have a clue about what they said. I'm a very innocent bystander because this ball was brought to me nearly 40 years after I had hit it for the Six Sixes."

At some stage, I knew I was going to have to ask the $64,000 – or rather the £26,400 question – because it had often come up during conversations I'd had during the course of Operation Howzat? I wasn't surprised by the indignant reply I received from Sobers:

"When that ball was sold for £26,400, did you receive any of that money?"

"Me?"

"You."

"Look, look, look, look, look…now look, now listen…I have nothing else to say to you. You can go and do what you like because I never thought you were going to ask me a question like that."

"I just wanted to ask you because – "

"How can you dare to ask me the question?"

"I ask you the question because it's a question which has been asked of me by people as I've been investigating this story. I'm simply asking you the question."

When he'd finally calmed down, Sobers confirmed that he had "got no money" from the sale of the ball. He said he was sick and tired of being contacted about the controversy:

"I wash my hands of it. I did what I thought was honest. All my life, I played cricket honestly, I tried to do all the best things with my life and as far as I was concerned, I was doing the right thing."

As the interview meandered on its way, Sobers took time out to criticise Christie's for their handling of the sale:

"The people that auctioned it, why did they not do research into it before auctioning it? That is what you should find out. That is where it has gone wrong. Why didn't the people who auctioned it look into it to make sure?"

Fair question – and one, I assured Sobers, that I wanted to put to Christie's at a later date. He repeated that he had both believed and trusted Miller when she'd told him how the ball had come into her possession via John Gough:

"It wasn't something that just popped up. This was somebody

who had had the ball for a long time. I haven't done anything wrong. I haven't done anything out of the ordinary. I did what an honest human being would do for a person who was in trouble."

His repeated use of the word 'honest' resonated with me because, as Sobers had already observed, he'd always played the noble game of cricket in the right spirit – and been renowned and respected for doing so. Over the years, I'd read countless tributes to him which cited both his talent and his impeccable approach to the game. I particularly remembered one comment by E.W. Swanton in his 1972 autobiography, *Sort of a Cricket Person*:

> There is a tradition of good sportsmanship in West Indies cricket,
> long established, which has never weakened. Garry Sobers is its
> perfect expression.

Sobers was adamant on four key points – he had given the ball to John Gough after hitting the Six Sixes in 1968; Basharat Hassan had mentioned Jose Miller's connection with the ball to Sobers some years before she'd asked him to sign the certificate of provenance in 2006; when they'd met at the Nottingham hotel, he had questioned her closely about its authenticity before signing the certificate and he couldn't remember the make of the ball or how many balls had been used in the over. As the interview drew to a close and I thanked Sobers for his time, his parting comments struck a particular chord:

"No problem, no problem. I just want you to understand. Whatever I do, I do it in the belief that it is true and, in honesty, I don't do anything to defraud anybody. I have never in my life and I will never stoop to do things like that."

Just as I'd put down the phone at the end of an exhausting, exhaustive and ultimately exhilarating interview, an email from Matthew Paton arrived in my inbox. It seemed the head of communications at Christie's had decided to pull up the drawbridge:

> We have duties of confidentiality towards our seller that prevent us
> from disclosing information which is not already in the public
> domain. However, if you wish to send us copies of the materials to
> which you refer I would be happy to forward them to Christie's legal
> department.

Paton had not only declined to answer my "specific questions", he'd also wrongly cited standard client confidentiality rules: Jose Miller had been publically identified as the ball seller since 2006. He'd also made the mistake of trying to fob me off with an offer to me to send my evidence to him before he then forwarded it to the auction house's legal department. I now knew it was time to involve the Christie's chairman and the Queen's nephew – Viscount Linley – in the Six Sixes ball mystery but the next stage of Operation Howzat? would have to wait a little longer. For the moment, I wanted a second opinion on the Sobers interview. After I'd played my dictaphone recording to Chris Davies down the phone, he confirmed my gut feeling that Sobers had not been party to anything underhand. He'd perhaps been more than a little naïve – by signing the certificate of provenance without knowing or even looking at the ball's make and, at least to my mind, too willingly accepting Miller's assurance – but that was about it. At this time, I was also in regular contact with Lawrence Booth, the editor of *Wisden* who was interested to know how my article was taking shape. Buoyed by his email comment – "Congrats on getting hold of Sobers – that's a massive development" – I suggested employing the successful Bonhams' tactic again. When Lawrence agreed that I should send a round-robin email of complaint to the company's hierarchy in light of Paton's latest response, I set about gathering together the necessary information.

I discovered that Lord Linley had been Christie's chairman since December 2006 – just after the Duke ball had been sold. I knew that he also ran his own furniture shop, Linleys, in London and I managed to find a personal email address from his website. I then searched online for the work addresses of half a dozen members of the Christie's executive management team – ranging from the deputy chairman, Charles Cator, to managing director Jane Hay, to the chairman of their South Kensington saleroom, Nic McElhatton. My email – to which I attached some of my evidence and my recent correspondence with Paton – focused firstly on what I called Paton's "dismissive and disrespectful" attitude towards me. I explained that during my investigation, I'd contacted a variety of organisations – including the Metropolitan Police's Art and Antiques Unit and the Trading Standards Institute – and a host of individuals like Sir Garfield Sobers and the former head of Christie's sporting memorabilia, David Convery:

All of them have been helpful – apart from Mr Paton who displayed
a worrying reluctance to address the pertinent issues. In fact, I consider his attitude to have been obstructive – and not one which casts
Christie's in a very good light.

From the outset, Mr Paton's reasoning has been spurious, disingenu-
ous and irrelevant.

As well as cataloguing my concerns about Paton's response to my
enquiries and the role of Rupert Neelands in the sale, I explained
why I wasn't prepared just to send copies of my evidence to
Christie's as Paton had suggested. I wanted to discuss my material
face to face with someone in a prominent position at Christie's –
not an unnamed person in the legal department. I then summed up
the crux of the matter:

> While the signed certificate of provenance and the contributions of
> the two cricket club archivists are obviously important, the overall
> responsibility must surely lie with the auction house selling the ball
> and compiling the – hopefully accurate – lot notes. Sadly, in this case,
> the notes are riddled with errors – leading me to believe that
> whoever wrote them carried out the research of the ball's prove-
> nance in a less than diligent manner.

I emphasized the importance of reputations – Christie's, Sobers'
and mine – in the investigation and made it clear that, despite
Paton's best efforts, I would not be deflected from my search for
the truth as I wrote the *Wisden* article and this book:

> I do hope that as a result of this email, Christie's will be able to help
> by addressing my concerns about its historical and present day
> conduct. As the most prestigious auction house in the world, I know
> that accuracy and attention to detail are two watchwords on which
> Christie's pride themselves and my investigation has solely been con-
> cerned with uncovering the truth.
> As the editor of *Wisden*, Lawrence Booth, remarked to me yesterday,
> the sale of the ball – and Christie's involvement in it – is "just not
> cricket."

Two days later, while reviewing the progress I'd made with my list
of interviewees, I decided I ought to complete my Nottinghamshire
hat-trick. Having made contact with Hassan and then spoken to
Sobers, it was time to pay a visit to Jose Miller at her home in West

Bridgford. It would be fair to say that our relationship didn't get off to the best of starts. Having confirmed that my letter had arrived, I rang to ask if I could come to interview her about her involvement in the Six Sixes ball story. I didn't record the conversation but, from the notes I made, she accused me of "creeping around" Hassan's home at night. Apparently, his daughter had seen me looking for his house number when I'd hand-delivered the letter to Sobers. Miller was also unhappy about the implications of the use of the phrase "fraudulent act" in my letter. I explained that my evidence strongly suggested that one had taken place and I defended my policy of writing to the nine people connected with the sale and then ringing them for an interview.

Miller said she'd like to meet me but, for the first time in her life, she'd decided to take legal advice about whether or not to agree to my request. She would be seeing her solicitor on Monday morning and I could ring her later that evening to find out the result. I explained that if he advised her not to be interviewed, there would be a big hole in the *Wisden* article and my book and readers would be left to draw their own conclusions. She repeatedly referred to her dilemma about seeking legal advice by stressing she had nothing to hide but then, when apparently on the point of agreeing to meet me, she would revert to being in two minds about seeing her solicitor.

She said she'd had about 80 minor operations on her oesophagus because of a disorder she'd suffered from since the age of four and she complained that the Six Sixes controversy was doing nothing for her health – for which I apologised. I explained that I was having problems getting information out of Christie's.

"Like all big organisations," I continued, "they're...-"

"...closing ranks," she said.

Miller insisted that the Duke ball was the one given to her by John Gough which, in turn, had been passed on to him by Garry Sobers in 1968 – even when I informed her that it was the wrong make, a Duke rather than a Surridge. When I told her I was simply looking for the truth, she replied: "The version I have got is the truth." She briefly recalled travelling down to Christie's in London with her partner, Angus Hall, a retired Co-operative Society manager, in August 2006 and although she didn't remember the name of the person they'd met, she said she'd try to find the consignment document which contained his signature. As I put down the phone and began drawing up my list of questions for Miller, an email arrived from Sarah Charles in the Christie's dispute resolution department. She noted, incorrectly as it happened, that I wasn't keen to involve the legal department but said she thought it was the appropriate part of the organisation to consider and address my concerns. After saying she'd take up my complaints against Paton with him, she turned to the "substantive issues" I'd raised in my email:

> We do of course take very seriously any allegations regarding authenticity of items sold through Christie's. You refer to a significant amount of video, audio and documentary evidence which you would like us to consider.
> Although I understand that you are reluctant to submit that to the Legal Department, I invite you to reconsider, so that we can review for ourselves the evidence you have obtained and give proper consideration to the concerns you raise.

Howzat? While not as spectacular as the response I'd extracted from Bonhams, it was a result of sorts in that I would now at least be dealing with a name – as opposed to an anonymous member of the Christie's legal department. As her email had arrived late on a Friday afternoon, I felt it best to leave replying to Charles until the following Monday. I spent most of the weekend transcribing the Sobers interview – all 13 pages of it – and on my return from watching some football on TV at a local pub on the Sunday, I found a phone message from Miller asking me to ring her back. When I did, I discovered that she'd be happy to see me after all.

"It's absolutely ridiculous for me to be seeking legal advice when I've got nothing to hide," she said, "when all I know is the truth."

I agreed and we arranged to meet at her home on the following Tuesday. We discussed the possibility of my taping the conversation: I stressed I wanted to have a record of it in "the interests of accuracy" but she wasn't very keen. I said I could take notes but I'd prefer to leave my dictaphone running on the table. Recording our conversation would mean there could be no dispute about what I would write in my article and this book. We agreed to resolve the matter on the day.

Any hopes I'd entertained of a successful outcome to my discussions with Sarah Charles the next day were dashed from the moment she began speaking. I explained that she'd misunderstood my attitude towards involving the Christie's legal department: I knew it was necessary – it was simply that I wasn't prepared to send my evidence to Paton who would then forward it to an unnamed individual in the department. Once again, I politely requested a meeting at which I could present my evidence but she insisted that she would review it by herself: I didn't need to be – and wouldn't be – present. I argued that some of my evidence – like my only DVD of the Six Sixes over – was too valuable to send in the post so I was happy to come to London to explain its importance but she was having none of it. It was her way or no way. Take it or leave it. I felt I had no alternative but to accept the offer of a review. The next day, I sent her the evidence I'd emailed to Lord Linley – including the 1968 Glamorgan newsletter confirming the ball used in the over was made by Stuart Surridge and not Duke & Son, and three *Nottingham Evening Post* cuttings. I also attached my detailed research into the false claims in the lot notes about the number of balls used in the over and the assertion that Duke & Son were supplying balls to Glamorgan at the time – as well as a transcript of BBC interviews with two former Glamorgan opening bowlers, Malcolm Nash and Tony Cordle. I explained that John Parkin, who'd been standing at the other end during the over, had also confirmed that one ball had been bowled.

I stressed the urgency of the situation in light of my *Wisden* commission, repeated my offer to travel to London for a meeting and said I was looking forward to hearing from her soon. Pigs might fly. It was to prove the start of the latest – and last – of a series of extremely frustrating pieces of correspondence as Operation Howzat? headed towards its conclusion.

Putting a shine on a scuffed ball

Truth will come to light...at length truth will out.

William Shakespeare, The Merchant of Venice

For once, I wondered if The Bard had got it right. Had the world's greatest playwright, so often the source of so much wisdom, made a mistake by including the 15th century saying in Act 2 Scene 2 of his "most excellent history"? Was Launcelot's observation to his father Gobbo as they discussed their relationship not accurate after all? Despite all the efforts to hide it, would the truth about the Six Sixes ball eventually come to light?

As my investigation approached its denouement, this just was one of a number of questions I kept asking myself. Every time I ticked off another name on my interviewee list, I wondered if I would ever completely solve the mystery. Had my search for the truth about the ball been worth it? Did it really matter what had happened? By speaking to Jose Miller, I at least now knew that I would be returning to the source of the controversy, to the woman who, quite literally, had set the ball rolling when she'd decided to sell it via Christie's in 2006. And, for the first time, I would be encountering one of The Gang of Nine in the flesh. I'd always felt that a face-to-face meeting rather than a telephone conversation would give me a better idea of a person's character. That option wasn't always available, as in the case of Garry Sobers and, I suspected, the present and former Christie's contingent, but I was pleased at last to have the opportunity to pursue my enquiries in person.

Before heading off to Nottingham, I emailed Ashish Singhal to let him know that, via Viscount Linley, I'd established contact with Christie's and they were giving my evidence "proper consideration." I suggested he should dispatch the contract, the ball and the certificate as soon as possible and I was mildly encouraged by his description of the news as a "very good and positive move" – before taking his promise to send me the contract by courier later in the week with the usual large pinch of salt.

When I arrived at West Bridgford, Angus Hall opened the door and took me through to a conservatory at the back of the house where I was introduced to Jose Miller. As a couple of terrier dogs yapped and snapped around my heels, I sat down opposite the couple as they settled themselves on another sofa, before accepting the offer of a cup of tea from Miller's sister, Pauline. Almost immediately, Hall produced a piece of paper, a sort of contract, through which I had to promise to seek their permission before using any material from our discussion. Frankly, I was quite taken aback. When I explained why I wouldn't be signing it – there was no way I'd be handing over editorial control of Operation Howzat? to anyone – we quickly agreed that a pair of dictaphones should be placed on the table between us so we'd both have a full record of our conversation. After that encouraging moment of compromise, an interview lasting nearly three hours got underway. Via more than 60 questions, Miller, in considerable pain because of her debilitating oesophagus condition and with more than a little help from Hall, patiently responded to my methodical investigation.

I thought it best to begin at the beginning so Miller explained that her connection with the ball dated from her working relationship with John Gough, who'd become secretary of the Nottinghamshire Supporters' Association in 1967. The following year, Miller was recruited as his assistant when the association opened The Tavern, which was situated around the back of the main pavilion. The pub, later demolished during redevelopment, was an important part of the fabric of Trent Bridge during the late 1960s when sports writer Duncan Hamilton first visited the ground. In *A Last English Summer: The Biography of a Cricket Season*, he admitted that he always recalls that period of his life whenever he goes to Trent Bridge now. "The doors to the Old Tavern are flung open," he wrote, "and I can smell the beery warmth from it. The glare of its neon bulbs breaks into the gentle darkness of mid-evening." It was a convivial and welcoming environment which Gough and Miller were delighted to have helped create.

"I was working alongside John from the time The Tavern opened," recalled Miller. "We were doing the glasses. I worked lots of hours that I didn't get paid for, but I loved it."

When Garry Sobers arrived to play for the county in that same year, they both got to know him well. In fact, Miller introduced Sobers to his first wife, Pru Kirby, an Australian, and was invited to their wedding in Nottingham in 1969. After being brought back from Swansea, the Six Sixes ball had been on display in the window of the branch of the South of England Building Society in Market Square in Nottingham before finding a permanent home in the supporters' association's office, near The Tavern. Contrary to popular belief, the ball was never kept in the Eddie Marshall lounge bar, a more formal function room alongside the main Tavern bar, where the association used to regularly meet. Miller replaced Gough as secretary when he retired in November 1975 and a review of the year on the county's website notes that there had been "few better known faces at Trent Bridge," than Gough's. "He worked all hours to build up The Tavern into what it is today." Miller inherited a staff of 20 to continue running the pub and she was also responsible for fundraising.

"The first time I saw the ball," she said, "it was in John's office on a window sill with a little bit of a card saying it had been used in the Six Sixes over. Garry had signed it and there was also a purple Rest of the World cricket jacket which he'd given John after captaining the international side in the 1970s. John kept it in a little wardrobe in his office. I never looked at the make of the ball, to be honest. To me, it was just a cricket ball. John was retiring, I was taking over his job and one day he was clearing out his office.

"'Which one do you want?,' he said to me, "the ball or the jacket?'

"'Are they yours to give?' I asked.

"'Garry gave them to me,' John replied.

"'Well… the jacket will get moths in it so I'll have the ball,' I said. I remember like it was yesterday. I wrapped it in a bit of lace cloth, took it home and put it in my make-up drawer."

According to Miller and Hall, the ball stayed there for more than 30 years until it was consigned to Christie's. As her health deteriorated, Miller decided to sell it and put the money towards the cost of building a 'clean' room extension to her home. She'd written to Sobers in 1994 asking him to verify the ball and give her permission to sell it. After not receiving a reply, she'd put the idea on the back burner until 2006 when she feared her oesophagus problem had become much worse.

"We knew everything had to be spotless in the room we were to have built," she explained, "because I would have to be on a drip. So I thought I'd see if I could get anything for the ball. I ran into Basher Hassan and told him I was trying to get hold of Garry. He asked why I'd not contacted him – he said he could have sorted it for me – and we agreed that the next time Garry came over, Basher would arrange to for me to have a reunion with him."

Miller confirmed that the meeting took place at the Beeches Hotel in Nottingham in the summer of 2006. As she and Hall waited in reception with the ball and the certificate of provenance, Sobers came down from his room.

"We shook hands," recalled Miller, "and I felt he was a bit more distant than when I'd been invited to his wedding but then I hadn't seen him for a long time. But he seemed pleased to see me and said he was sorry to hear that John Gough had since died.

"A friend of mine, Diane, who's very good at fancy writing, had drawn up the certificate of provenance. The first thing I said to Garry was this: 'Would you like this ball back? Take it back, it's yours. I've got medical problems but I don't feel comfortable about selling it without your permission.'

"'No,' he said. 'It belongs to you – you have it.'

"Garry looked at the ball, closely examined it and saw his signature on it. He then looked at the certificate and said he wasn't happy with the wording. I'd called it a 'cracked' cricket ball and Garry said 'it isn't a crack, it's the seam.' So he said I would have to get another one done."

The significance of the signed certificate of provenance in the Six Sixes ball mystery cannot be overstated. It was a key part of the Christie's authentication process and the sale wouldn't have taken place without it. So, despite Miller's obvious discomfort and, at times, faltering voice, I thought it was important to question the couple in more detail about the hotel conversation with Sobers in 2006. It became clear that the ball's history but not its make had been mentioned during the discussion.

"When Sir Garfield asked you to take out the word 'cracked', did he ask you if you were sure about the authenticity of the ball?"

"We were asking him," said Miller and Hall together.

"So you asked him – and what did he say to you?"

"He said 'yes – that's the ball I gave to John,'" said Miller. "'That's the ball.'"

"Garry says he asked you if it was the ball that he had given to John Gough."

"No…" replied Miller. "I told Garry about the day John retired, about the Rest of the World jacket and the ball and John asking me which one would I like."

"But he's saying to me that when you spoke to him, he questioned you and said 'are you sure this is the ball?'"

"No, he didn't," said Hall. "I was there and he didn't say that. It was down to him…"

"So you took the ball and a certificate of provenance to him and you were basically asking him 'is this the ball?'"

"Yes," Miller and Hall replied.

"I never gave it a thought," added Miller. "You're going to think I'm thick but I didn't realise that cricket ball was going to be worth so much. And I didn't ask Garry 'is this the ball that you hit around St Helen's in Swansea 38 years ago?'"

"Why would she ask him when she'd had it in her possession for about 30 years?" said Hall.

As I listened to their version – and compared it with the Sobers one – it seemed to me that when Sobers and Miller had met in 2006, they'd both been looking for reassurance from each other that the ball was genuine; that it was the one given in 1968 by Sobers to Gough before he'd passed it on to Miller on his retirement. Both had presumed it to be the correct ball because of its association with Gough. Miller's recollection of the choice she'd made between it and the purple Rest of the World jacket in 1975 had simply strengthened their mutual belief that it was indeed the one used in the over. As a result, neither of them had queried its authenticity and both had assumed it was the real thing. It almost seemed to be a case of "the blind leading the blind" in that nobody appeared to be certain of – or too concerned about – the ball's manufacturer.

"Garry now says," I continued, "that he knew nothing about the make of the ball in 1968 or 2006 and he trusted you – he took your word?"

"Right," said Miller, before turning to Hall. "I've got to be truthful Angus – I never really looked at it or turned it upside down."

"We know nothing about the ball's make," said Hall.

"I'm telling you the truth as I know it," insisted Miller.

"What do you say about the fact that the ball hit by Sir Garfield was a Stuart Surridge whereas the ball that was…"

"I don't know anything about it at all," replied Miller.

"Not a clue," said Hall.

"Not a clue. Not. A. Clue," confirmed Miller.

I was trying to be firm but fair with my questioning but I realised that my forensic approach was taking its toll on Miller, who regularly gulped down small measures of liquid painkiller and iced water during the course of the interview. At this stage, I thought it would be appropriate to reveal my evidence about the ball's provenance. During a short break, I presented the couple with a copy of the 1968 Glamorgan newsletter in which a report of the Six Sixes confirmed the ball had been made by "the firm of Stuart Surridge." When they'd both read it, I explained how this single sentence had alerted to me to the authenticity discrepancy in 2008. Once my suspicions had been aroused, I'd felt obliged to try to get to the bottom of the matter.

"I can understand your point of view," said Miller, "but I know nothing about the make. I didn't realise the importance of it to be truthful – it was just a cricket ball."

"I think the duty was on Christie's to verify…" said Hall.

But before we moved on to discuss the involvement of the auction house, I asked Miller to explain how the amended certificate of provenance which she'd taken to Christie's had been signed by Sobers in 2006.

"Garry was going to London within a couple of days," she said, "so I brought the original certificate and the ball back and told Diane that I needed help. I said I wanted her to leave out the word 'cracked' because Garry wasn't happy with it. Diane drew up another one overnight and then Basher's wife, Anne, got it signed by Garry for me the next day."

After briefly discussing the history of the ball and then making an appointment by telephone with Christie's, Miller and Hall had driven down to London in early August to formally consign the ball to the auction house. Hall, in particular, remembered the day well. It was his birthday and they'd had a difficult journey to the capital after he'd taken a wrong turning at Hanger Lane in Ealing. As a result, they'd got completely lost and arrived late for their appointment. Once at the saleroom in Old Brompton Road in South Kensington, the couple had been met by a member of staff who took them, along with the ball and the certificate of provenance, into a small room. At this stage, I knew it was time to ask another one of those $64,000 questions: who was the person they'd dealt with on the day? At first, neither Miller nor Hall could remember his name. I'd suspected as much – after all, it was more than six years ago – so I'd brought along half a dozen black-and-white photos of the three specialists listed in the Christie's catalogue for the sporting memorabilia auction held in November 2006. I'd printed off the photos of David Convery, Max Dunbar and Rupert Neelands from the Convery Auctions, Manchester Jewish Museum and Christie's websites respectively. I didn't mention any of the three by name and I had two copies of each photo so that Miller and Hall could consider them separately during the impending identity parade.

"No," said Miller when I showed her Convery's photo. "It wasn't him," she said after looking at the Dunbar one.

"No, I don't recognise any of them," remarked Hall, after I'd given them both a photo of Neelands. Miller agreed with him.

"Well…it's one of them," I said.

"Is it?" asked Miller.

"Yes," I insisted.

"Has he changed?" said Hall.

"No, no."

Not for the first time during Operation Howzat?, my heart was starting to sink. Perhaps I'd got it all wrong? Perhaps none of the Christie's specialists was involved? Then again, Convery had already told me that Dunbar and Neelands had catalogued the sale and, as the head of the Christie's sporting memorabilia department at the time, he should surely know? It was important to stay calm.

"It definitely wasn't him, was it?" said Miller to Hall as she pointed at the Neelands photo. "Too old – he was younger than that. He was small and dark if I remember."

I suddenly recalled part of the phone conversation I'd had with Miller while arranging my trip to West Bridgford. She'd mentioned seeing the man who had dealt with the ball's consignment on the day of the actual auction four months later.

"You said he'd been on the phone when you arrived for the auction and he'd nodded to you?"

"Yes," Miller replied. "He nodded to me."

"These are the three people," I said, pointing to the photos, "and one of them handled the sale, met you and then was involved in writing some lot notes for the ball."

I suspect that my mention of the erroneous lot notes must have triggered something in Miller's mind – something she'd seen written down on the Christie's consignment agreement.

"I think there were some initials on it," she said, "and I think they were DWB. It looked like the signature scribbled on the receipt when we got it – I think it was DWB."

Now we were getting somewhere. This sounded promising.

"What about Dunbar?," Hall suddenly chipped in. "Would that make any sense?"

It certainly would. It made an awful lot of sense. Howzat? The umpire's finger was on the way up.

"Thank you," I said to Hall. I wasn't the only person to be delighted by his vital recollection.

"Ooh! you've remembered! Well done!," cried Miller – and not for the only time.

"I had a terrible day but… "

"Angus," I said. "You've hit the nail right on the head."

"Well done!," exclaimed Miller.

"That's all I can remember," said Hall.

"Before I do anything," I continued, "which one of these is this man Dunbar?," referring to the photos of the Christie's specialists.

"Well the most likely one is this one," replied Hall, picking up Dunbar's photo.

"This is the man," I said, "who, when I rang him in May last year, refused to answer my phone call. And when I asked about the ball through someone else in his office, the reply I got was 'no comment'."

"Well done!," said Miller. "Well done!"

Well done indeed. And just to confirm the identification, Hall began to rummage around in his pile of documents for their copy of the consignment agreement. When he couldn't find it, he said he'd email it to me but I suggested he could return to his home – about 20 minutes away – and bring back the relevant piece of paper so off he went. The two dictaphones were switched off, I sat back in the sofa and accepted the offer of a top-up from Pauline Miller. It was time for a small celebration – not with champagne but a nice cup of tea. I breathed a sigh of relief in the aftermath of one of the biggest breakthroughs in Operation Howzat? so far.

It was while we were waiting for Hall to return that I made another hugely significant discovery – one which would justify all the time and effort expended during the previous nine months in trying to track down the ball's movements. As we sat sipping tea, I asked Miller about her relationship with Basharat Hassan, the conduit between her and Sobers. In accordance with her oft-stated policy of telling the truth, Miller revealed that, when the cheque from the ball's sale had finally arrived from Christie's, she'd had to give Hassan some of the money. The full details would emerge later in our recorded conversation. For the moment, I was slightly more interested in examining the paperwork which would unequivocally confirm the Christie's contact who'd handled the ball's consignment and who then, I assumed, had written the infamous and inaccurate lot notes.

Twenty minutes later, Hall returned to West Bridgford with a veritable treasure trove of transaction testimony. It contained not only the Christie's consignment agreement but copies of the remittance advice, cheque and settlement statement. Miller had been in the right area with her recollection of the initials of the person involved – DWB was in fact MWD. They were there in black and white, alongside his estimate of the ball's worth – between £5,000 and £8,000 – and although I didn't know his middle name, Max Dunbar's signature, "for and on behalf of Christie's", was there for all to see on the consignment agreement. There was no doubt about it: Dunbar was our man. DRS had done the trick. The evidence had been reviewed and confirmed the umpire's original decision. Hot spot had picked it up: definitely out – and Dunbar was back in the pavilion. The rabbit had returned to the hutch.

When we began recording again, I asked the Miller and Hall about their initial meeting at South Kensington and, in particular, Dunbar's questions about the ball.

"He asked me where I got it from," Miller said, "how I got it and I said I worked at Trent Bridge, my boss retired and I took over – the same story really."

"Right. Let me ask you two questions: did you tell him that the ball was the last of three used in the over?"

"No. I didn't know…"

"I wouldn't have a clue," said Hall.

"Fine. Second question, again, a crucial one as you'll see in a moment. Did you tell them that Glamorgan were being supplied with balls made by Duke & Son in 1968?"

"No," replied Miller.

"Absolutely not," said Hall. "Max Dunbar didn't ask us any of those two questions but I never thought he really believed who we were."

I then handed them both a copy of the Christie's lot notes containing the two erroneous statements about the number of balls used in the over and Glamorgan's ball suppliers at the time.

"I've heard all sorts of theories about how many balls were used, and how many the umpires put in their pockets," continued Hall, "but we didn't know and Dunbar never asked."

I felt it was essential that the couple realised just why the Duke ball was not the genuine article so I also explained that the TV footage of the event confirmed that Malcolm Nash bowled only one ball.

"When you were at Christie's, did anyone involved in verifying the ball mention it or, in your presence, look at any TV footage of the Six Sixes over?"

"No," said Hall.

The couple then told me more about their meeting with Dunbar. It hadn't lasted long. They hadn't been impressed with him – "we just thought he was an office boy" – or their treatment – "we didn't even get a cup of coffee." They'd not been present at the meeting between Christie's and Andrew Hignell, the Glamorgan archivist who'd travelled to London to verify the Six Sixes event; "I'd never heard of him until I read his name in a newspaper report," said Hall. I then returned to the involvement of Sobers' agent in the sale of the ball:

"Do you know if either Basharat Hassan or Garry Sobers contacted Christie's by telephone during that time?"

"After we'd been to London," said Miller, "I asked Basher to confirm who I was. I mean, I just didn't want Max Dunbar to think that I was a barmaid that worked at The Tavern and who'd said 'I'll have that ball'. I wanted Basher to confirm who I was and how I'd got it so I said 'would you or Garry get in touch with Christie's and please tell them how I got it – and tell them that it's the ball?'"

"To the best of your knowledge, Basher did that and he confirmed the story about Garry, John Gough and you getting the ball?"

"He told me he had phoned," said Miller, "and he told me it was strictly OK. I wouldn't have gone within a thousand miles of this chap Dunbar if I'd have known that there was something not right."

I then fast-forwarded to 15th November 2006 – the day the couple had travelled back down to South Kensington for the auction of the ball. They'd felt that a final figure of somewhere around the £5,000-£8,000 estimate would have been enough to kick-start building work on the proposed 'clean' room and they were also expecting to receive some inheritance money following the recent death of Miller's uncle in America. As the bids went from the reserve price of £5,000 to the hammer price of £22,000 and the mystery buyer won the battle for the ball, the pair couldn't believe what they were witnessing at their very first auction:

"I was gobsmacked," said Miller.

"Unexpected result!" recalled Hall.

"I wanted the auction to start again so I could take it in," confessed Miller. "To me a cricket ball is a cricket ball, to be honest."

"But it must have been beyond your wildest dreams when you realised you'd got £22,000?," I asked.

"It was a real better figure than we thought," replied Hall.

Although the overall cost of the ball, including a 20 per cent buyer's premium, came to £26,400, Miller revealed that she'd received only £18,815.75 of the £22,000 – with the rest of the hammer price going to Christie's via a 10.68 per cent commission (£2,761.25p), a 1.5 per cent loss or damage liability (£330) and the cost of an illustration (£30). After Miller had rung Christie's to complain about the delay in payment, the cheque finally arrived nearly seven weeks after the sale – followed closely by a phone call from Hassan:

"He said he wanted the same amount that Christie's had," recalled Miller.

"It was a percentage amount," added Hall.

In the event, Miller gave Hassan a cheque for £3,763.15, actually 20 per cent of her net total and £1,000 more than Christie's took in commission. The cheque, along with the relevant paperwork and a note to Hassan and his wife, Anne, was hand-delivered by Hall to Hassan's nearby home in West Bridgford. How had the couple felt when Hassan asked for money – did they feel they owed him anything?

"No", replied Miller.

"He didn't do much," added Hall.

"But he did facilitate the signing of the certificate of provenance?" I said.

"I did think that without his help…," replied Miller. "Now when we discussed it yesterday morning, Anne couldn't remember anything about it. But I sent her some flowers for taking the trouble to get the second certificate signed in 2006 because I knew she must have scurried around to get it done – I'm sure Garry was going to London pretty soon – and I got the certificate back signed properly the next day.'

"His request for money came out of the blue," said Hall.

"I possibly thought 'Well… that's a bit of a cheek', to be honest," added Miller.

"Have you ever spoken about that cheque before?"

"Not since but he has over the last few days when I've seen him about four times. I said to him: 'Basher, I'm telling the truth. Whatever, I am telling the truth.'"

"And what did he say to you?"

"We must all tell the same story."

"There is no story," said Hall.

It was time for me to start wrapping up the interview. The clock was ticking and the couple had provided me with some very valuable information but there were still important questions to be asked, not least about the proposed 'clean' bedroom which had been needed because of Miller's condition. It transpired that the conservatory in which we were now sitting was mainly built with her £15,000 proceeds from the sale of the ball. After undergoing several endoscopies to deal with her problem, Miller was now able to swallow food more easily and for the moment, her diet was no longer restricted to liquids and trifles.

"In 2006, I was thinking it was going to be horrible and I thought I had to have a 'clean' area. I had an operation in 2012 to help but there's going to be a time when I've got to be fed every day."

"We haven't been out for a meal for 12 years," said Hall, "but the treatment of Jose's condition last year now enables her, although she's still in terrible pain, to eat a chip – something which you and I never think twice about doing. There wasn't so much of a need to convert part of the space into a 'clean' area so we've ended up with a conservatory."

"It was never used as a 'clean' room because I wasn't ready to die at the time," added Miller, whose condition has considerably worsened over the last six months.

During our conversation, while acknowledging their key role in providing the signed certificate of provenance, Miller and Hall were still critical of Christie's for what they consider to be the auction house's less-than-diligent approach to verifying the ball's provenance.

"I'm very annoyed," said Hall, "after hearing and reading about the ex-Glamorgan players being up in arms before the date of the auction. If they approached Christie's and were given the bum's rush, we have been betrayed."

"I'm really annoyed, I'm really upset," said Miller. "This controversy has made me more ill – the stress makes my condition worse. I've had no sleep at all. When it started and there were bits about me in the paper, I felt like going out with a black bag on my head. This is also about my good name."

As the interview drew to a close, I realised that another $64,000 dollar question was looming large on the horizon – this time about the £15,000 profit Miller had made from selling the ball. I told them about my trip to Chester during which I'd managed to persuade Bonhams to withdraw the ball from their sporting memorabilia auction in May 2012 and I then asked the first in a series of preliminary questions:

"Do you still maintain that the Duke ball you sold at Christie's was used in the Six Sixes over?

"I can only say this," replied Miller. "I wouldn't have tried to go to Garry…if I knew that something was not right, I wouldn't sell it would I?"

"It never crossed our minds that it wasn't, because of the history," said Hall.

"What do you say, Jose, to the person who paid £26,400?"

"I feel really sorry for him," replied Miller. "I think it's absolutely terrible that he's paid for a cricket ball that's worthless. I think it's awful."

"A man called Bernard Shapero bought it on behalf of a man living in India. He paid £26,400 for a ball that frankly isn't genuine. Do you have any views about whether you should do anything now in terms of helping to right this wrong? Do you feel maybe that you should pay any of the money back? You say you feel sorry for the person. Do you…?"

"Well…I feel sorry now I hear what you're telling me about Christie's who I relied upon to authenticate it all," replied Hall.

"It's six, nearly seven years since you took it to Christie's in good faith. What do you feel now should happen? If somebody said to you 'well…you ought to pay back some of the money – '"

"The man should have his money back," Hall immediately replied.

"Do you agree with that Jose?," I said.

"I don't think I should be made to pay back Basher's share," she said. "In fairness, he should cough up. But what I've had, I will give back…"

"Christie's should cough up," said Hall.

"If something was done that's not right, I'll give it back," repeated Miller.

"You would give the money back – your £15,000?"

"Yes," they both said. "I would like to meet the man in India who bought the ball," added Hall.

"This is about my good name here, to be honest," said Miller.

As I made my way home, I was very pleased with the way my first face-to-face interview in West Bridgford had gone – and hoped that the next one with Hassan would prove just as fruitful.

The next day, all hope of a TV documentary about the Six Sixes mystery disappeared when Tony Roe, from the *Inside Out* programme in Nottingham, confirmed a complete lack of interest from his superiors in the BBC East Midlands region. Not to worry. Onwards and upwards.

I then decided to ring the Peter Wynne-Thomas, Nottinghamshire CCC's archivist and historian, an author of more than 50 cricket books and an all-round good egg. A recent tribute on the Association of Cricket Statisticians and Historians' website described him as having been "at the forefront of the game's researchers for some four decades." He has "always been prepared to share his knowledge and findings with others, and has been particularly supportive of new writers and researchers." I couldn't agree more. Like his counterpart at Glamorgan, Andrew Hignell, Wynne-Thomas had always been very good to me – from the moment in 2007 when he told me about Jose Miller's connection with the Six Sixes ball. Whenever you visit his Trent Bridge haven of tranquility, he can be found, head in a book or scorebook, beavering away alongside other enthusiasts who have popped in to make use of the library. He's a cricket nut with a sense of humour; old school but someone who has embraced new technology – up to a point. On his Twitter account, @Wizipedia, Wynne-Thomas describes himself as having an "irrational love of cricket and typewriters. Medical textbooks have completely failed to discover a cure, cartoons do give temporary relief." His 260-odd followers are fed a regular stream of cricket stats such as "Gary Sobers scored 247 more first-class runs in his career than Australian legend Don Bradman." I'm not sure a lot of people know that – I certainly didn't. Wynne-Thomas still uses his typewriter for books, reports and letters and although he's actually never posted anything on the internet himself, his vast knowledge base is being mined for a new website, www.history.trentbridge.co.uk.

I wanted to talk to him about his role in the sale of the ball because he and Andrew Hignell had consistently been thanked by Christie's for their contribution to the authentication process. I knew that the two archivists had spoken on the phone before Hignell went to London to view the ball in 2006 but I wondered if Wynne-Thomas had had any other input? During a recorded conversation, he confirmed that he'd never seen the Six Sixes ball, despite reports at the time that it was destined for the Trent Bridge museum. In fact, the ground didn't have one in 1968 but two glass cases, containing memorabilia mainly from the 19th century and up to the Second World War, had been kept in the Long Room. I mentioned the wrong make of the ball and the lot notes assertion that three balls rather than one had been bowled by Malcolm Nash. Wynne-Thomas said he'd not been contacted by Christie's before the sale, he didn't know what Hignell had said during his meeting at the sporting memorabilia department in London but he remembered the phone conversation with his Glamorgan counterpart.

"I think we talked about whether one or more balls had been used in the over," he told me. "It's a long time ago but I'm sure the make of the ball wasn't mentioned."

"In response to any press enquiries about the ball," I said, "Christie's put out a press release citing the certificate of provenance and the help they received from the two archivists. How do you feel about that?"

"I'm not bothered about it. All I told them, through Andrew Hignell, is what I've told you. As far as I'm concerned, I've never seen the ball but the story I'd heard seemed to be pretty convincing: that the ball that had ended up with the Notts supporters' association was the ball that was used in the match. It just seemed a logical thing to happen. Jose Miller assumed it was the right ball. There's no reason why she shouldn't have thought that that was the ball that was used by Sobers."

As I listened back to the interview, I realised that despite his wealth of knowledge about the history of cricket, Wynne-Thomas had been a peripheral figure in the authentication of the Six Sixes ball. When I switched my attention from Trent Bridge in Nottingham to the SWALEC Stadium in Cardiff, I swapped one refreshingly frank archivist for a distinctly disinclined one. Once again, Glamorgan's 1st XI scorer and statistician, who'd now become the curator of the Museum of Welsh Cricket, began to behave rather strangely. When Hignell answered his direct line, I introduced myself and he kept repeating his name as well as "Glamorgan Cricket" – as if he couldn't hear me very clearly or even at all; almost as if no connection had been made. He seemed to be suggesting that there was something wrong with the line. It sounded clear as a bell to me so I made it plain that I could hear him perfectly well and then he suddenly hung up. When I immediately rang back, Hignell's answerphone clicked in so I left a message, then sent an email asking him to contact me to discuss his role in the Six Sixes ball mystery which I'd outlined in my round-robin letter. Why did I have this feeling that Hignell didn't want to talk to me?

I then rang Basharat Hassan to set up our long-awaited interview but after I'd explained that I was now ready and able to see him, he declined my invitation to meet. In the course of an often heated conversation, Hassan said he wasn't willing to speak to me. It took a short, sharp text message half an hour later to change his mind:

> Having spoken to Sir Garfield, Jose Miller, Peter Wynne-Thomas and Christie's, I now have some very important questions I would like to ask you – either face to face or on the phone. I would urge you to take the opportunity of speaking to me: the right of reply is a crucial part of fair, balanced and objective journalism.

Hassan rang back almost straightaway and, as I was arranging a convenient time and place for us to meet, an email arrived in my inbox from Hignell. It was a classic 'thank you but no thank you' response in that he acknowledged my messages and letter and confirmed that he'd held a meeting with Christie's in 2006:

> However, I do not think that it is appropriate that details of what, at the time, were private conversations should be passed on to a third party.

I wasn't sure why but this "I don't want to be interviewed business" was starting to catch on. As I was already back in touch with *Wisden* editor Lawrence Booth about the progress of my interviews, I thought it would be appropriate to run Hignell's reply past him. I believed it should be challenged and Lawrence agreed that I should email Hignell to explain the latest situation and highlight the possible implications of his refusal to be interviewed. I pointed out to Hignell that he'd already revealed details of his Christie's discussions twice to a third party – me – and that despite his repeated reluctance to help, I'd since discovered the identity of the person he'd met in London. I mentioned the ongoing Christie's review of my evidence and my interview with Peter Wynne-Thomas about his meeting with Hignell in 2006.

> As well as the world's leading auction house, this case involves the reputation of the world's greatest ever all rounder and, through you, the good name of Glamorgan CCC. I'm very worried about the effect such a negative response to the questions I would like to ask you will have on the wider cricketing family and I'm also concerned that it will not portray the county in a particularly good light. Having just spoken to *Wisden*'s editor, Lawrence Booth, I would urge you to reconsider your decision and agree to answer my questions – either face-to-face when I am in Cardiff next week or on the phone. Truth, transparency and accuracy are at the heart of this story and the right of reply is a crucial part of fair, balanced and objective journalism.

As with Hassan's text message, this email did the trick – if only temporarily. Within minutes, I received an encouraging reply from Hignell:

> Thank you for the greater information you have sent. Please can you forward your questions in advance to me, and I will arrange a time to see you next week. Will ring you back shortly as my landline has a fault.

Within seconds, my mobile rang – it was Hignell on his mobile – and during a perfectly amicable discussion, I updated him with the progress I was making with my *Wisden* article and the sequel to *Six of the Best* to be published later in the summer. When I brought up the three-ball theory which the late Glamorgan scorer, Bill Edwards, had often mentioned when talking about the Six Sixes, Hignell said that while clearing out some of Edwards' possessions recently, he'd come across some old balls with faint signatures on them. I inferred that he was saying he'd found evidence to support the three-ball theory but I ignored his remark and moved on to provide him with a brief history of my investigation, including my preliminary contact with the Metropolitan Police's Art and Antiques Unit and the Trading Standards Institute. When Hignell said he'd found my round-robin letter "alarming", I explained that everyone involved in the sale had received one. I was simply searching for the truth – in particular, I just wanted to know what he'd said to Christie's in 2006. After confirming that he would see me in Cardiff sometime during the following week, Hignell asked if I'd be happy for someone to take notes during our meeting. I readily agreed and said I would send him details of my availability. He said he would keep looking for the notes of his meeting at Christie's. I heard nothing over the following weekend and then, just after nine o'clock on the Monday morning, this email arrived in my inbox:

> Thanks for your subsequent email and phonecall. I have now taken legal advice on this matter and, as a consequence, I will not be able to meet up with you.

Ah well. I'd given it my best shot. As I said in my reply to him, I thought it was important for Hignell to have the opportunity to give his version of events. As I reflected on his equivocation, I realised it was entirely his prerogative whether he talked to me or not but I still wasn't quite sure why he was behaving so bizarrely.

It had been quite an intense afternoon and I felt I needed to take a short break from following up my round–robin letter. Next stop? India. It was time to talk to Neville Tuli, the chairman of the Osian's Group, a.k.a. The Mystery Man, who'd bought the ball via Bernard Shapero at Christie's in 2006. Of all the characters I'd come across during the course of Operation Howzat?, the Indian art impresario was by far the most intriguing – and not just because I'd had to work so hard to find out who he was. I really wanted to know why he'd paid such an outrageously high price for a cricket ball. On the grounds of client confidentiality, Shapero had refused to reveal his identity and I'd been reluctant to approach Tuli for fear that he might complain to Shapero which, in turn, might have alienated The Book Man. But once Shapero was aware that I knew about Tuli's involvement, I felt free to contact the ball's original buyer directly. I hadn't been totally happy with a profile of him I'd written for the book because it had been culled largely from internet articles about his career. Although I'd included quotations by Tuli, I'd written it 'blind', without having access to a much wider range of information, because I'd not been able to speak to the man himself and I was keen to rectify the situation as I checked both the profile's accuracy and its tone.

Via email, the Osian's Group's communications vice-president, Supriya Chawla, agreed to put half a dozen key questions to the company's founder and driving force. I was also granted a longer interview at a later date. Within a day, an email arrived from Tuli explaining his association with the ball. He confirmed everything Chris Davies and I had managed to glean during Operation Howzat? – and a little bit more. The final cost to him of acquiring the ball had not been £26,400 but £27,170 because of the £770 in VAT Tuli had paid on the buyer's premium. He explained that Shapero had bid on his behalf before for books, photographs and prints and said the bat and ball were "part of a vast knowledge-base for our museum which was/is being created on the fine and popular arts, cinema, culture and related aspects, with a focus on India and Asia, amid a larger historical framework."

When the glass casket had arrived at New Delhi Airport, Tuli con-firmed that "the economic downturn, our severe liquidity crunch, plus the 15% import duty chargeable as we had taken an import licence for the bat and ball" meant it stayed in customs along with many other objects. "Though demurrage was being paid monthly", it was auctioned in November 2009:

> My logistics team were later approached by some gentleman (I do not know his name) after the auction to re-sell the bat and ball at about 1.5 times our cost. We had no liquidity to spare so the items were lost forever. It was really very sad, but with so many economic difficulties, it was accepted as part of the process.

I agreed with him: the fate of the Six Sixes ball was very sad. Its authenticity had been disputed and then disproved and instead of being given pride of place in a sporting memorabilia collection, the ball had ended up being retrieved from an airport's assortment of unclaimed goods. Its confinement in New Delhi had also proved embarrassing for Tuli but he clearly had nothing to hide. The same could also be said of Peter Wynne-Thomas, Jose Miller and Angus Hall. In fact, the couple's response to Operation Howzat? had gone a long way to restoring my faith in human nature. Their commitment to telling the truth about their association with a scuffed and discredited cricket ball had brought back some of its shine. To my mind, their willingness to return the money they'd made from its sale spoke volumes. Miller was obviously unwell; she'd found the whole controversy deeply unsettling but her determination to give her side of the story shone through every answer. From the outset, she had protested her innocence and I felt there was no reason to doubt the veracity of her recollections. As Operation Howzat? moved towards close of play, I wondered if I would be able to extract some similarly candid disclosures from other members of The Gang of Nine – ex-Christie's employees David Convery and Max Dunbar, and the man formerly known as Garry Sobers' agent, Basharat Hassan. It was time to find out.

Hopping around in a hot spot

Men occasionally stumble over the truth, but most of them pick themselves up and hurry off as if nothing had happened.

Winston Churchill

They say a change is as good as a rest – and so it proved once I'd finally made contact with Neville Tuli. My belated correspondence with the original ball buyer had done the trick. The welcome break from following up my round-robin letter meant that I returned to the task refreshed and re-focused. With the end in sight, I was now over halfway through interviewing the nine people who had, in some way, been involved in the sale of the ball: five down, four to go.

Having refused to speak to me nine months earlier, I realised that Max Dunbar was unlikely to have changed his mind but I drew up a list of questions all the same as I prepared to ring him. He'd been chief executive officer of the Manchester Jewish Museum for nearly two years and I was fascinated to discover a report about his appointment in the Jewish Chronicle Online. It revealed that in what was described as a "short but colourful career", Dunbar had been a photographic curator for the National Portrait Gallery before joining Christie's. He'd then gone on to run the World Rugby Museum at Twickenham and administer an Everton FC memorabilia collection in Liverpool before taking up his present post. The story also explained that, while at Christie's, Dunbar had "handled the sale of the 1871 silver FA Cup – the world's most expensive piece of sports memorabilia" which fetched £420,000 in 2005. Why, I wondered, was no mention made of the fact – now confirmed by Jose Miller's consignment agreement – that Dunbar had also personally supervised the sale of the world's most expensive cricket ball for Christie's a year later? The inclusion of that historic event on his CV would surely have added even more colour – not to mention prestige and kudos – to an already "colourful career." Ah well. Perhaps I'd be able to find out during the interview? On the other hand, perhaps not…

I rang Dunbar on his direct office phone line and he confirmed that he'd received my letter and email explaining my investigation. I made notes throughout our conversation and switched on my dictaphone so that I would have a record of my questions and my reaction to his replies. From the outset, Dunbar made it clear that he didn't want to talk about the Six Sixes ball. I told him he'd been named as the person who'd handled the sale by the woman who had consigned the ball in the summer of 2006. He immediately referred to me to Christie's via Matthew Paton, the communications director, and to David Convery, the auction house's former head of sporting memorabilia. Whenever I pressed Dunbar about his involvement, he said it had happened six years ago – "it's no longer something I can talk about" – and said he was running a new organisation now. When I said I'd like to "record an interview with you or come and see you because you are a key person in all this," he again referred me to Convery.

"Well…he says you catalogued it," I persisted.

"He was the head of department," replied Dunbar. "It was his responsibility."

"But, surely, that's no excuse? I will have a word with him. He's on a list of people I'm trying to ask for their version of events."

Dunbar repeated his stance by again referring me to Christie's and saying he couldn't talk about something that happened so long ago.

"But your name is being mentioned by everybody," I continued, "and if you decline to be interviewed or to answer some pretty basic questions, then I'm not very sure what sort of impression is going to be given. All I'm really asking you is – where did you get the information about there being three balls in the over and the Duke – "

Dunbar interrupted me and continued to stick to his script. As soon as he mentioned the sale catalogue, I interrupted him:

"Yes…but who wrote the catalogue? Who wrote the catalogue notes – that's the key thing because there are two fundamental errors in there. 'Three separate balls were used in the over' – that's not true because one ball was used in the over – and the other one is that 'Duke & Sons were supplying balls to Glamorgan County Cricket Club during this period' and that is untrue. And what I'm trying to do is to find out who gave that information to whoever wrote the lot notes – because they're both wrong and I have evidence to prove it. The ball has already been withdrawn from a Bonhams auction on the strength of my evidence so I'm asking you to answer those questions – where did you get the information?"

Dunbar then reprised his argument about the sale happening a long time ago before he'd begun his new job in Manchester so I jumped in again:

"It's not that long ago – it's six years ago and -"

But Dunbar was on a roll. He repeated the party line about Convery, Christie's and his unwillingness to comment.

"You can't – I'm sorry – you can't forget your past. Something's gone wrong here. Are you able to tell me who wrote the lot notes?"

When he declined to, I knew Dunbar was keen to end the conversation so I made one final attempt:

"Can you tell me who you got the information from?"

Dunbar again refused to tell me and said he had to go so I bid a not very cheery farewell: "You haven't heard the last of this. Sorry mate. OK. Bye-bye."

It was no idle threat because I was felt sure that Dunbar's involvement with the sale would re-surface some time in the future but my immediate concern now was an interview with the seventh member of The Gang of Nine – Sobers' agent in 2006, Basharat Hassan, who I'd arranged to meet in Nottingham in two hours time. The agreed venue was the Larwood and Voce pub, which lies inside Trent Bridge, but when we discovered it was closed until midday, Hassan suggested we should find somewhere else. Through his connection as a club committee member, we were able to adjourn, along with Hassan's wife, Anne, to the Derek Randall Suite in the Hound Road Stand at Trent Bridge. The place looked familiar and I soon recognised it as the venue for one of the *Six of the Best* talks I'd done with John Parkin a couple of years earlier. As we settled ourselves around a table, Hassan ordered some coffee and I explained why I'd sent the letter: I wanted to speak to him about the ball sale for my *Wisden* article and also for this book – the follow-up or sequel to *Six of the Best*. I thanked him for agreeing to see me and as a pair of dictaphones were placed on the table, I began my attempt to get to the bottom of Hassan's involvement in the Christie's sale in 2006.

The two-hour interview had all the makings of a Six Sixes ball version of 20 Questions – or rather 120 questions – with many of the answers consisting of brief denials. Hassan confirmed his earlier recollection that when he'd arrived at the Beeches Hotel in Nottingham in 2006, Miller and Sobers were already discussing the ball. "That's the first time I ever saw it," Hassan assured me. He recalled Sobers asking for the wording of the certificate to be changed because the ball's seam had been described as 'cracked' but Anne Hassan denied helping to facilitate the signing of the new, re-written certificate the next day. "I had nothing to do with this ball whatsoever," she declared, "apart from hearing the story of it."

"I'm told Jose had to make a correction," I continued. "She had to take out the word 'cracked', she took it back to her friend, Diane, and the next day, she's saying that you Anne helped – "

"You mean the certificate to take to Garry?," asked Hassan.

"I haven't seen any certificate," said his wife.

"I can't answer you that because I can't remember it at all," added Hassan. "I know the certificate was signed by Garry – I know that."

Hassan maintained that he first realised Miller's ball was made by Duke & Son via my recent round-robin letter. He didn't know the make of the ball actually used in the over in 1968 and after I showed him the Glamorgan members newsletter confirming it was a Surridge, he produced a reply which was to pop up prominently during the interview: "I wouldn't know that."

Hassan insisted that his involvement with the Six Sixes ball had ended at the hotel meeting he'd helped to set up for the certificate to be signed. He said he hadn't gone to Christie's or had any contact with them before the sale – despite Miller's contention that she'd asked him to ring the auction house to endorse her and Hall. I pressed him again:

"So you – I need to get this clear Basher – you didn't ring Christie's?"

"I did not ring Christie's at all."

"Not at all?

"No. I finished at the Beeches. I didn't ring Christie's. I'm sure I didn't ring Christie's. It was a long time ago."

"Jose said – and Angus, her partner, said – that they wanted you to say: 'Look…this woman knew Garry Sobers, she was secretary of the Nottinghamshire Supporters' Association.' She wanted you to vouch for her and she says that you rang them – "

"I can't remember Grahame – I'm sorry about that."

I then presented Hassan with a copy of the Christie's lot notes, and highlighted the false statements about the number of balls used in the over and Duke & Son being Glamorgan's ball suppliers at the time. Again, he was adamant: he didn't know how that incorrect information had been supplied to Christie's – he certainly didn't speak to anybody there. He said he'd not been playing in the game at Swansea in 1968 and when I suggested that somebody had been "telling porkies" by viewing the TV footage but not spotting that the same ball was used for the whole over, he said he had "nothing to do with this." He'd only seen the footage on the TV news, he wasn't happy that the ball his client had said he'd hit for Six Sixes had proved not to be genuine and he had no idea why someone would lie about the make of the most famous ball in the history of cricket – "it seems strange to me," he observed.

As I ploughed my way through my list of questions, Hassan's short answers meant I was making pretty good progress and I wasn't too downhearted by his succession of negative replies. In fact, I was quite happy to continue, safe in the knowledge that another $64,000 question was quietly lurking just around the corner. The interview rumbled on through a variety of issues: Hassan insisted he didn't know how Sobers could have said in May 2006 that only one ball was bowled and then been party, through signing a certificate of provenance, to a Christie's statement that three balls were used six months later; the pair had never discussed the make or the number of balls bowled and he denied that, as Sobers' then agent, he was guilty of what some people might describe as a dereliction of duty by letting Sobers sign the certificate without being 100 per cent sure of its authenticity. In short, like Manuel in *Fawlty Towers*, he knew nothing – about the ball, its make, the lot notes, what Sobers had or hadn't said about the number of balls. Hassan's regular refrain of "I wouldn't know" or "I don't know" or "I have no idea" reflected his response to my enquiries – a curious mixture of ignorance, inertia and indifference. As the question about any personal profit he'd made from the ball sale drew nearer, I must admit to becoming genuinely excited about how he would react. When I asked Hassan if he thought the sale of the ball smelt "a bit fishy", he replied "I wouldn't think they would lie, would they?" I declined to answer. When the interview moved on to the £22,000 hammer price the ball fetched at Christie's in November 2006, I knew the moment had arrived – and I made sure I flagged up its importance:

"Now this is a crucial question. Did you receive any of the money for your help in facilitating the signing of the certificate of provenance?"

"No," replied Hassan. "I'm not going to speak about that at all. No."

"You haven't received any money. Did Garry Sobers receive any of the £22,000?"

"I've no idea. I don't think so – because she had all the money."

"Jose had all the money? Right. But surely you felt you were entitled to some part of the hammer price because you had arranged for your client to sign a certificate of provenance which proved very crucial in the run-up to the sale? You had facilitated the signing of that certificate, and without it, the ball wouldn't have been sold for a world record price so – "

"No."

"It was understandable, some might say standard business practice, that you would want your cut – either for yourself or your client or for both?"

"No."

"So you didn't ask for – and you didn't receive – any of the money that Jose Miller received from Christie's for selling the ball?

"No."

"You received nothing?" Hassan nodded in approval. "Well…I have it on very good authority from a journalist colleague of mine that, in fact, you did ask for money, and that you were paid some by Jose Miller. Now I need an answer – is this true or not?"

"The money from where, from where?

"From the sale of the ball. She was given £22,000 – she was probably given less than that because Christie's still had to take something off – and I have it on good authority from a journalist colleague of mine that you did ask Jose Miller for money, and that you were paid some by Jose Miller."

"I did not ask for any money."

"You did not ask for any money? And were you paid any money?"

"I was paid but I did not ask for any money."

"Right. Hang on. So Jose Miller said to you 'here Basher, have some money'?"

"I was surprised."

"Right. So you did not ask Jose Miller for some money following the sale of that ball by Christie's?"

"No."

"How much did you receive from her?"

"I think it might have been about four grand."

"Four grand?"

"Yes. That would have been like a commission. If I was going to have it."

"Yes. So she gave you about four grand. How was the payment made – in cash or a cheque or bank transfer?"

"Cheque."

"And was it made out to you or Basher Promotions?"

"I'm not sure."

"How much of that money did you give to Garry Sobers?"

"I didn't give him any because Garry wouldn't have any."

"He wouldn't have any?"

"He said he didn't want any money from it at all."

"Right. Well. He tells me he received nothing. He said he was simply doing Jose Miller a good turn because she had medical bills to pay. Does Garry know you were paid four grand by Jose Miller?"

"Doubtful. No."

"How do you think he'd feel if he did know?"

"I don't think he would say anything anyway."

"He wouldn't be very happy would he?"

"No. Because he knows I do a lot of work for him anyway."

"But I don't think he'd be very happy about his agent pocketing four grand and him receiving nothing surely?"

"I don't think so. I think he wouldn't say anything."

I then raised the question of the phone call Hassan had made to me in March 2008 while I was writing *Six of the Best* which, in effect, had launched Operation Howzat? During that short conversation, a transcript of which I produced and then read to him, he'd twice said that "Garry wouldn't like it" if I talked to Miller about the ball. When I'd asked him why, he'd said she'd recently been ill and it would only upset her. Despite that, I'd inferred that Hassan was warning me off because, for some reason apart from Miller's illness, he didn't want her speaking to me about the ball. I believed he was trying to put pressure on me by saying that the world's greatest all-round cricketer would prefer me not to contact Miller. When I put that interpretation to Hassan during our interview, he said the comment related only to Miller's illness before offering an alternative reason: "Garry hates to keep talking about the Six Sixes." He then denied that he'd made the phone call because he was afraid Miller might tell me something about the ball. When I suggested it was because she'd paid him nearly £4,000, Hassan declared he had "nothing to hide." He denied that he'd been trying to warn me off before producing another reason for making the call to me in 2008: it was to "see how my book was going." I then raised the subject of the Six Sixes dinner held in Cardiff later that year when the former Glamorgan all-rounder, Peter Walker, interviewed Sobers in a Q & A session. Hassan admitted that he might have issued some pre-event instructions to the organisers or to Walker about not mentioning the ball to Sobers – "don't talk about it because he gets upset about it."

Hassan later accepted that my mention of his part in the process by which the ball had arrived in Christie's in *Six of the Best* was simply an acknowledgement of his role in facilitating the signing of the certificate of provenance by Sobers in 2006. When I raised the subject of the effect the Six Sixes ball controversy was having on Jose Miller, Anne Hassan suddenly interrupted and accused me of accusing her husband of fraud. As Manuel used to say in *Fawlty Towers*, "she go crazy", citing my round-robin letter and saying she didn't like my attitude. I quickly defended sending the letter to The Gang of Nine and the general approach of my investigation:

"You don't like my attitude," I said, "because I'm asking one or two awkward questions. I accept that and I'm sorry but I've asked Sir Garfield – did he get any money from the £22,000? Do you think

I liked doing that? I must just finish. Basher. Finally, how do you see this being resolved? Somebody has paid £26,400 for a ball that is a fake. As somebody who was involved – although I'm not accusing you of anything and I'm not saying you knew the make of the ball – I'm asking you, how do you, as a cricket man, see this whole thing being resolved?"

"I don't know," said Hassan. "I don't know what to say and where to start. It's very difficult. I don't know if it was the right ball or not. I couldn't tell you anything."

Once tempers on both sides had cooled down, I showed the Hassans some more of my evidence which covered the make of the ball and scuppered the suggestion that three balls had been used in the over. I then put forward my theory that the original Surridge might have somehow become mixed up with some Dukes on its return to Nottingham in 1968. We again discussed how the authenticity controversy might be settled and I knew there was one more question I needed to ask Hassan. It was similar to the one I'd put to Miller and Hall nearly a week earlier. How would he feel about returning his share of the £22,000 to the person who'd bought the Duke ball at Christie's?

"I would give my money back," Hassan immediately replied.

"You would?"

"Simple as that."

"No doubt about that?"

"No. Listening to it, I don't know if it's a fake ball or the right ball but if this is causing problems, then he can have my commission money back."

"But you do understand that the ball is not the ball – I've convinced you?"

"I'm still not sure."

"You're still not sure?"

"Not sure."

"Oh right. But that would be the decent thing to do wouldn't it?"

"From my point of view, yes."

"Just one final thing. How do you feel that Christie's have behaved in all this, in the sense that they were ultimately the people who were saying 'this ball is the real thing.'?"

"I'd like to know what Christie's were doing. Christie's should have done more research on it; if there was any doubt, they should have pulled the ball out."

With that, the interview ended and we left Trent Bridge. Once again, a visit to West Bridgford had paid rich dividends. Little by little, the truth about the Six Sixes ball was gradually emerging but I hoped there was still more to come, especially about the mysterious and elusive writer of the Christie's lot notes. On my return from Nottingham, I emailed Max Dunbar in Manchester asking him to re-consider his refusal to discuss his involvement and to answer some questions about the lot notes. They covered his rejection of first-hand testimony about the ball's make from Peter Walker and Malcolm Nash, Andrew Hignell's non-definitive answer about its authenticity, the TV footage of the over and David Convery's role. In the light of Miller and Hall's comments about Christie's' handling of the sale, I also posed this question:

> I know there was disquiet about the ball's authenticity leading up to
> the auction and at the auction. A month later, the *Independent on
> Sunday* ran a story seriously questioning the ball's provenance.
> As no money had changed hands in December 2006, why didn't you
> review the sale in the light of this new evidence?

I wasn't surprised when Dunbar failed to respond but I had expected some sort of acknowledgement to an email I then sent to Sarah Charles in the Christie's dispute resolution department. After I'd lodged my complaint about the attitude of their director of communications, Matthew Paton, she'd been reviewing my evidence for a week but my request for a progress report fell on deaf ears. Another email I fired off to Ashish Singhal about the non-arrival of the contract a couple of days later produced a similar response. Patience was a great virtue, and I knew I had to show lots of it. I referred to my interviewee list again: seven down, two to go – the man who was running the Christie's sporting memorabilia department in 2006, David Convery, and the auction house itself.

After Convery had already named Dunbar and Rupert Neelands as the two specialists specifically involved in the sale of the ball in his two emails, I wondered just how he would respond to my request for an interview? Three days later, I set up my dictaphone to record all my questions and reactions as I rang the offices of Convery Auctions in Blackburn near Edinburgh. This conversation proved even shorter than the one with Dunbar – it lasted just over a minute. I introduced myself as "Grahame Lloyd, Six Sixes ball business" and thanked him for twice getting back to me.

"I'm very grateful for your help," I continued, "but since receiving your last email, I've spoken with Max Dunbar and Christie's and they've both referred me to you as head of the department at the time. And they say you were responsible so I'd like to ask you a couple of questions if I could?"

Convery said that, as he'd already explained, he'd had nothing to do with the sale of the ball. He'd been involved in "another private matter" at the time and he didn't work for Christie's anymore. Like Dunbar, he made it obvious that he didn't want to talk about the ball and said that I'd have to take it up with Christie's. As he prepared to ring off, I jumped in:

"Yes, but you – hang on! Excuse me! We have a man who paid £26,400 for a ball which isn't genuine. I've taken it up with Christie's. You were responsible because you were head of the department and all I'm looking to do is find out who wrote the lot notes – Max Dunbar or Rupert Neelands?"

"It wasn't me that wrote the lot notes for that ball," replied Convery.

"So was it Max Dunbar or Rupert Neelands? Who supplied Max Dunbar, who I know handled the sale – ?"

At that point, Convery hung up and I realised I had to give up. The two former Christie's employees who, apart from Rupert Neelands, I suspected knew most about the sale, would simply not play ball. I'd tried to persuade them to talk but, like Hignell, they'd refused to help me. Despite overwhelming evidence to the contrary, Dunbar was in denial about his role while Convery had been co-operative via email but inconclusive on the phone. My subsequent email to Convery was very much along the lines of the one I'd sent to Dunbar. I asked him a series of questions – including one that had been bugging me for the best part of a year:

> Why doesn't the sale of the ball feature in your impressive list of
> achievements on the Convery Auctions website? It was surely a huge

feather in your cap and sales like that are very good for business in terms of attracting new customers but you appear to have air-brushed it from your personal history?

By this time, I realised that my investigation into the Six Sixes ball mystery was drawing to a close. Eight down, one to go: it was time to turn to the last name on my list, Christie's, in the person of Sarah Charles. The one remaining question now was simple: would Christie's acknowledge that the ball they'd sold was not the genuine article and hold their hands up – or would they wash their hands of the whole sad and sorry saga? The dispute resolution department of the world's most prestigious auction house was to be my final port of call as Operation Howzat? reached its climax.

Over and out

The responsibility lies with the captains for ensuring that play is conducted within the spirit and traditions of the game. The umpires shall be the sole judges of fair and unfair play.

Law 42, The Laws of Cricket

It was just what I needed. Not exactly a kick up the backside – more a gentle reminder. I'd spent the best part of the next weekend in front of my computer transcribing the two face-to-face West Bridgford interviews when an email pinged into my inbox – not from Ashish Singhal or David Convery or Max Dunbar and not, sadly, from Sarah Charles. The sender was Lawrence Booth and his message, as usual, was brief and to the point:

> I hope you're well. I just wanted to check on how you were getting on. I've just had a *Wisden* meeting in which it was made clear that we need copy asap. Will you be in a position to get something to me over the next day or two?

My reply was equally concise. Everything was in hand and the finished article – complete with responses from all but one of The Gang of Nine – would be with him by the next day. I told Lawrence I was still waiting to hear from Sarah Charles but I was on the case. His short reply included a comment which just about said it all: "Bloody Christie's!"

As *Wisden*'s editor or captain, Lawrence's unstinting support had been a huge source of encouragement to me from the moment he'd commissioned my article about the Six Sixes ball mystery. Later during the summer of 2012, he'd made the headlines himself after breaking the "Textgate" story which exposed England batsman Kevin Pietersen's behaviour during the second Test against South Africa. Writing for the *Daily Mail*, Lawrence had revealed that the South African-born batsman had made uncomplimentary comments about England captain Andrew Strauss and his team-mates in text messages sent to members of the opposition. The story would land Lawrence the Sports Journalists' Association's Scoop of the Year award in March 2013. He'd showed his commitment to me by immediately agreeing to courier the Duke ball back to Britain at the end of England's winter tour of India and I was grateful to have him in my corner during the latter stages of Operation Howzat? Lawrence had been monitoring my progress with the nine interviewees for my *Wisden* article and had recently asked for some accompanying photographs of the Six Sixes over and the ball. As well as locating them, I was pleased to be able to email him my article the next day, albeit without a comment from Christie's. When I'd rung their dispute resolution department, one of Sarah Charles' colleagues had told me she was on a week's holiday.

"Sarah's dealing with your enquiry and will be in contact on her return on Monday," said Karla Sheerin-Griffin. "She's speaking to whoever is involved – I've heard her on the phone to them – and it hasn't been left by the wayside."

Half an hour after sending off the article to Lawrence, I unexpectedly heard from The Space Man. At long last, he'd found time to produce a copy of the draft contract for the Duke ball's return from India. Bearing in mind his track record, I suppose I shouldn't have been surprised to discover that the document bore little relation to the one I'd drawn up some weeks earlier. In fact, it was a ludicrous mixture of legalese and false statements. The Six Sixes Curse of the Inaccurate had struck again – big time. As I politely pointed out to Ashish Singhal by return of email, the contract contained "one or two errors" about alleged assurances I'd given him about gaining a refund, interest and other damages from Christie's. When I read the clause "In case of any dispute, the courts in India will have jurisdiction", I realised that this was a contract destined never to be signed. You couldn't make it up but they – The Space Man and his corporate lawyer – had done just that. Once again, Singhal's appreciation of the spirit of cricket had let him down badly. The sole judges of fair and unfair play would have ruled this contract out of order without having to refer to any decision review system. I told Singhal I would forward the document to Bernard Shapero and let him know The Book Man's response.

Three days later, Lawrence Booth emailed me with an update on my *Wisden* article which, he said, was in need of a "resounding final paragraph." In the absence of a comment from Christie's, he suggested that we might have to include something along the lines of "at the time of writing, Christie's dispute resolution department had failed to respond to my queries". It would have been very frustrating not to have completed the story but there wasn't much I could do until Sarah Charles returned from holiday. Lawrence then sent me his edited version of the article – "my sense is this does the job at a decent lick, with the caveat that we still need that final paragraph" – and asked for my observations and clarification of a couple of points. We then exchanged emails as the finishing touches were put to the article before it was sent to *Wisden*'s lawyer. Things seemed to be progressing smoothly until I received Lawrence's next email in which he flagged up a potential problem. He said it had emerged after he'd shown the article to one or two colleagues, including his co-editor and consultant publisher. They were concerned that the Christie's angle was incomplete which meant there were "worrying implications for our plans to publish." As I read on, I had the distinct feeling that things were about to unravel:

> I think, on reflection, that this is more of a problem than I initially gave credit for. I'm sorry to alarm you at this late stage, but my colleagues are right that this is an issue we need to be careful about.

We discussed the development on the phone the next morning as Lawrence prepared to begin proof-reading the 2013 edition of *Wisden* with his colleagues at the typesetters in Suffolk. He explained that because "The Bible of Cricket" had always been primarily a source of reference, it wouldn't be possible to include a story which had no conclusion. When cricket lovers referred back to this particular *Wisden*, they would be expecting to read the story of the Six Sixes ball mystery in its entirety – complete with a definitive ending. I couldn't disagree. I also understood that my article could well be out of date by the time *Wisden* was published in early April if it included a holding sentence about Christie's failure to respond and, in the meantime, the auction house had actually deigned to produce a final verdict. I realised that Operation Howzat? had now reached a crucial point and that unless Christie's contacted me soon, my article would be pulled. I immediately rang Sarah Charles but was told she wasn't available. Later that afternoon, this email arrived in my inbox:

> I am sorry I missed your call earlier this afternoon. I acknowledge

receipt of the material you have provided. I was away last week and was unfortunately unable to complete my review before I left but am taking it forward this week.

The next morning, I managed to speak to her on the phone when I stressed the urgency of the situation. As well as looking for a response to my evidence about the Duke ball which I'd submitted three weeks ago, I explained that there were two particular sections in my article which needed addressing: David Convery's revelation that Max Dunbar and Rupert Neelands "would have catalogued that sale" and criticism of the way in which Christie's had handled the ball's auction in 2006 from Garry Sobers, Jose Miller and Angus Hall. I said I couldn't understand why her review was taking so long to complete. Surely three simple phone calls to Convery, Dunbar and Neelands would have sorted out everything? She asked for any criticism of Christie's to be sent to the legal department rather than to communications director Matthew Paton so I later emailed her the relevant sections of my article. I explained that with the deadline from the *Wisden* printers just two days away, I'd be grateful for a "swift response."

As I waited for her reply, I re-established contact with Bernard Shapero. During a brief phone conversation, I explained the latest *Wisden* situation and the refusal by Convery, Dunbar and Hignell to speak to me. Although he seemed genuinely pleased – and grateful – when I told him that Miller and Hassan were both prepared to return their share of the £26,400, Shapero admitted that he wasn't very happy about receiving money from an ill woman. He agreed with my view of Ashish Singhal's draft contract for the ball's return so I emailed The Space Man to effectively conclude our negotiations. I said his contract was "inaccurate, unnecessarily complicated and needs to be simplified" and we would only proceed on the basis of the "perfectly adequate" original version which I'd sent him.

Just over 24 hours later, any lingering hopes I might have entertained of seeing my article in the 150th edition of *Wisden* disappeared completely when I received this email from Sarah Charles in the Christie's dispute resolution department:

Thank you for your email. It is difficult to comment on extracts

taken out of context and, as I explained to you, my review is not yet complete, but we would like to make the following statement:
The ball was sold at auction with a certificate of authenticity from the batsman who purportedly played it. We take matters of authenticity very seriously and are reviewing the material that has been provided to us.

Once again, the signed certificate of provenance had proved pivotal and, surprise, surprise, the review of my evidence was still going on. I immediately rang Lawrence Booth to let him know and then began to reflect on the timetable I'd followed. Had my desire to refrain from approaching The Gang of Nine for as long as possible, in the hope of securing some TV or radio documentary interest, been to blame? Should I have begun the process much earlier and thus given Christie's more time to consider my evidence? Perhaps; but given their propensity to procrastinate, I knew there would have been no guarantee that they would have responded any sooner even if I had. Despite an intense feeling of frustration, I managed to contain my disappointment as I considered my response. I was confident that the quality of my material would eventually vindicate my position; that short-term pain would be eclipsed by long-term gain. I knew it was important to keep my composure – and my powder dry – as I composed my reply:

Thank you for your email and the statement Sarah.
As you know, as well as my *Wisden* article, I'm also writing a book about the Six Sixes ball and I'd like to know when this particular dispute is likely to be resolved by Christie's.
Can you tell me when your review of my material will be completed and if I will have the opportunity to come to London to discuss the matter with you?

Later that day, Lawrence sent me a copy of the *Wisden* lawyer's report on my spiked article, along with his apologies that our arrangement hadn't worked out. The legal summary highlighted one or two points that, had the Christie's issue been successfully resolved, would have needed changing before publication but I was delighted with the overall summary of "leave the facts as known to speak for themselves." That had been my approach from the outset and I knew that the facts would indeed make themselves heard within the pages of this book later in the year. My article may have bitten the dust because Christie's had been dragging their heels but I knew I'd soon be back on the front foot. In fact, the *Wisden* setback served only to strengthen my resolve to see Operation Howzat? through to the end. While Christie's prevaricated, I would persevere. I settled down to complete this record of my attempt to unravel the riddle of the Duke ball.

There were one or two loose ends to be tied up – such as the final response from Christie's, a progress report for Bernard Shapero and the formal cessation of negotiations with The Space Man. A week after I'd sent him my ultimatum about the contract covering the safe return of the Duke ball from India, Ashish Singhal emailed me with his reply:

> I have just returned to office yesterday from a business trip and had time to discuss your email. We tried to honour our commitment of sending you the ball but we shall not be prepared to proceed without a legal binding agreement.

In truth, I'd not expected anything different and, in a way, I was relieved that The Battle for the Ball was finally over. The Duke definitely wouldn't be coming back to Britain now and, as I explained to Singhal, it would form no part of any discussions I might have with Christie's. As I prepared to cut all ties with The Space Man, I couldn't resist firing a parting shot across his bows, based on his most enlightened yet ultimately futile observation during our protracted negotiations:

> We too are happy to abide by a legally binding agreement but it has to be accurate. Sadly, your version is not – as I clearly explained to you in my email of 12th February. Why have you not been able to address my concerns about the errors which I highlighted in that email?
> You once told me that "whatever the truth is must prevail and we should all be happy to abide by it." As I have said many times during our correspondence, truth lies at the heart of this matter and any contract must be truthful before it can become legally binding – wouldn't you agree?

Needless to say, I received no reply. As part of my largely dormant relationship with Bernard Shapero, I felt obliged to keep him up to speed with any developments. Following my exchange of emails with Christie's and Singhal, I suggested that Shapero might like to speak to one of his regular contacts at the auction house or approach Sarah Charles himself in an attempt to move the matter forward. His failure to respond led me to believe that The Book Man was, perhaps understandably, losing interest.

Having received no reply to my last email from Christie's, I made two attempts in March to elicit a final response from Sarah Charles. When I rang her at her office, I was told she was in a meeting but would call me back. When she didn't, I carried on writing this book before contacting the dispute resolution department again a week later. This time, I was told she wasn't in but I was given her mobile number and advised that I could ring her at home. During our conversation, she told me that she'd "pretty much finished" her review of my evidence and that "internal talks were taking place." Alleluia! At last, it seemed some sort of progress was being made. I was encouraged to hear that the DVD of the Six Sixes had been looked at but when I asked when her review would finally be completed, she wasn't prepared to put a time limit on it. She said she didn't think Christie's would be giving a formal statement to a journalist so I had to correct her by reminding her that I was also the author of seven books. I said that as a result of working on my eighth for the best part of a year, I'd like a response from Christie's to my concerns about the ball's authenticity as quickly as possible.

During the discussion about a press statement, the dispute about my earlier treatment by Christie's communications director, Matthew Paton, re-surfaced. Charles maintained that I'd suggested in an earlier conversation that I didn't want to pursue my complaint against Paton so I was forced to correct her once again. I said that while the review of my evidence had always been my priority, if a press statement were to be issued, I presumed Paton would have to be involved simply because of his role, so our fractious relationship would then have to be addressed. I mentioned the six weeks she'd now spent reviewing my material and expressed my surprise that my offer to travel to London hadn't been taken up. I said again I intended to pursue the matter and we agreed that I should ring back in a week's time. As it happened, I wasn't able to phone on that particular date as my book-writing gathered momentum and took priority.

Towards the end of March, I contacted Supriya Chawla, at the Osian's Group in India, about the extended interview she'd promised me with Neville Tuli. I also needed his help in re-writing my earlier profile of him based on some articles I'd read on the internet. Through not being able to speak to him directly because he was Bernard Shapero's mystery client, I didn't feel comfortable with the portrait I'd painted of Tuli. It was unsatisfactory, ill-informed and not fully formed. I also wanted to make sure I'd not made any fundamental mistakes and I was happy for Supriya to forward the extract to him – "not for Neville's approval but for confirmation of the facts." At the same time, I was hoping Tuli would be willing to help me produce a more rounded assessment of his career. In the event, he did just that and I realised that my interpretation of his role in India's cultural history needed to be revised – which it duly was. In a most illuminating and thought-provoking email, Tuli corrected one or two factual errors and filled in the gaps in my understanding of Osian's, his interest in sport and, "more importantly, history, in all its forms", as he explained his personal mission statement:

> Everything one has done over the last 20 years has been in a clear historical context of building love and respect for the histories of the subject in the minds of the Indian public, hand in hand with financial respect for the tangible objects which defined that history, as it is because of this neglect that the Indian sense of identity of the individuals and the nation as a whole remains incomplete and insecure.
> Without the security of a solid history behind you, every civilization will shiver and falter in times of crisis.

I was intrigued to learn that this "mediocre cricketer and brilliant footballer" had been a lifelong fan of Lancashire County Cricket Club and Spurs and knew a lot about the histories of other sports such as golf, motor racing, boxing, athletics "let alone horse racing." As I re-read Tuli's email, I was impressed by the way in which he'd gently reprimanded me for my lack of knowledge. I also appreciated his phlegmatic and relaxed attitude to my role as a journalist and writer, despite the "blind spots" he'd noted in my extract. I positively warmed to him when I read remarks like "but you are fully entitled to your view" and "obviously, you are absolutely free to write as you deem fit." In short, Tuli had put me in my place while putting me at my ease. He understood that the freedom of the press meant I could write what I liked as long as it wasn't defamatory. For my part, I wanted to amend my initial profile and, as a result of his email, I sent him a series of follow-up questions. I specifically wanted to find out if, having heard about my evidence which questioned the Duke ball's authenticity, Tuli would now be taking up the matter with Christie's.

Friday 5th April was always going to be a significant milestone on my particular 2013 calendar. Not only did I turn 60 but the date marked the first anniversary of Operation Howzat? It had been a full year to the day since John Parkin had rung me with the news that the Duke ball was up for sale at Bonhams. As the date approached, I suddenly had a brainwave: why not check with Christie's to see if their patently exhaustive review of my evidence had finally produced a result? It would be a fitting finale to my investigation if I could complete the circle a year after it had all begun. But would I at last be able to elicit a conclusive reply from Christie's? It seemed like a good idea at the time so, with pen poised to make my usual contemporaneous notes of the conversation, I rang Sarah Charles in the dispute resolution department again. This was one dispute that I really wanted to see resolved but it seemed that my concern wasn't shared by Christie's. Sadly, it was the same old story. I explained that my *Wisden* article had been dropped because of their inadequate and inconclusive response before the printers' deadline but that my enquiries were continuing. I'd recently made contact with the original Duke ball buyer in India and would be trying to find out how he proposed to take the matter forward. In return, Charles told me she had nothing to report – apart from this earth-shattering revelation:

"The results of my review have been passed to someone within Christie's and I'm waiting to hear from them."

I revealed that while I was obviously very disappointed not to see my article appearing in such a prestigious publication as *Wisden*, it could be included in an online version of the almanack in June and my book about the Six Sixes ball mystery would be published in the late summer. So, although the immediate pressure had been lifted, I still needed a definitive decision from Christie's. She said that, as a result of my phone call, she would chase it up. I decided there and then that I wouldn't ring her again until the book had been completed and, with that, I returned to my keyboard to put in another shift at the typeface.

As well as working on the manuscript, I knew I would soon have to put on my publisher's hat. My 'To Do' list included obtaining quotations from printers, registering the book with the relevant publishing authorities, briefing my designer and collecting photographs from people like Sushant Nigam, Ashish Singhal and Neville Tuli in India, Jose Miller in Nottingham and Bernard Shapero in London. I also had to approach Matthew Engel, a former *Wisden* editor, about writing the book's foreword instead of Lawrence Booth. Having commissioned my article and then agreed to courier the Duke ball back from India, I felt the current *Wisden* editor had become much more involved with the Six Sixes story than I'd anticipated at the outset. It would be more appropriate for the foreword to be written by a completely independent authority on the game. Having provided me with a perfect preface for *Six of the Best* and recently delivered an exceptional eulogy at the funeral of the esteemed sportswriter Frank Keating, Matthew was the obvious candidate and readily accepted my invitation.

There was still one outstanding issue to be resolved before I returned to Christie's for their final verdict on my evidence. What was Neville Tuli going to do? After all, he was the man who'd paid £26,400 for a cricket ball which clearly hadn't been bowled in the Six Sixes over. Would he be interested in trying to get his money back? It turned out that the chairman of Osian's Connoisseurs of Art preferred to answer my follow-up questions by phone rather than email so I agreed to ring his office in early May. Tuli's passion for the history of India, particularly its cultural heritage, coursed through the hour-long interview as he expanded upon the account of his association with the ball which he'd provided three months earlier. My interest was three-fold: I was looking for more information about the Christie's sale in 2006 and the subsequent e-auction of the bat and ball three years later. Looking ahead, I wondered if Tuli would decide to approach Christie's after examining my evidence. At the start of the interview, he confirmed that he'd not been aware of the pre-auction disquiet about the ball's authenticity amongst certain ex-Glamorgan players.

"As the bidding went up and up," I said, "before reaching the hammer price of £22,000, were you at all worried about the cost of acquiring the ball? What were your thoughts as you spoke to Bernard Shapero on his mobile phone?"

"You don't think like that," Tuli replied. "That's not how you build collections. Those thoughts didn't really arise. Yes, obviously after £15,000, I was curious but, at the end of the day, there is no other country but India that would have loved that ball, because over here we are passionate about cricket. It's like anything: why does any object achieve a certain price? An intangible quality is not something you can just judge like that – it just doesn't work like that."

"The final price of £26,400, or $50,000, is a world record: were you at any time worried that you had paid over the odds for what, after all, was only a cricket ball?"

"It's not only a cricket ball. It's a piece of history and an important piece of history. From the point of view of paying what is a world record – there are thousands and thousands of items we've bought for world record prices."

When I raised the subject of who had actually paid Christie's for the ball in November 2006 – Shapero or Osian's? – Tuli was keen to put the record straight:

"Bernard never paid anything – we paid. He was the agent on the phone. Sometimes if I'm not there personally, I ask the agent to bid. Bernard is an old friend and he said he'd do it on our behalf and that was convenient. Otherwise, all payments are made directly from Osian's to the auction house. If this one was made directly to Bernard's account and he then paid Christie's, our accounts department would know that. That's not something I get involved with."

According to Tuli, the Six Sixes ball had stayed in London for 18 months after the sale because of Osian's liquidity crisis and the time taken to sort out the relevant import licence paperwork. A year after the start of Operation Howzat?, it had never been fully explained to me just why the display case containing the antique bat and the Duke ball had been sold by the IGI Airport in an online auction in November 2009, another 18 months after its arrival in India. Tuli didn't seem totally clear about the process either and, during our interview, he again claimed that Osian's had been paying demurrage charges to the airport during that period. The Airports Authority of India allows import cargo to be stored for free for three days before a standard rate based on weight and length of stay is levied. But if an item isn't claimed or cleared from the confines of the airport within a month, it can be sold through an e-auction. Tuli's financial problems meant that money was tight when the ball arrived in New Delhi in the summer of 2008.

"The whole world has gone through a liquidity crunch," he recalled, "and we were affected by it more than others because we had invested in a large amount of assets which were not for sale and were relatively illiquid. Obviously, the cash flow started going down because the market started falling. There were huge amounts of items imported and the demurrage charges and duties were piling up."

When I mentioned the law covering the sale of unclaimed or uncleared goods after 30 days, Tuli warmed to his theme:

"Those things are fine but if you keep on paying your demurrage charges, then customs have no reason to dispose of your items. At the end of the day, it's when you've defaulted or when you're saying that you won't pay. We were continually paying the demurrage charges. I didn't deal with the customs – one of my officers did and he definitely kept on reminding me. There were a whole lot of things, not just the bat and ball, and I said 'just keep on paying the demurrage charges and ask for as much time as possible and we will pay'. And we've paid for virtually everything we ever bought; iron-ically the bat and ball were two of the few things that ever got auctioned. I'm not saying that customs did something that was wrong: they were well within their rights to hold the auction, despite the continued payments of demurrage. I'm just saying that, given the items were cricket-related, maybe they seemed easier to dispose of in an auction."

When I approached the IGI Airport for a response to Tuli's expla-nation – and, in particular, his demurrage payment claims – it seemed as if the Six Sixes Curse of the Inaccurate had struck again. His version of events was robustly disputed by general manager (cargo), Sushant Nigam, a fount of much knowledge throughout Operation Howzat? He insisted that the letter of the law under the provisions of the 1962 Customs Act in India had been strictly followed by airport officials and confirmed that "the imported consignment becomes ripe for disposal after 30 days of its landing if not claimed or cleared by the consignee." The 18-month delay between the display case's arrival at the airport and its subsequent sale was the result of "so many procedural formalities for conducting an e-auction which makes the entire disposal process a time-consuming one." Dealing with the glass casket was also postponed because there were so many other cargo items which needed to be disposed of.

"Mr Tuli's claim that his company kept on paying demurrage charges but did not collect the cargo due to financial reasons does not make sense," said Nigam. "It is illogical. Whom did he pay? The airport has no record of any payment based on factual information collected from the available documents. Demurrage charges for this particular consignment were not paid and there was no request to hold it back from being auctioned.

"Why did Mr Tuli not respond to written notices sent to him about his unclaimed cargo? His company even ignored notice of the intended auction of his goods given through three newspapers and the airport website. In this regard, all legal formalities were properly completed and Indian Customs directions were complied with.

"Mr Tuli also had the opportunity to obtain Customs permission to shift this cargo to any other public bonded warehouse until final clearance at lower demurrage charges but he chose not to take it."

Having lost the ball by way of the e-auction, Tuli recalled that Osian's had then been approached about the possibility of buying it for a second time. Again, one of his officers, rather than the company's founder himself, dealt with this latest development. Ashish Singhal's unsuccessful attempt to sell the ball back to Osian's for about $20,000 – approximately £15,000 – was described by Tuli as an "exorbitant amount" beyond the costs the company had already incurred at the airport.

"I haven't a clue if we were, as Singhal claims, prepared to pay only $8,000," said Tuli, "but we'd already bought the ball – how much more money were we going to lose? We probably didn't have the liquidity at that time; there were other priorities."

"Did you ever know how much Ashish Singhal paid for the bat and ball in the glass casket at the e-auction?"

"No. I think my officer did tell me something but I can't remember exactly. He said it was something very, very ludicrous."

"I understand it was 72,000 Indian rupees which, at the time, was about £940 for the pair?"

At this point, Tuli was unable to suppress a giant guffaw. "My God. What a world!? What a world."

"The ball is now universally acknowledged not to be the real thing. How do you feel about that seven years after you bought it at Christie's?"

"It's sad, very sad, more than anything because it creates this kind of lack of faith in history and in the due diligence of auction houses. As someone who's been to an auction house and runs one, I know that everyone tries their very best to do as much homework as possible and obviously sometimes everyone gets stretched."

"What do you think about Christie's role in this business, in that the ball is the wrong make and in their lot notes, they claimed that three balls were used in the over rather than one – as the BBC TV footage conclusively shows?"

"They must have done their research after all. It is Christie's whatever's said and done and Christie's and all great auction houses make mistakes. They're 200 years old and you have to respect the due diligence they do. Mistakes are still made but I don't think they would have done it at all deliberately. It could be shoddy research but beyond that I wouldn't point fingers."

"Should they have done more research into its origins before selling it?"

"Well…we all can. Anyone who makes a mistake in life can do more research. Even if you speak to everyone in the world and write the finest book on a subject, someone, 10 years from now, can come up with some new evidence."

When I revealed more details of the pre- and post-auction disquiet in Britain, and particularly in Wales, Tuli's mood became less phlegmatic and less conciliatory. I explained that some former Glamorgan players had questioned the ball's authenticity before it was sold but their protests had been ignored. Then an article in the *Independent on Sunday* had raised the question of the ball's make nearly three weeks after the auction and a full month before the vendor, Jose Miller, had received her cheque from Christie's.

"Well…that's a different matter," said Tuli. "At least they should have alerted us because, obviously in India, we don't get to hear these things. We promptly paid after 20 days. Basic etiquette demands informing the buyer if there is anything like that in a public newspaper so at least Bernard Shapero should have been informed if Christie's didn't know that it was Osian's and myself buying the ball."

"Do you think Christie's have any duty – whether it be moral, legal or otherwise – to repay you your money?"

"One of the reasons Osian's are in debt is because we have placed moral and ethical standards beyond the legal standards and, by and large, the world just doesn't seem to respect those things. I don't know what to expect from the world. The last three years have taught me that whether the mistake is yours or not, you take the consequences and move on – that's what leadership essentially is. And in a world that is getting more and more difficult, I don't know what to expect from others."

As a result of our conversation, Tuli said he would be forwarding my evidence about the Duke ball's authenticity to his lawyers, although I stressed that the opportunity for some sort of remedial action had passed because the Christie's five-year 'bring back' rule had expired. After revealing that the Osian's art fund debts were gradually being paid off – "it will take a few more months and whatever time it takes, we'll get it done" – Tuli spoke enthusiastically about the launch of his company's knowledge base and research engine, theosianama.com, in August 2013 and an auction of memorabilia from India's cricketing heritage in September 2013. I later wrote a catalogue article about the Indian involvement in the Six Sixes phenomenon through two of the four batsmen to have achieved the feat – Ravi Shastri and Yuvraj Singh.

Over the last 45 years, the names of Sobers and Nash have been inevitably and indelibly linked to that famous over at Swansea. The former West Indian skipper resents being primarily remembered by many people for his remarkable feat but what about the ex-England triallist, the other half of the cricketing combo which sounds like a comic double act or a country and western duo? When scorn starts to be poured on his part in the famous cricketing landmark, Malcolm Nash can point to a successful county career in which he collected nearly 1,000 first-class wickets – not to mention countless free dinners. But what irks him most is the sale of what he always refers to as the 'ball' – in inverted commas – by Christie's in 2006. It still rankles with him and he's determined to set the record straight. His last delivery in the over which made history at St Helen's may not have been a very good one but at least it wasn't a 'wrong 'un' or a 'no-ball.' It was a Surridge not a Duke and the only one he'd bowled to Sobers during that over.

Towards the end of June, I met Nash for the first time. After spending 22 years in Canada and the United States, he'd decided to come home to Wales to be closer to his family. In North America, Nash had mainly been involved in sports marketing before joining a company making recycled plastic landscaping products. He'd also worked widely as a cricket coach but it was while he was driving school buses in Florida that the heart condition which was to prompt his return came to light. Now living near Swansea Airport on Gower, not far from his daughter, Amba, he agreed to meet me at his new home so that I could bring him up to speed with Operation Howzat? After spending an hour or so explaining my evidence and the current situation, I asked, in the style of the late Eric Morecambe, what he thought of it so far?

"I'm just surprised that the whole series of events hasn't been concluded," Nash admitted. "I was obviously on the wrong end of a severe hiding from, if not the best batsman then certainly the greatest all-rounder in the world, and people said 'hey, how did you feel at the end of that over, what was it like?' and I said 'it was just another day in my life.' And that's really what it was.

"'But with the ball being smashed out of the ground so many times, how did you feel?' people then said. 'I felt OK about it' I replied. 'I learnt a lot and that helped me in my development from thereon.' But what happened is this: the ball came up for auction and I heard it was a Duke and I said to myself 'we never used Dukes'. We certainly didn't use them in Swansea or Cardiff or Llanelli or Pontypridd – we used Surridge. And I'm still amazed why people want to dispute the fact that we used a Surridge and not a Duke. All I know is that I bowled all of my career with Glamorgan using Surridge balls – apart from one, maybe two years in the Seventies."

So Nash had reaffirmed his long held belief – and, by now, the generally accepted one – that the ball sold in 2006 was the wrong make. What about the three-ball theory espoused so confidently in the Christie's lot notes – that the auctioned one was the third and last to be bowled in the over?

"The first two balls went out of the ground but they came back," Nash said. "We used the same ball for all six deliveries and it was charred and scarred and scuffed but we never changed it. It never got lost until the last ball and it was then returned a day or so later.

"It's worth noting that Christie's have never bothered to call me or spoken to me or been in touch with me to say 'you were the guy who bowled that ball. Can you verify what it was that you bowled and how many balls did you use in the over?' Nobody has ever asked me personally that question other than you, Grahame, when you were writing *Six of the Best*."

Nash then recalled a phone conversation he'd had with Peter Walker, the former Glamorgan all-rounder, before the auction of the ball in 2006 when the seam bowler was living in the United States.

"'Nashy, do you know that the ball that you bowled in '68 is being auctioned?'

"'That's interesting,'" I said.

"'It's a Duke.'

"'It can't be.'

"'What?'

"'You ought to know better than that, Hooky [Walker's nickname]. We only ever used Stuart Surridge. We didn't use a Duke ball.'

"I can't remember the whole conversation verbatim," said Nash, "but I believe I said to Peter that we needed to get in touch with Christie's to let them know that we never used Dukes. They ought to review it because the ball I bowled was definitely a Surridge. 'What they do about it,' I said to him, 'I don't know.' Peter said he would get in touch with them.

"Now I'm back in Wales, I can certainly do something positive about it because you're talking in person to the guy who was actually there on the field and propelled the ball. If all parties concerned have an interest in what's going on, they can come and talk to me about that as well. Or if not, I will certainly go and talk to them at some time in the future and ask them why they're so adamant that a Duke was used when it wasn't. And I'll wait for that answer."

Whenever the Six Sixes are discussed, Nash is invariably criticised for continuing to attack Sobers, to try to get him out, with his part-time, left-arm orthodox spin. Even as the record-breaking feat loomed larger on the West Indian's radar, Nash refused to bowl defensively by firing the ball wide down the leg side or outside the off stump in an attempt to stem the flow of runs. Forty five years later, his only regret is that he didn't bowl over, rather than around, the wicket, a tactic which might have trapped Sobers leg before wicket or bowled him.

"Looking back, I think maybe that would have been a better option. I changed tack with the last ball: it was a seamer, again from around the wicket, and it turned out to be a rank long hop which went further than any of the others.

"The interest in such a well-travelled ball is still going after nearly 50 years and I would actually really like to see a conclusion to all of the nonsense that's going on now. This isn't the first conversation I've had about the Six Sixes – it happens ever year. I doubt if it'll be the last because there's obviously unfinished business here."

I knew how Nash felt.

Stumped at stumps

*A reputation once broken may possibly be repaired, but the world
will always keep their eyes on the spot where the crack was.*

Bishop Joseph Hall

Operation Howzat? was approaching its denouement. Eighteen
months after I'd been alerted to the Bonhams sale of the Duke ball,
the game was almost over. After all the trials and tribulations, the
twists and turns, it had come down to the last wicket. Would I be able
to bowl out the opposition and win the match? It was, as it so often
is in Twenty20 and one-day games, and occasionally in Ashes Test
matches, "squeaky bum time" – to quote British football's most successful manager, Alex Ferguson.

From the start of my investigation, I'd realised that Christie's were
always going to be backwards in coming forward with a definitive
response to my evidence. History showed that the auction house
usually declined to comment about the ball's origins before referring
to the signed certificate of provenance and the role of the two cricket
club archivists. I thought they would be treading even more warily in
light of my material and the importance of the over in sporting
history. And as I'd worked my way through the various interviews, I
realised that Christie's reputation wasn't the only one on the line. At
the other end of the food chain, Jose Miller, the woman who had
enabled the auction house to make just over £7,500 from the sale of
the ball, had twice referred to the importance of her "good name"
as she recalled her version of events. One remark in particular – that
she felt like going out "with a black bag on my head" when all the
Duke ball publicity kicked off – really resonated with me. I was no
judge and certainly not a jury but I must admit I had no reason to
doubt her account because honesty and transparency seemed to illu-
minate every answer that both she or Angus Hall had given me. It
was clear, more than ever, that I was now dealing with a story about
not only the reputations of Miller and Christie's but about those of
the people in between – from Garry Sobers and Basharat Hassan to
Max Dunbar, David Convery and Rupert Neelands to Andrew

Hignell and Peter Wynne-Thomas – and, as the teller of the tale, to me. We all had an interest in the Six Sixes ball mystery because we all had the same thing to lose: our integrity, our standing or station in our own section of society or, as Miller had put it, our good name. Some members of The Gang of Nine had chosen to put their heads in the sand, others to front up and explain their involvement with the controversial sale: each to their own and all that.

As I waited to hear from Neville Tuli in India before contacting Sarah Charles at Christie's, I began to reflect on the implications of my investigation. What precisely had been achieved? What untoward or irregular behaviour had I actually uncovered? Had the whole thing been a complete waste of time, did it really matter and would anybody be interested in reading about it?

When my enquiries began, it seemed to me – not unreasonably – that there could have been a connection between some or all of the members of The Gang of Nine who, in their different ways, had been associated with the auction in 2006. Some had benefited financially, one or two had enjoyed having their egos massaged and others had seen their reputations enhanced. Conversely, and regrettably, some, like Garry Sobers and Jose Miller, felt their good names had been besmirched as a result of their involvement in the sale. But as I'd tracked down the ball's movements since 1968 and presented my findings to the nine people involved, I'd come to realise that most of them had been acting independently of each other. My material may have appeared to suggest that a fraudulent act had taken place before the ball was sold in 2006 but as I collected their responses, I realised there was no hard evidence linking all nine with each other. It seemed to be a story of blissful ignorance and innocence, naivety and even stupidity; of incompetence, perhaps even negligence; and of less-than-diligent research, probably opportunism – but not of fraud. There appeared to be no grand conspiracy. While no plot had been hatched involving all or most of The Gang of Nine, I still felt deeply uncomfortable about the process by which the ball had been consigned to, and then sold by, Christie's. There was something not quite right about the verification procedure, in particular the ball's lot notes, and the roles played by David Convery and Max Dunbar left a bad taste in the mouth.

How significant was Andrew Hignell's contribution to the debate about the ball's authenticity and how important were Basharat Hassan's widespread and persistent denials and then his subsequent admission when I'd asked him if he'd received any money from its sale? These two questions would have to remain unanswered but in my quest to put right a palpable wrong, I was pleased that two of the three beneficiaries of the sale – Jose Miller and Hassan – were prepared to return their money. And I was delighted to have been able to lift the cloud of suspicion hanging over Garry Sobers, an honourable man whose reputation had been compromised by the shortcomings of others. In my view, he should have been more inquisitive before putting his name to the infamous certificate of provenance but consider this: why had he declined to sign the original one presented to him by Miller at the hotel in Nottingham? Because the Duke ball wasn't a "cracked cricket ball" – it was a normal one with a regular seam. Sobers may have been indifferent as to its make but at least he'd wanted to make sure its description was accurate. He'd wanted it to be correct, in the same way that he'd thought he'd been doing the right and proper thing by helping Miller to sell her prized possession in 2006.

Like Malcolm Nash, I knew the ball sold at Christie's was an imposter; it wasn't all it was cracked up to be. But although a considerable number of other facts had come to light as a result of Operation Howzat?, I felt sure that I hadn't uncovered 'the whole truth and nothing but the truth.' Frankly, I doubted if I ever would. As I prepared to ring Sarah Charles in the Christie's dispute resolution department, I fervently hoped that the unwritten 43rd Law of Cricket covering the exercise of common sense would prevail: just be sensible and do the right thing.

Two days after meeting Nash, I realised that Neville Tuli would not be taking up the matter with Christie's any time soon. Because the sale had taken place in 2006 and the Christie's five-year 'bring back' clause had now expired, I'd always suspected as much and this email from the head of the Osian's Group simply confirmed my view:

I have not had the time to look into this matter after passing the docs to the lawyers. Our Legal and Compliance Team are on the matter, and they will take forward as they deem appropriate. I am sure your research makes the position very clear and they will initiate action on the relevant matter as time permits.

On Friday 5th July, three months to the day after I'd last spoken to Charles, I thought I'd have another go. This book was virtually written and the production process was well underway. All that was needed now was a response from Christie's. I made it clear from the start that, "in the interests of accuracy which is right at the heart of this matter", I would like to record our conversation but Charles immediately refused my request. She didn't like the idea of her "off the cuff" comments being taped but she said she would give me a statement. I pointed out that none of the other major interested parties had objected and surely the best way to guarantee a 100 per cent verbatim account would be to record our conversation? Again, she declined so I decided to use my dictaphone to make sure I had a copy of my questions and I wrote down her replies in note form. Sadly, it was another one of those circular conversations in which the party line was strictly followed. It lasted 10 minutes but produced little information; there was plenty of heat but not too much light. To avoid any misunderstanding, I took my time as I began with the crucial question:

"You've had my material for more than five months and the last time I spoke to you in early April, you said: 'The results of my review have been passed to someone within Christie's and I'm waiting to hear from them.' I would hope by now that you've heard from them and you can provide me with a response to my belief that the ball Christie's sold for £26,400 was not the one bowled in the actual over by Malcolm Nash in 1968?"

Sadly, my hopes were dashed by a very disappointing reply because, once again, "answer came there none". Charles explained that she had indeed passed on her review of my evidence to "someone within Christie's" but he wasn't in the office at the moment. In the end, I didn't receive any statement but her position could be best summarised as follows:

"I have followed our process but I don't have any feedback from the person I passed my review on to. I haven't got anything to tell you, I haven't got any answers but let me find out for you next week."

Throughout the conversation, I calmly expressed my amazement that Christie's had been unable to produce a response to my disquiet about the ball's authenticity. I reminded Charles of our last conversation in April during which she'd promised to "chase up" the matter; I said she'd had enough time to respond and I then asked her who she'd given her review to. She declined to reveal his name.

"I find it incredible that an organisation like Christie's cannot give me an answer. I have waited and waited. I have written the book and I'm waiting for an answer to my simple request from Christie's."

After Charles had refused to answer my question about the identity of the author of the erroneous lot notes, I decided it was important to make sure my record of our conversation was completely accurate.

"Hang on, I'm writing this down. 'I haven't got any of this…'"

"You don't need to write it down," she replied.

"I do need to write it down because I'm getting more and more concerned that Christie's, frankly, are dragging their heels. I have a book that's coming out – as I've told you for the last five months – and I'd like a response. If you've done a review, surely you can tell me a little bit about it?"

"I haven't got any of this in my head," Charles said. "I completed the review some time ago and I can't remember the details off the top of my head."

"Don't you have a filing system? Can't you look into the file now as you're talking to me and say 'this is the result, these are the people that I spoke to'? Are you able to tell me – did you speak to any of the specialists?"

Charles declined to reveal if she'd spoken to either David Convery, Max Dunbar or Rupert Neelands and again refused to tell me the name of the person at Christie's who'd been given her report. When she suggested that I ring her again in a week's time, I politely pointed out the urgency of the matter. I explained that I had editorial and print deadlines to meet and I insisted that I should ring her after the weekend.

"Two o'clock on Monday gives you, I hope, enough time to find out what Christie's response is to this," I said. "I don't think that's unreasonable."

As I put down the phone, I experienced a distinct feeling of déjà vu. I briefly considered sending another email to Lord Linley, the Queen's nephew and the chairman of Christie's, but felt, on reflection, that it would only prolong the process rather than bring it to a conclusion. I knew I needed a response from the company to finally wrap up Operation Howzat? Five minutes before I was due to contact Charles on the following Monday, she rang me to explain that she'd not been able to speak to her colleague yet because he'd not appeared in the office. We agreed that I would ring her 24 hours later and when I did, I was told by a colleague that Charles was attending an off-site meeting. I asked if she could contact me but heard nothing and knowing that she didn't work on Wednesdays and Thursdays, I rang her office again on the Friday – only to be told that she was attending a meeting away from the building. I then sent her a text asking her to ring me but received no reply.

On Monday 15th July, I decided enough was enough. I was under pressure from my designer to complete the manuscript before forwarding it to the printers and it was time to end the waiting game. When I rang her office, I discovered that Charles wouldn't be in until later so I asked her colleague to pass on a message: could she ask Charles to ring me as soon as possible and to check her computer's inbox? I then wrote and sent the following email:

> In my view, a response from Christie's is both in the public interest and of interest to the public. People who buy items from your auction house need to be reassured that those items have been through a rigorous process of verification before being offered for sale and cricket lovers around the world are interested in this ball because it was part of one of the game's most iconic moments.

I explained that I was also looking for a response to my complaint about my treatment in January by the Christie's director of communications, Matthew Paton, and after reminding Charles of our correspondence – or rather lack of it – during the last 10 days, I cut to the chase:

> I have to tell you that time has now run out. I think any reasonable person would conclude that I have given Christie's ample time to respond to my concerns – I simply cannot wait any longer. My book

is going to be published this summer and editorial and printing deadlines mean that I need a response by five o'clock today. That is the
cut-off point and any response given to me after that time will not
be included in the book.

 The book will contain a record of my correspondence with
Christie's since my initial contact through Matthew Paton in January.
It will reflect Christie's reaction to my concerns and will also include
a list of questions which I have wanted to put to Christie's since
January but have not been given the opportunity to ask.

At four minutes to five, an email from Charles arrived in my inbox.
I was disappointed but, in truth, not really surprised by its contents.

Thank you for your various messages. As you know, I had referred
this matter on internally. I have now heard back and can inform you
that Christie's wishes to make the following statement:
 Christie's takes issues of authenticity very seriously and, as a result
of Mr. Lloyd's inquiry, has investigated again the details around the
sale of this cricket ball. The ball was consigned to Christie's in 2006
with good provenance and with a signed certificate from the
batsman Sir Garfield Sobers "that this signed cricket ball was bowled
during the over in which I [Sobers] hit Six Sixes off Malcolm Nash".
Christie's has not found evidence or knowledge of any wrongdoing
that helps to shed any light on the subsequent controversy identified
by Mr Lloyd.

My complaint against Paton for what I considered to be his "dismissive, disrespectful and obstructive" attitude had been completely
ignored and my evidence had been met with a dead bat and then
kicked into the long grass, pushed aside and hidden in the hope that
it would be forgotten or ignored. The BBC TV footage showing
the Surridge ball used in the over being returned was apparently of
little or no consequence – as was the testimony of Malcolm Nash,
the bowler who'd held it in his hand before every delivery and that
of Peter Walker, the fielder standing closest to Nash during the
famous over, who'd complained about the Duke ball's provenance.
This was just part of the evidence described by Bonhams as "compelling and conclusive" when they'd withdrawn the disputed ball
from their sale in May 2012.

I would have liked to have questioned Christie's about their statement and the comment by the ball buyer, Neville Tuli, himself an auctioneer in India, that the controversial sale created "a lack of faith in history and the due diligence of auction houses." I would have liked to have asked Christie's about the role of their three sport specialists, especially the writer of the incorrect lot notes, and the decision not to abort the sale, or at least put it on hold, following the *Independent on Sunday* article casting doubts on the ball's authenticity just over two weeks after the auction. And I would liked to have known their response to the view of many people connected with the ball – especially Malcolm Nash – that Christie's hadn't done their homework properly once it had been consigned. Sadly, it would not be possible. Despite my best efforts, the last wicket hadn't been taken. The game was over, stumps had been drawn and Operation Howzat? had finished. I was disappointed that the 43rd law of cricket had been disregarded; common sense had not prevailed and I felt that an opportunity to do the decent thing had been passed up. I emailed Charles to thank her for her reply and immediately set about putting this book to bed.

But there was one question, perhaps above all, that I'd been hoping to put to Christie's through her, one which now had to remain unanswered: in light of the response from the ball seller, Jose Miller, and Garry Sobers' then agent, Basharat Hassan, to the possibility of returning their money from the sale, would Christie's follow suit? Given the uncertainty – to say the very least – about the ball, were they prepared to pay back the £7,500, including the 20 per cent buyer's premium, they'd made from the sale to Neville Tuli? It didn't seem a huge amount, certainly not in the grand scheme of things and especially when I re-visited the press release written in January by Matthew Paton which had trumpeted Christie's yearly results and revealed record sales figures for 2012 of £3.92 billion.

When I tried to find out just how much money is being made by Christie's, I became engulfed by a financial fog. As a private company owned by French billionaire Francois Pinault, the world's leading auction house doesn't report profit or loss but produces sales totals twice a year, based on completed public and private transactions, including fees. When Christie's announced their 2012 sales figures, chief executive officer Steven Murphy confirmed to the Reuters news agency that the auction house was in the black. When asked whether it was more profitable now than when he joined in late 2010, he replied: "I can say that we're very happy. There's wind in our sails."

During a phone interview with Scott Reyburn, the London-based art market correspondent for Bloomberg News, Murphy explained why contemporary art sales had risen by 10 per cent. "It's not non-collectors looking to move cash into art. Existing clients are spending more and many of our new bidders have previously bought from dealers and art fairs. They like the transparency of auctions."

Ah yes. Those transparent Christie's auctions. Like that of the Duke & Son cricket ball sold for a world record £26,400 on 15th November 2006 as part of sale 4104 run by the sporting memorabilia department at South Kensington. The torch of transparency that Operation Howzat? has shone onto that troubling transaction shows that Jose Miller is willing to return her £15,000 to Neville Tuli; Basharat Hassan is also prepared to pay back his share of nearly £4,000; but Christie's, despite a mountain of evidence which proves that the Duke wasn't the actual Six Sixes ball, have stood by their vexing verification process. After re-investigating its sale, they have not found "evidence or knowledge of any wrongdoing that helps to shed light on the subsequent controversy" so the question of refunding the £7,500 that the auction house made from lot 173 doesn't even arise.

The day after I received their final response to my evidence, Christie's announced their half-yearly results for 2013. As well as confirming their expansion into China, the press release also revealed that the company would become the first international auctioneer to host sales in India – the home of the notorious ball, its owner and part-time collector Ashish Singhal and art impresario Neville Tuli. An inaugural auction of contemporary art would be taking place in Mumbai in December 2013 as "a reflection of the strong momentum in the domestic art marketplace, the increased international appeal of Indian art and the growing participation of Indian collectors across international sale categories." There's clearly no holding the world's leading auction house; they're doing a roaring trade and look to be heading for another bumper year. During the first six months of 2013, Christie's global sales increased by nine per cent over the same period in 2012 to £2.4 billion…

Afterword

First of all, let me apologise. To anyone who made the innocent mistake of asking me the simple question 'How's it going?' during the last 18 months, all I can say is 'I'm sorry.' If being boring had been an Olympic sport, I would have struck gold; no problem, no contest. I am to boredom what Usain Bolt is to sprinting. If I had a pound for every pair of glazed-over eyes I've encountered, and then ignored, throughout the duration of Operation Howzat?, I would never have had to write this book to earn a living. But the fruits of my labour don't include either a medal or money (just yet) – only the extraordinary story of the Six Sixes ball.

From the moment I heard that the disputed Duke was up for sale again, I just felt compelled to tell the tale, to put down on paper my quest for the truth about the world's most famous cricket ball. And although along the way, I know my obsession has severely tested my relationships with friends, family, colleagues and acquaintances – as well as with people I've hardly known at all – I hope everyone will think that this dark cloud has eventually produced a particularly silver lining. Like pregnancy, a book's gestation period can be both tiring and tiresome but the end result justifies all the effort; the gain is well worth the pain. I trust that a story which may have bored in the telling has beguiled in the reading. It is complicated, even complex – which inevitably rules out brief explanations – but it is as comprehensive as I could possibly have made it.

I'm indebted to a number of people who have either had to put up with me "banging on about that bloody ball", read parts of the manuscript or given me much appreciated encouragement as I've hacked my way through the undergrowth. They are: Lorraine Bewsey, Rob Bradley, Robert Bradley, Elaine Elvidge, Beti George, Trevor Haylett, Eric Lloyd, Ric Metcalfe, Michele Murphy, Mike Murphy, John Parkin, Carolyn Puzzovio, Enzo Puzzovio and Pat Rook. A number of the photographs in this book are reproduced by kind permission of their copyright owners and I'm grateful to Nev Adams, BBC Cymru Wales, Huw John, Jose Miller, Peter Wynne-Thomas, Bernard Shapero, Ken Smith, Dennis Sosnowski,

Mike Taylor, Chris Vaughan and Tony Woolway for their help.

I would also like to thank the following people for their contributions: Lawrence Booth, Alex Capon, Sarah Charles, Supriya Chawla, Shrishti Choudhary, Alexander Clement, Parin Desai, Vishal Dhori, Clive Ellis, Charles Hanson, Dominic Howell, Richard Lewis, Giles Lyon, Rachael Morley, Malcolm Nash, Sushant Nigam, Bernie Nyman, Matthew Paton, Tony Roe, Julian Roup, Mike Scott, Ashish Singhal, Nisha Susan, Robin Turner, Neville Tuli, Peter Walker and Alan Williams. Special mention must be made of Bernard Shapero who played an important part in my ultimately abortive attempt to secure the Duke ball's return from India. When I provided him with an update towards the end of Operation Howzat?, I could sense that his patience was starting to wear a little thin. My painstaking attention to detail had, it seemed, turned me into a right pain in the neck:

"You've rung me at least 100 times," he opined, "I've seen you twice –"

"No, only once."

"It seems like twice!"

Sorry to have been such a nuisance, Bernard. I'd like to thank Basharat Hassan, Jose Miller, Garry Sobers and Peter Wynne-Thomas for agreeing to be interviewed about their connection with the ball. I'm particularly grateful to Jose and her partner, Angus Hall, for their willingness to take me into their confidence and then provide me with some significant documents and photographs for the book. I hope my investigation hasn't proved too stressful at a time when Jose has been suffering from ill-health and I only wish that some of the other people involved in the sale of the ball could have been as co-operative.

I'm also indebted to the hard work put in by Chris Davies, who I barely knew at the outset of Operation Howzat? but who has become a valued friend. As befits the great-grandson of the legendary strong-man, Eugen Sandow, he has been an archetypal tower of strength, uncovering vital information and lending enthusiastic support as the incredible story unfolded. A tick and a gold star must also go to Dave Simmonds whose editing skills proved priceless once the manuscript was completed. Chapter after chapter, he carefully kept my literary excesses in check, reigned in my occasional tendency to over-write and generally offered me some very sound editorial advice. Simon Hicks has once again brought all his experience as a designer and editor to bear on my fourth book as an author-publisher and I'm especially grateful to Matthew Engel who, with his thoughtful contribution, has now completed a hat-trick of forewords to my cricket books. It goes without saying that any errors are entirely my responsibility.

One of the unexpected pleasures of writing this book has been the process of selecting the epigraphs at the beginning of each chapter. I've re-acquainted myself with E.M. Forster, discovered more about writers such as Mark Twain, Rudyard Kipling and Alice Walker and learned a lot about Rabindranath Tagore, he of the memorable sunsets, stars and tears saying, so beloved by Ashish Singhal. After choosing part of the cricket song, *Willow the King*, as the book's opening epigraph, I was fascinated to learn more about Edward Bowen, who wrote the lyrics for this celebration of the battle between bat and ball. Not only was he the first master at the classics-obsessed Harrow School to identify himself completely with sports and games but he helped to set up the English Football Association and bagged a pair in his only county championship match for Hampshire against Somerset in 1864. Ah, the joys of cricketing trivia…

Quotations about truth have inevitably featured prominently in these pages and I was particularly pleased to come across a whole collection of them by Winston Churchill. One has been used as an epigraph and I've saved another until the conclusion of this book:

The truth is incontrovertible. Malice may attack it, ignorance may deride it but, in the end, there it is.

Amen to that. A less subtle remark was regularly uttered by Churchill during the dark days of the Second World War when he used to end almost every phone call with the acronym "KBO." It stood for "keep buggering on" and perfectly summed up the great statesman's spirit of perseverance and determination. I suppose it was a variation on a theme articulated by another wartime leader, General Joseph Stilwell: "Don't let the bastards grind you down". That I haven't allowed that to happen has, as usual, been partly due to the support of my children, Tom, Becca and Alys. "Don't worry Dad," Becca assured me as the climax to Operation Howzat? approached, "it'll all be worth it in the end." I hope you think she was right.

Bibliography

Aye, John, *In Praise of Cricket* (Frederick Muller, 1946)

Bailey, Trevor, *Sir Gary* (Collins, 1976)

Forster, E.M., *A Passage to India* (Edward Arnold, 1924)

Hamilton, Duncan, *A Last English Summer: The Biography of a Cricket Season* (Quercus, 2010)

Heffer, Simon, *The Daily Telegraph Century of County Cricket: The 100 Best Matches* (Sidgwick & Jackson, 1990)

Lewis, Tony, *Playing Days* (Stanley Paul, 1985)

Lewis Tony, *Taking Fresh Guard* (Headline, 2003)

Lloyd, Grahame, *Daffodil Days: Glamorgan's Glorious Summer* (Gomer, 1998)

Lloyd, Grahame, *Six of the Best: Cricket's Most Famous Over* (Celluloid, 2008)

McLellan, Alastair, *The Enemy Within: The Impact of Overseas Players on English Cricket* (Blandford, 1994)

Sobers, Garry, *My Autobiography* (Headline, 2002)

Sobers, Garry, (with Brian Scovell), *Sobers: Twenty Years At The Top* (Macmillan, 1988)

Swanton, E.W., *Sort of a Cricket Person* (Collins, 1972)

Tagore, Rabindranath, *Stray Birds* (Macmillan, 1916)

Walker, Peter, *It's Not Just Cricket* (Fairfield Books, 2006)

Extracts were used from the following magazines and newspapers: *Antiques Trade Gazette, Daily Express, Guardian, Herald (Scotland), Independent, Independent on Sunday, Lincolnshire Echo, Mail on Sunday, Nottingham Evening Post, Playfair Cricket Monthly, Sunday Times, Tehelka, Times, Western Mail* and *Wisden Cricketers' Almanack.*

The sparknotes.com website

The Cricinfo website

The Jewish Chronicle Online

Bloomberg News

Reuters

The 1968 Glamorgan County Cricket Club Members Newsletter

The 1968 and 1969 Glamorgan County Cricket Club Yearbooks

Index